W9-DDD-139

JAN WONG'S CHINA

ALSO BY JAN WONG

Red China Blues: My Long March from Mao to Now

JAN WONG'S CHINA

Reports From a Not-So-Foreign Correspondent

Jan Wong

To Ilona,
Enjoy!

人Wong 黄明珍

Doubleday Canada

Canadian Cataloguing in Publication Data

Wong, Jan
    Jan Wong's China: reports from a not-so-foreign
    correspondent

Includes index.
ISBN 0-385-25902-6

1. China – Politics and government – 1976–   . 2. China –
Social conditions – 1976–   . 3. Wong, Jan. I. Title.

DS779.2.W646 1999   951.05'9   C99-931393-2

Jacket photographs by Photonica *(top)*/Masterfile *(bottom)*
Jacket design by Mario Scaffardi/Victory Design
Text design by Heidy Lawrance Associates
Map by Bernard Bennell
Printed and bound in the USA

Published in Canada by
Doubleday Canada, a division of
Random House of Canada Ltd.
105 Bond Street
Toronto, Ontario
M5B 1Y3

BVG 10 9 8 7 6 5 4 3 2

The photographs on pages 181, 281, and 297 appear courtesy of the *Globe and
Mail* and may not be reproduced without permission of the *Globe and Mail*.

For Ben and Sam

Contents

Acknowledgments ix
A Note About Chinese Names xi
Prologue 1

 1   Tiananmen 9

 2   Waterdown Village 35

 3   Big Mound Village 51

 4   Going Postal 71

 5   State Sloth 91

 6   Serve the People 109

 7   Foreign Devils 125

 8   Blue China Reds 139

 9   The Dalai Lama's Revenge 157

10   Farting at Ferragamo's 181

11   Pandora's E-mail 193

12   Great Leap into the Driver's Seat 209

13   In the Chinese Closet 223

14   The New Opium Wars 239

15   Holding Up Half of Hell 259

16   Love Thyself 281

17   China's Little Emperors 297

Epilogue 315
Index 323

Acknowledgments

John Pearce, editor-in-chief of Doubleday Canada, who first approached me to write *Red China Blues,* also inspired this book. Lesley Grant edited the manuscript with a sure touch and made invaluable suggestions. Michael Cohn was everything a literary agent should be.

For allowing me to draw upon my articles and photographs published in the *Globe and Mail,* I'd like to thank Earle Gill, the paper's Editorial Business Manager, William Thorsell, editor-in-chief, and Michael Doody, vice-president and general counsel of Thomson Corp. For my book leave, I'd like to thank my *Globe* editors, Cathrin Bradbury and Sarah Murdoch. Johanna Boffa in the library provided emergency research. Paula Wilson in the photo library tracked down old negatives. Bernard Bennell drew the map. Stephen Strauss, as usual, maintained the flow of office gossip so I never felt lonely working at home.

Mel Mencher, my former professor at Columbia's Graduate School of Journalism, explained exactly how I could – and why I should – make a final research trip to China in 1999 *and* still meet my tight deadline.

As a foreign correspondent in China from 1988 to 1994, my two closest friends were Catherine Sampson of *The Times* of London and Lena Sun of the *Washington Post.* Both were generous with their insight and information. They were also tremendous fun, even during the darkest days.

For help on this book, I'd also like to thank other friends and colleagues in China, especially Ben Mok, Jaime FlorCruz, Susan Lawrence, Jim and Cathy McGregor, Jane Su, Joan Hinton and Sid Engst. Kathy Wilhelm, a former Beijing colleague in Hong Kong, sent me data promptly. Joanne Lee-Young in Hong Kong generously provided notes on her experiences.

I also thank my Chinese friends in China. You know who you are. It's best if the government doesn't.

In the United States, my matchmakers, Betty Zheng and Simon Hui, helped me, as always.

In Canada, my mother and my Aunt Ming read early chapters and encouraged me. When my obsolete printer sputtered, Cheuk Kwan helped me print out the second draft. In Toronto, Janet Brooks expertly read and corrected not one, but two, drafts.

My cousin-in-law, Colleen Parrish Yao, reeled off witty sub-titles at the drop of a hat, including the one we finally chose. She is assured of a job in publishing if she ever tires of managing a multi-billion-dollar pension fund.

In Toronto, Mercedita Iboro kept the household running smoothly, noting when we ran out of bleach and mayonnaise and remembering the boys' dentist appointments. This book would not have been possible without her.

Nor would have it been possible without my husband, Norman. Fat Paycheck thought up the main title, helped me refresh old memories and hustled the boys off to karate lessons each weekend so I could work in peace.

And my boys. Every writer/mother should have angels like them. Ben, nine, and Sam, six, understood deadlines. And they were completely understanding one weekend when they had to eat hot dogs and chips and watch three videos in a row. I feared my maternal neglect would scar them for life – until Ben one day said that he, too, wanted to be a writer.

A Note About Chinese Names

To help readers cope with odd-sounding Chinese names, I have often tagged on titles, such as "Architect Zhang" or "Snakehead Yan" or "Migrant Worker Zhao." Occasionally, I have translated names, primarily as a memory aid, but also because knowing the meaning will help readers understand the culture and context. Parents, for instance, often named children according to the political movement of the day. My friend, Zhou Yue, whose name means "Great Leap" Zhou, was so called because she was born during the 1958 Great Leap Forward.

I have used pinyin, the official system of romanization in China. It is generally pronounced as it looks, with a few daunting exceptions. *C* is pronounced *ts*, *q* is pronounced *ch*, *zh* is pronounced *j* and *x* is pronounced *hs*. I don't expect anyone to remember that, so I often put a word's pronunciation in brackets right after, for instance: *guanxi* (gwaan-see). With pinyin, some common English spellings have changed. Mao Tse-tung becomes Mao Zedong, Peking becomes Beijing and Chungking becomes Chongqing. In a few cases, I have kept the well-established English spellings: Chou En-lai, Canton and Nanking.

Family names precede personal names in Chinese, which is just another indication of the importance of the collective over the individual. With only about a hundred family names in common use – and 1.3 billion people – many people in this book have the same surnames. The reader can assume they are not related, unless otherwise stated.

In a very few cases, I have changed names to protect people. Reporters are supposed to let the reader know when. I have not. The reason is I'd rather keep the Chinese authorities guessing.

The exchange rate has fluctuated over the years. I have tried to convert any yuan figures by the exchange that prevailed at the time. All dollars are U.S. dollars.

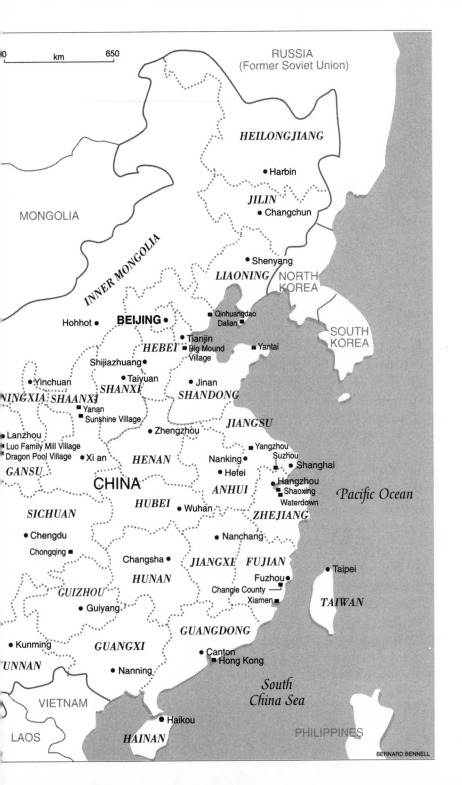

km

RUSSIA
(Former Soviet Union)

HEILONGJIANG

● Harbin

JILIN
● Changchun

MONGOLIA

INNER MONGOLIA

● Shenyang

LIAONING   NORTH
KOREA

Hohhot ●   **BEIJING** ●   ■ Qinhuangdao
Dalian ■

SOUTH
KOREA

● Tianjin
HEBEI   ■ Big Mound
Village   ● Yantai

Shijiazhuang ●

● Yinchuan   ● Taiyuan   ● Jinan

NINGXIA SHAANXI   SHANXI   SHANDONG

■ Yanan
■ Sunshine Village   JIANGSU

● Lanzhou   ● Zhengzhou
■ Luo Family Mill Village
Dragon Pool Village   ● Xi an   ■ Yangzhou
Nanking ●   Suzhou

GANSU   HENAN   ● Hefei   ● Shanghai

CHINA   Hangzhou ●
ANHUI   ■ Shaoxing
Waterdown

HUBEI   ● Wuhan   ZHEJIANG

SICHUAN   *Pacific Ocean*

● Chengdu

Chongqing ■   ● Nanchang

Changsha ●   JIANGXI   FUJIAN
HUNAN   ● Taipei

Fuzhou ■
Changle County —
GUIZHOU   Xiamen ■   TAIWAN

● Guiyang

GUANGDONG

● Kunming   GUANGXI   ● Canton
■ Hong Kong

UNNAN

● Nanning   *South
China Sea*

VIETNAM

LAOS   PHILIPPINES

● Haikou

HAINAN

BERNARD BENNELL

JAN WONG'S CHINA

Prologue

Top: Nanny Ma and Ben in 1990.   Photo: Jan Wong

Bottom: Author and family – Norman Shulman, Ben and Sam (in carriage) in Tiananmen Square, 1994.   Photo: Lena Sun

"**D**o you want to adopt a baby girl?"

I put down my chopsticks and stared at Nanny Ma.

"Yes," I blurted, at the same moment as my husband, Norman, yelled, "No!"

It was August, 1994, and I was ending my six-year posting as China correspondent for the Toronto *Globe and Mail*. Right after lunch, I would be heading for Beijing's International Airport.

At home in China, we always lunched with Nanny Ma, a never-ending fount of everyday gossip. Her presence also enabled us to dine with our toddlers, Sam and Ben, without the normal parental pain of retrieving the broccoli they tossed overboard.

"What do you mean, 'adopt'?" I asked Nanny Ma, ignoring Norman. It was her maid's baby, she said. Actually, it was her maid's uncle's wife's baby. As my mind raced, the journalist in me silently noted: *In the 1990s, even my maid had a maid.*

The maid and her aunt were from the provinces, part of an estimated 100 million peasants streaming into China's great cities looking for work. They were mostly young, vigorous – and fertile. And nobody was in charge of monitoring their menstrual cycles. Taking advantage of this loophole in Beijing's one-child policy, the aunt was having babies at regular intervals. This latest was her third – and her third daughter.

In a culture where peasants prized sons and dismissed daughters, no one had to explain that the couple didn't want her. *I* did. But how could I smuggle a baby out of China and into Canada? I briefly considered wearing a Snugli under a really loose blouse. Then my gaze fell on Sam in his highchair, blissfully dumping his milk on the floor.

My one-year-old didn't need his passport – not at that exact moment. I was returning to Toronto alone to supervise the move. Sam, Ben and Norman would join me two weeks later, enough time to get Sam a new passport. It might just work. All newborns look alike, so Sam's scrunchy-faced passport photo would work fine. And who could tell a baby girl from a baby boy? I figured an infant strip search at Canadian Customs and Immigration was statistically remote.

Norman, who had suffered too many sleepless nights as a father, was still spluttering. I glanced at my watch. Ten minutes just wasn't enough time to adopt a baby.

An hour later, in the Beijing airport departure lounge, I couldn't help noticing six foreign couples, each snuggling a Chinese baby girl. They were part of the happy flood of Westerners adopting infant girls from China. As our plane took off, I felt bereft. During the long flight to Toronto, I watched the parents pacing the aisle, soothing their brand new daughters.

I thought about the baby girl then, and long after I returned home. In addition to my six years as a foreign correspondent, I had spent six much earlier years in China as a gullible Maoist. After my Beijing posting, I took a leave in Toronto from the *Globe* to write a memoir, *Red China Blues, My Long March from Mao to Now.* During my research, I discovered that my own grandmother had been abandoned on the streets of Canton a century ago. Her father, a peasant, couldn't, or wouldn't, feed her and her baby sister. He carried them into the city in two willow baskets, balanced on a bamboo shoulder pole. Luckily for my grandmother and my great-aunt, someone took them in, gave them each a year's education and refused to bind their feet. My grandmother ended up marrying and coming to Canada at age 16.

The little baby girl I left behind would be five by now. I think about her often. Does anybody hug her? Does anybody love her? Does she have enough to eat? Is she even alive? At that last lunch with Nanny Ma in Beijing, I never thought to ask her name. But in my mind, I called her the Ten Minute Baby. Because, if I had just had enough nerve, I could have had a baby in ten minutes.

Reporting on China was not just another assignment to me. I cared deeply about the country of my ancestors. It was where I had misspent my radical youth, where I had eventually come of age and where I had found my American husband, a draft dodger who chose to flee to China during the Vietnam War. Norman Shulman arrived in Beijing in 1966 and learned to speak fluent Chinese. He went by his Chinese name, Shu Yulu, or Fat Paycheck Shulman. It was an ironic moniker, considering that for most of his years in China he earned about $1 a day.

My Chinese name was Bright Precious Wong. My own links to China reached back more than a hundred years. One grandfather arrived in Canada from Guangdong Province at the turn of the century. The other came even earlier, in the 1880s, one of several thousand coolies who helped build the Canadian Pacific Railway.

As a third-generation Canadian, born and raised in Montreal, I grew up speaking English, learning French and avoiding Chinese. Then, my teenage years coincided with the Great Proletarian Cultural Revolution of 1966–1976. I became fascinated by the mysterious events breaking out on the other side of the world. At McGill University, I majored in Asian studies. I also dreamed of changing the world, like so many other students at the time with the exception, perhaps, of those in engineering.

Based on zero knowledge, I became a fervent Maoist. In 1972, I traveled alone to China during my summer vacation. I was 19. I pestered the authorities to let me stay and study Chinese. To my shock, they agreed. And that was how I became the first Canadian to study there since the Cultural Revolution. I made widgets in factories, transplanted rice in paddy fields, read Marx and Lenin, snitched on class enemies and did my best to be a good little Maoist. But by the time I left in 1980, Chairman Mao was dead, the Cultural

Revolution was finished and capitalism was taking hold. I was no longer a True Believer.

Still, China had seduced me, as it has seduced so many others. I planned to return one day as a journalist, and I did. In 1988, I became the *Globe*'s 13th Beijing correspondent. I was the bureau's first female and the first to speak Chinese. More importantly, I was the first with a complete Cultural Revolution wardrobe.

I chronicled my Maoist misadventures in *Red China Blues*. That book was really about me. I wanted to write another book, about China. October 1, 1999, was the 50th anniversary of the People's Republic. As the date approached, my publisher suggested reprinting my best dispatches. But I wanted to write a bigger book, certainly based on my stories, but incorporating the wealth of my 12 years experience in China. And I wanted to report on the latest changes, too. In 1999, I planned a trip back to revisit old friends and forbidden places.

But would Beijing issue me a visa? After my reporting there, authorities condemned me as a "traitor." *Red China Blues*, with its detailed recounting of the Tiananmen Massacre, angered them too. I knew, because the Chinese Embassy in Ottawa demanded that TV Ontario bar me from a reception to which I'd already been invited. The public broadcaster obeyed, even though the reception was to mark the broadcast of a documentary I'd hosted. When Miro Cernetig arrived in Beijing for the *Globe and Mail* in 1998, authorities combed through his shipment of household goods and confiscated just one item: *Red China Blues*.

So it seemed like a bad idea to apply for a Chinese visa in Canada. I wondered if I could get one in Hong Kong. It was a long way to go on a wing and a prayer, but I figured my chances were better than even. Hong Kong was the busiest gateway into China. My Canadian passport, renewed since my stint in Beijing, had no telltale markings exposing me as a bourgeois journalist. And I had one unusual circumstance, which I'll keep a secret. Maybe I can take advantage of it again next time.

Two days before I left, an independent filmmaker in Toronto called. Robin Benger proposed accompanying me with a camera-man named Alister Bell to make a documentary marking China's

50th anniversary. I'd worked hard to learn accentless Chinese so I could operate incognito. Did I really need a pair of six-foot white guys tagging along, loaded down with cameras, lights, a tripod, radio mikes, headsets, batteries and tapes? But it would be an adventure, too. Impulsively, I agreed.

My boys hate when I travel. But as Ben, eight, fell asleep that last night, he said sweetly, "I hope China lets you in, Mom." The next morning at dawn, I left without waking Fat Paycheck or the kids. Over cappuccino at the airport, Robin, Alister and I discussed the project for the first time. Then, paranoid about being overheard on the plane, we split up and didn't regroup until Hong Kong.

The former British colony had changed dramatically since I had last been there covering the July 1, 1997, handover. In March, 1999, the place was depressed. The humongous new airport was eerily empty. The stock market had plunged. Real estate prices were down. Department stores were deserted, despite 90-percent-off sales. Tourism had dried up, or rather, the free-spending Americans and Japanese had disappeared, replaced by mainland Chinese on cheap package tours.

The next morning, I dropped off my passport at a travel agency recommended by a friend. It accepted my $25, no questions asked, for a rush, same-day tourist visa. On blind faith, I bought a ticket to Hangzhou for the next morning. All day, I wondered if my visa would come through. When I got back to my hotel that evening, an envelope was waiting. I tore it open. Just my passport. Good. A note would have been a bad sign. With trembling fingers, I paged through it. There was the visa, so big it occupied the whole page. It said "tourist," in Chinese, in deep blue ink with the ornate red five-star seal of the People's Republic of China.

The next day, I flew to Hangzhou, the capital of Zhejiang Province, on the southeast coast of China. Standing in line at the "frontier inspection," I felt my heart beating too fast. My palms were sweaty. Would the unsmiling border guard notice my damp passport? Gingerly holding it by my fingertips, I handed it over. He typed my name and birthdate into the computer. I held my breath. Then he reached for a stamp. I was in!

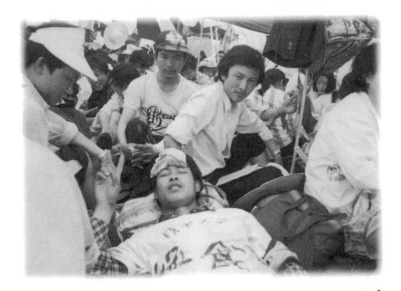

1

Tiananmen

Top: Hunger-striking students in Tiananmen Square in May 1989.

Photo: Yan Yan

Bottom: In Tiananmen Square in March 1999.   Photo: Robin Benger

"**B**right Precious!" my old roommate screamed over the telephone. Paranoid about tipping off the authorities that I would be slipping into China, I had given Zhang Hong (Scarlet Zhang) no advance warning that I was going to be in Beijing. We quickly made a date to have dinner.

That March afternoon in 1999, she met me on the side of the road and gave me a big hug. Even though I was half an hour early, she was already waiting for me. Just like the old days at Beijing University, when she was plucked from her history class to take care of me, a bumbling foreigner who could hardly speak Chinese, Scarlet somehow still felt responsible for my well-being.

On the way up in the dingy elevator, she told me she was working at the National Library of China. I'd brought her a copy of *Red China Blues* from Canada. She told me she'd already seen it, in the library's special section for Western books about China. Anyone could read my book, she said, providing they didn't take it out of the library. (So much for the Chinese police confiscating Miro's copy.)

Scarlet had already leafed through it, but couldn't read it. She didn't know English. "The only thing I regret," she said, "was that they told me to speak Chinese to you and I obeyed. I should have learned English from you."

We were 19 years old back in 1972. We had been a good match: naive, idealistic and eager to please. Scarlet had obeyed the Communist Party and I had tried my best to fit into Maoist China. Her thick glossy braids had become a simple bob. Her voluptuous figure, which she once masked with a baggy Mao suit, was decidedly middle-aged. Now she wore loose-fitting pants and a plain sweater.

Her life had changed dramatically from our days as revolutionary roommates, freezing together in our badly heated, whitewashed dorm, surviving on rationed rice. Like millions of Chinese, Scarlet was absorbed by the home-decorating craze sweeping the country. She poured me tea, then gave me a tour of her two-bedroom apartment. She and her husband had renovated every inch, installing a granite countertop in her tiny kitchen, polished wood floors in her living room, halogen pot lights, elaborate molding, built-in bookshelves and armoires, carved wooden doors, Italian ceramic tile and, in her bathroom, a pale aqua Kohler toilet and matching pedestal sink. She had been thwarted in only one item: a giant General Electric refrigerator. "It was too big to get through our front door," she said.

I couldn't imagine how she could afford such luxuries on her librarian's salary. But it turned out her husband had taken early retirement from the Ministry of Forestry, where he had been a wildlife photographer. At 55, he had started several businesses. One of them was a company making wildlife films. Zhang Congmi used his old contacts at the Ministry of Forestry to obtain permission to film in restricted zones. At the moment, he had five camera crews in several Chinese provinces filming everything from endangered animals to famous scenic spots.

But his big money-maker was importing wildlife from Africa. Spotting a trend in China's soaring ownership of private cars, he realized there would be a demand for places to go on family outings. "Now everybody wants to drive around in safari parks," said Zhang Congmi. Again, relying on his contacts in the Ministry of Forestry, which had jurisdiction over endangered species, he had imported 12 elephants at $22,500 each and 14 giraffes at $17,500 each. Because he had to squeeze them onto Boeing 757s, he only took animals under one year of age.

Zhang Congmi boasted of having 30 employees and a fleet of 14 cars. Scarlet's apartment renovations, he said, had cost $15,000, a fortune in Chinese terms. They'd just bought a 3,000-square-foot villa on the Shandong coast. And their only child, Mao Mao, was in university, studying television filmmaking. Her tuition, nearly $1,000 a year, would have strained a lot of family budgets. For them, it was nothing.

Scarlet and her husband invited me out for Mongolian Hot Pot with a friend who owned a brand new Toyota Previa minivan. After gorging on simmered mutton and beef, pickled garlic cloves and warm sesame buns, we drove in the darkness through Tiananmen Square. Suddenly, their friend remarked, "Here is where the tanks passed over. It's freshly paved. You can't feel the ruts anymore."

The square itself was under "renovation." That March, workers were laying new pink granite paving stones at a snail's pace. The entire square had been effectively sealed off, boarded up around its entire perimeter with ten-foot high sheets of blue-painted plywood. The official excuse was that the square needed to be refurbished for China's 50th anniversary that October. "I laughed when I heard that Tiananmen wouldn't be fixed until July," said Scarlet, who had done her share of renovations.

Every Chinese knew that meant the square wouldn't re-open until well after June 4, the tenth anniversary of the Tiananmen Massacre. The authorities were terrified of protests, or even the thought that someone might lay a wreath in the square.

"Of course, people remember, Bright Precious," she said. "I myself will never forget what happened. But we remember in our hearts. Violence isn't the way to change China. We will *heping yanbian* (evolve peacefully)."

As Beijing University history graduates, we both knew what that meant. "Peaceful evolution" was what Mao had always feared. It was why he claimed China needed the Cultural Revolution to shake things up. It meant evolving so peacefully that you didn't care anymore about class struggle, only about pale aqua pedestal sinks.

The 1989 Tiananmen mass protests caught everyone by surprise. That spring, few anticipated where the demonstrations would lead.

After all, the economy was humming. But when you don't have to count every grain of rice in your bowl, you become much less of an animal and much more of a human being. And the more you feel like a human being, the more you want to be treated like one. Their first taste of the West only whetted their appetites. Put another way, when Chinese ate Big Macs, two hours later they hungered again – for freedom.

Tiananmen started with a funeral. Nobody was particularly heartbroken when Hu Yaobang, a former Party chief, died on April 15, 1989. But mourning an expired Communist leader was the only way to organize a demonstration without getting into trouble. "It began with a single death," I wrote in my dispatch to the *Globe*. "It could end with many more." Cautious editors back in Toronto cut the second sentence. I'm sure they thought: *She's getting melodramatic. Been there too long.*

By the time the tanks occupied Tiananmen Square seven weeks later, hundreds, perhaps thousands, were dead. In *Red China Blues*, I estimated the final toll at about 3,000 because of the density of the crowds that night and the battlefield weaponry deployed.

Earlier that spring, the students had launched a gentle hunger strike in Tiananmen Square. Singing songs and waving banners, they demanded freedom, democracy and an end to corruption and privilege. No one advocated overthrowing the Chinese Communist Party. Only when the government ignored them did they up the ante. Some began to call for Deng Xiaoping's resignation.

Paralyzed by infighting, the government did nothing. Deng wanted to crush the impertinent demonstrators. His heir apparent, Party chief Zhao Ziyang, disagreed. The Communist Party, Zhao believed, could only save itself by liberalizing the country. Meanwhile, millions of ordinary Beijingers joined the students. So did students from the rest of China, who streamed into the capital or staged copycat hunger strikes at home.

It took several weeks, but Deng finally managed to purge Zhao. Then he imposed martial law. The students, who had already called off their hunger strike, remained defiant. So did the populace of Beijing. We were all naive. No one believed the People's Liberation Army would shoot the Chinese people in cold blood. As spring turned to summer, many began drifting back to campus. Even with martial law in force, some foreign correspondents believed nothing more would happen. A few even left for a vacation.

That's why the massacre surprised everyone. Few, myself included, understood at the time that Deng was crushing the last bit of dissent within the government. It was a warning, written in blood, to anyone in power who still supported Zhao Ziyang and his political reforms. The students – and the ordinary citizens of Beijing – were mere pawns.

On a hot Saturday night in June, the People's Liberation Army rumbled into the capital in trucks, tanks and armored personnel carriers. Years of brainwashing had seemingly washed all reason from the minds of the Chinese people. That night, they stood their ground, and died.

I spent the evening of June 3 interviewing protesters. Around 12:45 a.m. on June 4, I retreated to the nearby Beijing Hotel, just minutes before the first troops rolled into Tiananmen Square. From the hotel balcony, I counted the ambulances, timed the volleys and watched the blood-soaked pedicabs transporting the wounded to safety. I sat all night, and counted.

On Sunday morning, I watched stunned as a knot of survivors stood, a city block away, screaming curses at the soldiers. I saw the commander give the order to shoot. The soldiers, in formation across the north end of Tiananmen Square, raised their rifles. As the people turned and ran, the soldiers shot them in the back. Now it was broad daylight. I could easily count the dead and dying as they lay on the street, in front of my hotel balcony.

As I wrote in *Red China Blues*, I saw the people regroup and creep back to curse the troops again. The commander gave another order, the soldiers raised their rifles again, the people ran, and the soldiers shot them in the back. More died. All day, I watched as they crept back, cursed, and were shot again, and again, and again.

After Tiananmen, Beijing issued a Most-Wanted List of 21 student leaders. By fall, half had been arrested, three escaped overseas and the rest were still at large, trying to avoid a pervasive network of Street Committees.

Across China, 6.4 million cut-rate domestic spies formed a sinister Neighborhood Watch system. The spies were sometimes illiterate, mostly female and all retired. People dubbed them "the bound-feet brigade," even though foot-binding had ended decades earlier and most had normal feet. "You can't offend them or you're in big trouble," said one young woman, who had had two house guests interrogated by them.

A few months after the Tiananmen Massacre, I visited a Street Committee to see how it was assisting with the crackdown. "It's such a pity," Liu Fuwen (Cultured Liu) said with a sigh. "We haven't found any students on the Most-Wanted List. If we did, we'd turn them over to the police."

She was a 62-year-old grandmother, with wire-rim glasses, stiff gray hair and an ominous red armband. Together with her five deputies, all retired women wearing red armbands, Cultured Liu patrolled the alleyways of a West Beijing enclave called Place of Blessed Peace. She and her ladies were professional busybodies. Each month the government paid them a modest stipend to be the eyes and ears of the Communist Party. It was their job to know everything that went on in Blessed Peace (population 1,520). And they did.

Street Committees were part Ann Landers, part homespun thought police, part security guards. If you wanted to marry, go abroad or open a business, you needed their letter of recommendation. They even decided when you could have your first and only child. The previous year, China claimed its 1 million Street Committees had solved 7.2 million disputes and thwarted 120,000 murders and suicides.

The Communists did not invent the granny patrols. They merely perfected them. During the Tang Dynasty, a *baojia* system of collective responsibility grouped the population into 20-family cells. Each cell policed itself, and everyone was punished if one member committed a crime. In Blessed Peace, the ratio was virtually unchanged from the Tang Dynasty. The 24-member Street Committee oversaw 460 families, or 1 for every 19 households.

The little old ladies mediated family fights, they barged into homes to check for sloppy housekeeping and they took note of unreported overnight guests, who were supposed to be registered at the local police station. "We're not the police," said Cultured Liu, who retired from her job as a factory administrator five years earlier. "But we have a duty and responsibility to report things."

In 1989, many Blessed Peace residents didn't have home phones. The Street Committee levied a modest fee to use the one in its office. That way they could eavesdrop *and* make money. "How can we not know everything?" asked Cultured Liu, with a gentle smile.

Big Grandmother was watching, even when nature called. With indoor plumbing a rarity in Blessed Peace, the old ladies of the Street Committee squatted alongside everyone else in the neighborhood latrine. So they knew who was menstruating. More important, they knew who *wasn't*. That was useful for nipping out-of-plan pregnancies in the bud.

"Everyone calls me Auntie Liu," said Cultured Liu. "I've watched the neighborhood kids grow up. If someone has morning sickness, I know about it right away."

She'd never forced anyone to have an abortion, she insisted. Instead, she'd merely subtracted an available slot from the number of babies the government had allotted in Blessed Peace's quota for the following year. (Chinese friends scoffed. People rarely had a child without permission, but if they dared get pregnant without authorization, the Street Committee insisted on an abortion – and visited the couple nightly until they caved in.)

I accompanied Cultured Liu as she patrolled her neighborhood with her security chief, a sweet-looking grandmother named Yang Xiuying. A young woman passed by with a pot of rice. "Cooking dinner?" Cultured Liu asked pleasantly.

"Sure, sure," the woman answered with an ingratiating smile.

An elderly man cycled by. "You were out?" Cultured Liu asked. He nodded and waved. Cultured Liu wasn't particularly sociable. It was just her way of letting everyone know she was watching.

The Street Committee patrolled twice a day. For two years, Blessed Peace hadn't had a single burglary, Cultured Liu noted proudly. Suddenly, she and Granny Yang spied a couple of schoolboys on a brick wall surrounding the public latrine. "Jump down," Cultured Li ordered. The boys looked sheepish, but stood stock still.

"Here, I'll catch you," Granny Yang offered, stretching out her tiny arms. Looking mortified, the boys jumped off the wall and ran away.

Cultured Liu was on her second four-year term as Street Committee chief. She knew exactly who had voted for her last time, and who hadn't. The idea of a secret ballot puzzled her. Without a show of hands, she said, how would she know who supported her? Besides Granny Yang, her security chief, she had deputies for birth control, dispute mediation, welfare, health and women's affairs.

Fights erupted easily in the crumbling courtyards of Blessed Peace. Half a dozen families were crammed into space designed for one. In summer, when windows were open, one man's snoring could disturb his neighbors' sleep. One family's laundry could block another's entrance. "We handle the small fights. The big problems go to court," said Cultured Liu.

A few weeks earlier she'd overheard a husband and wife quarreling in their home. "I just happened to go by," she said. Naturally, she popped in. The wife, a music teacher, wanted her husband, an astronomer, to take her out for the evening. He preferred staying home to read. Cultured Liu leaped in. "I told him, 'No matter how busy your work is, you should go out with your wife. Take her to a movie. Go dancing.'" She then turned to the wife. "'If he's busy, go out less. Do more housework.'"

Back in her office, Cultured Liu told me that no one in Blessed Peace had taken part in the Tiananmen demonstrations. How was that possible? I asked. After all, millions of Beijingers had taken part and some of the biggest demonstrations occurred right near Blessed Peace.

"We see everything," she said testily. "You must believe me."

At 2.84 million soldiers, the People's Liberation Army (PLA) was the world's largest standing army, bigger than the armed forces of the United States and Russia combined. But with Beijing slashing defense spending to focus on economic development, the PLA was quickly becoming a ground force with obsolete weapons. One study estimated that by 1990 half of its military aircraft were no longer operational.

In 1997, China transferred half a million PLA troops to the People's Armed Police (PAP), the paramilitary force for crushing civil unrest. In 1999, President Jiang Zemin declared domestic stability to be China's number one priority. That same year, the PAP swelled to one million strong. Internal disorder, it seemed, was a bigger threat than foreign invasion.

Fighting spirit was another matter. Tai Ming Cheung, a military analyst in Hong Kong, estimated the army owned 15,000 enterprises by 1997, generating annual revenues of $10 billion and profits of $3 billion. The PLA got into pig farming, airlines, coal-mining, cellphones and professional basketball teams. With its headquarters and barracks occupying some of China's choicest urban real estate, it also got into five-star hotels.

Talk about secure accommodations. Like the Street Committees and their pay phones, the security forces could earn hard currency *and* keep tabs on foreign visitors. The luxury PLA-owned Palace Hotel had 2 nightclubs, 7 restaurants and 52 security cameras, including a few embedded in the ceilings of its elegant wood-paneled lifts. Unaware their every move was monitored, a foreign man and a Chinese woman hit the emergency-stop button. When they emerged after a brief tryst, the Chinese woman was arrested.

The PAP was a partner in the New World Hotel. The Ministry of State Security, which tailed dissidents and diplomats, owned the Kunlun Hotel. The Public Security Bureau, as the police were called, was an investor in the Ramada Asia Hotel. The Beijing Military Command owned Le Meridien Jinlang in Beijing. And in Canton, Norinco, the army's shadowy weapons dealer, owned the Cathay Hotel.

But the army shot itself in the foot. As security forces arrested students and patrolled the streets with AK-47s, they scared away the very tourists they needed to fill their hotels. In 1989, the Palace Hotel incurred heavy losses. The Meridien postponed its opening. And the Ramada offered half-price rooms and a 20 percent discount in its restaurants. When Norman and I took Ben to the Ramada for lunch one Sunday, we were its only customers. The doorman rushed across the vacant parking lot to help with the baby carriage. A bellhop insisted on carrying our diaper bag all the way to the dining room. There, we had our choice of thirty empty tables and five waitresses.

Sometimes, hotel guests got a glimpse of the classic paranoia of these unusual owners. When CNN aired graphic footage of the Tiananmen Massacre, the military partners switched off the satellite at the Palace. "The generals were terrified the local staff would see the CNN broadcast," said Ross Terrill, a Sinologist staying there at the time. The order upset the news-starved guests, he added. "People shouted at managers in the lobby."

As other hotels closed for lack of supplies during the Tiananmen Massacre, the Palace Hotel's military connection enabled it to remain open throughout. During the worst days, when foreigners were fleeing to the airport in flag-draped convoys, you could always count on Sunday brunch at the Palace. After surviving a drive-by tank shooting, I once consoled myself foraging among the ice sculptures for smoked salmon and steak tartar at the Palace's coffee shop buffet. "Probably we had good supplies. But I don't think it had anything to do with the army," Hans Brouwers, the general manager, said uncomfortably.

Not everyone was so discreet. The Beijing Ramada's general manager, Werner Schmidt, confirmed that its chairman, Wang Fusheng, was "an important guy in the police department." When Chairman Wang decided he wanted the hotel opened in seven weeks, it was. "Unbelievable. I would have bet any amount of money they would not have made it," marveled Schmidt, who had previously worked in Malaysia. In that southeast Asian country, the King was sometimes a hotel guest. Whenever there was trouble, Schmidt would say, "You want me to tell the King about my problems?"

So how did he threaten people in China? He laughed happily. "Here, I don't have problems." He drew my attention to the Ramada's 15 security cameras, and joked, "Who needs them? We are under the protection of the police!"

As the army made money, it grew less reliant on the central government. Beijing, concerned about this new-found independence, ordered the military to get out of business. By 1998, the PLA announced that the divestiture was complete. But it was too soon to tell if the PLA had truly renounced China's new money culture.

Certainly, it didn't get out of the arms business. Beijing became the third-largest arms supplier to the Third World, behind the United States and the former Soviet Union. Estimates put its annual arms sales at $2.3 billion. Despite signing the Nuclear Nonproliferation Treaty and the Missile Technology Control Regime, China was believed to have shipped M-11 missiles to Pakistan.

A Chinese effort to obtain American military technology extended over the Reagan, Bush and Clinton administrations. In 1998, Congress accused Beijing of stealing weapon designs from American nuclear laboratories and acquiring critical computer, ballistic missile, satellite and thermo-nuclear warhead technologies. Reports filtered out that China had also funneled money to the Democratic Party. Liu Chaoying, an aerospace executive, was alleged to be the conduit. Her father, Liu Huaqing, was China's highest-ranking general.

On April 15, 1990, the first anniversary of Hu Yaobang's death, soldiers practised bayonet thrusts on the edge of Tiananmen Square. For good measure, they screamed, "Kill! Kill! Kill!" The square itself was swarming with police, both plainclothes and uniformed. Suddenly, I noticed a man pulling a collapsible luggage cart toward the Monument to the People's Heroes. Soldiers shooed him away.

He was in his forties, neatly dressed in a Western-style blazer and jeans. I approached him and softly asked what he was doing in Tiananmen on so sensitive a date. "I came especially to Beijing for this. I came to mourn our great General Secretary Hu Yaobang." But it turned out he was commemorating those who died in the Tiananmen Massacre.

The man began untying a small plastic bag on his luggage cart. Inside were a few oranges, meant as an offering to the dead. Then he drew out a large white paper flower, with two streamers inscribed: "In mourning for Comrade Hu Yaobang. In memory of the heroes who died for democracy and liberty. Their spirits are immortal."

A small crowd gathered. The man pulled out a small white paper flower, which he began to tie to his left arm. A male bystander, holding a baby, helped him. I figured I had 20 seconds before the police grabbed him. "Who are you?" I whispered urgently, conducting the fastest interview of my life. "Where are you from? Why are you risking your life?" He was a mineralogist from Guizhou Province. "Aren't you afraid of getting arrested?" I asked.

He gestured at his luggage cart. "I've come prepared. I've brought all my things with me."

As if on cue, four uniformed police officers and several burly plainclothes security men pounced. "Come with us," a policeman ordered, grabbing him by the arm.

"What have I done wrong?" the man replied. "I'm just a scientist." He snapped open his attaché case to show them neatly mounted mineral samples. There was a minor scuffle as the police tried to grab the case. The man insisted on shutting it himself. With great dignity, he strapped it back on his luggage cart.

The police began pushing bystanders, ordering them to move on. No one did. But no one intervened, either. The police led the man across the square toward a waiting jeep, its engine revving, its red lights flashing. I trotted behind as close as I dared. "Where are you taking me?" I heard him ask.

"The Science Commission," one security man said, sarcastically. The mineralogist loaded his suitcases into the front seat of the jeep and then climbed into the back, wedged between two uniformed officers. A third policeman squeezed into the back. Then the jeep sped off.

In reply to questions from Western reporters, a Public Security Bureau spokesman said the man was mentally ill. I heard he was sentenced to ten years in prison. I felt terrible that I never got his name.

Authorities call it "the turmoil." The people call it "June 4th." Each year, from April 15, the date of Hu Yaobang's death, to June 4, the date of the Tiananmen Massacre, Beijing's security forces go on high alert. In 1991, on the second anniversary of the Tiananmen Massacre, I visited the Eternal Peace Cemetery, just outside Beijing, near the Western Hills. I'd heard some victims of the massacre had been buried here.

On that anniversary, the cemetery was eerily quiet. I soon found out why. Half a dozen police officers were standing guard over the tombstones. The Chinese were not allowed to mourn their dead. On that hot June day I scanned the gravestones, trying not to attract attention. I couldn't find what I was looking for, so I approached a lone gravedigger, hoping he wouldn't turn me over to the police. "Why have you come today?" he whispered. "There is a lot of surveillance." He glanced nervously around, then wordlessly led the way to one grave.

Her name was Wang Weiping. Unlike the other tombstones, which gave only the dates of birth and death, hers also stated that she had graduated from Beijing Medical University and was a gynecologist at People's Hospital. She was 24 when she died. Perhaps she was killed helping the wounded in Tiananmen Square. Perhaps she was shot on her way home from work – her hospital was near the square. Or perhaps she was one of the hundreds of thousands of demonstrators who had faced down the troops.

"Wang Weiping perished in the disaster," the inscription said. The gravedigger traced his finger over the Chinese characters carved into the granite. "Most of the gravestones don't put it so baldly," he said softly. "People don't dare."

Chinese custom calls for the family to visit the grave of a loved one on the anniversary of the death, each year for the first three years. Perhaps the police presence had kept her family away. "Not many families have come," the gravedigger said.

Someone, though, had paid Dr. Wang a visit a few weeks earlier. Two withered bouquets, bleached into dusty pastels by the hot spring sun, lay on her tombstone.

A few whispers. A nod. Then I was ushered into a back room while a beefy man kept an eye out for the police. Opium? Cocaine? Nope. The merchant reached into a cupboard and produced – a T-shirt.

This was contraband, Beijing-style. The forbidden T-shirt said, in Chinese, "I'm fed up. Don't bug me." Authorities had banned it and a dozen others. In the summer of 1991, it was now officially forbidden to be bored, alienated, nihilistic or sarcastic – or at least to say so on a T-shirt. "They banned everything that had a possible political meaning," said the merchant's wife, who lay sprawled, sipping a cup of cold tea, on the narrow bed in a back room.

With Chinese unable to mourn their dead, some bored, alienated, nihilistic and sarcastic university students had come up with the idea of protest T-shirts. The product just happened to coincide with a government propaganda blitz commemorating the 70th anniversary of the Chinese Communist Party.

People snapped them up, according to the *Beijing Evening News*, which approvingly called them "culture shirts" before it realized they were politically incorrect. "Your understanding of them depends on your cultural level," the merchant's wife explained, holding up a T-shirt with a classical Chinese phrase: "Heaven made me, so I must be of use." She said student dissidents wore that one to assert their self-worth in the face of mass expulsions and job blacklists.

Others, all in Chinese, said, "Sick and tired," "Everything's a failure," "Care only about getting rich," and "Life sucks." My favorite bore a standard Maoist slogan in handsome calligraphy, "Fear neither hardship nor death." Then, thumbing its nose at authorities, it added a flippant "And we don't fear YOU, either."

The Bureau of Industry and Commerce condemned the T-shirts as "decadent." It raided the factory that printed them, confiscating silk-screening equipment. Police also raided T-shirt shops. At the one I visited, the shirt censors had fined the merchant and confiscated his stock. But the merchant had more T-shirts tucked away, and continued to sell them, at inflated prices. The police returned and doubled the fine. The merchant had more T-shirts tucked away – and raised his prices again. The police were now demanding that he reveal his contraband source. "We're just going to say a salesman walked in and sold them to us," said the merchant's wife with a shrug. "How would we know who he was?"

Despite the ban, some people still wore them. I stopped a young man in sunglasses who sauntered by wearing the one with "I'm fed up. Don't bug me." To break the ice, I asked where he got it. He motioned toward a street of shops. "But they're banned now," he said, trying to save me a futile trip.

Was he a student or a worker? "I'm a soldier," he said, hastily adding that he hadn't taken part in the 1989 massacre. I told him I knew other soldiers who were ashamed to be seen in their army uniforms. Was that why he wasn't wearing his? True to the spirit of his T-shirt, he snapped, "Don't ask so many questions."

When pinning a white flower on your jacket got you ten years, what was the point of protesting? In the post-Tiananmen repression, people kept their opinions to themselves. Instead, they concentrated on getting rich. "People haven't forgotten," said Wang Dan. "June 4th is buried deeply in people's hearts, but there's no need to talk about it incessantly."

I first met Wang Dan at Tiananmen Square back when his idea for a hunger strike had galvanized a nation. Someone had asked him then if he was afraid of going to prison. He had just smiled. The night of the massacre, he was asleep in his dorm at Beijing University. When he learned he was number one on the Most-Wanted List of student leaders, he fled to northeast China, then doubled back to Shanghai and Nanking. He returned to Beijing, after naively convincing himself that he had committed no crime. On July 2, 1989, on his way to meet a Taiwanese journalist, a dozen plainclothes policemen waylaid Wang Dan on a busy street and pushed him into an unmarked car

At his closed-door trial, the thin, olive-skinned student was sentenced to four years in prison. He spent months in solitary confinement in Qincheng Prison, north of Beijing. Later he was transferred to Beijing Number 2 Prison, where he operated a knitting loom and made glass flowers. On February 17, 1993, the government released him on parole, four months early.

"I had no warning," he said, when I went to his parents' apartment to see him the day he was freed. Prison officials had simply called him back from his regular afternoon walk and told him he was free to go home. In a navy sweater, baggy gray pants and black cloth shoes, Wang Dan, then 23, looked much the same as in Tiananmen Square, minus his hunger-striker headband. His longish hair still tended to fall over his eyes. His only new item was a Chinese-made watch. "It's a present from my parents," he said. "I was not allowed to wear a watch in prison."

Sitting on the living room sofa, Wang Dan said his "greatest dream" was to continue the fight for democracy. "I have no regrets at all about anything I did, including the four years in prison. Perhaps I learned some lessons."

I went back to his home three months later, to see how he was doing. He now looked like a young entrepreneur. He was wearing a tie, contact lenses and, on his belt, a beeper. There was no contradiction, he told me, between the pursuit of wealth and the pursuit of freedom. Indeed, one was impossible without the other, he added.

"Without democracy, you can't protect your property. Without money, you can't build democracy," he said. "If I have a chance to go into business, I won't hesitate," he said. "But I don't see any opportunity right now."

During his years in prison, Wang Dan had marked each anniversary of the Tiananmen Massacre with a 24-hour hunger strike. That year, his first year back home, he said he would fast again. "I plan to do so every June 4th for the rest of my life."

I asked him if he had ever gone back to Tiananmen Square. He told me he had gone once, alone, at night. The memories had flooded back – the thrill of mesmerizing the crowds with his impassioned speeches, then the shocked pain of losing classmates who died in the crackdown. Wang Dan hadn't returned to the square since.

No one dared give him a job. Beijing University, where he had been a freshman in the history department, refused to take him back. He attended the university's 95th anniversary celebrations anyway. Plainclothes police dogged him every step of the way, including one overzealous agent who walked so close they bumped shoulders. Wang Dan never said a word. Neither did the agent.

On Qing Ming, the annual festival when Chinese tend the graves of loved ones, he and another student activist paid their respects to Wen Jie, a Tiananmen leader who died in prison of cancer. At the cemetery, six policemen stuck right beside Wang Dan and his friend until they gave up and left.

Mostly, he stayed in his parents' cramped fifth-floor apartment, strumming his guitar and listening to Michael Jackson tapes. To continue his education, he enrolled in a correspondence course at the University of California at Berkeley. In his bedroom, Wang Dan displayed two photos, one of Michael Jackson, the other of himself posing at an executive-style desk that belonged to a tycoon friend. "I sat in the chair to see how it would feel to have money," he said. He handed me his new business card. It said, "Wang Dan, Free Man."

Authorities rearrested Wang Dan in 1995 and sentenced him to 11 more years. Among his crimes: enrolling in that correspondence course. During his trial, I stood with other reporters outside a nondescript Beijing courthouse, catching a glimpse of him as he was whisked away in a police jeep. He waved jauntily.

History was repeating itself. Sixteen years earlier, as a news assistant for the *New York Times*, I had stood outside the same Beijing courthouse when Wei Jingsheng had gone on trial. The charge then was the same as for Wang Dan: "counter-revolutionary propaganda and incitement."

Both young men had enraged Deng Xiaoping. In 1978, Wei Jingsheng, then a 29-year-old electrician, had stuck up posters at Democracy Wall, daring to criticize Deng by name. My job back then for the *Times* included checking Democracy Wall, a dusty brick expanse not far from Tiananmen Square, where China's first dissidents were pasting up essays and commentaries. I remember how electrifying Wei's poster was. After a closed-door trial in which he served as his own defense lawyer, he was sentenced to 15 years.

Like Wang Dan, Wei Jingsheng was released on parole a few months early. And like Wang Dan, he didn't behave himself. During this brief period of freedom, Wei helped me connect with democracy activists in the provinces. He met frequently with reporters and dissidents. And he conferred with John Shattuck, the top U.S. State Department official in charge of human rights. On April 1, 1994, authorities re-arrested Wei Jingsheng and sentenced him to another 14 years in prison. The double draconian sentences transformed him into China's most prominent dissident.

Human rights activists abroad lobbied hard for Wei's release. In November, 1997, my successor, Rod Mickleburgh, called me in

Toronto to say that Wei Jingsheng had just been freed again, this time for "medical reasons," and was on his way to the United States.

"Medical parole" was a brand new tactic. It was a clever, face-saving way for Beijing to rid itself of the toxic waste of dissent while gaining approval ratings with Washington. As an extra bonus, China didn't even have to buy the one-way plane ticket. The U.S. State Department paid for it, business class, of course.

After Wei's arrival in New York, I made a date to meet him for lunch at a Manhattan restaurant called Jimmy Sung's. When Wei arrived, the Chinese staff was momentarily stunned. "It's such an honor to meet you," gasped a waiter, ushering us into a private VIP room. The maître d', who had seen the television footage of Wei reunited with his youngest sister and her infant son, beamed. "Your nephew has ears just like yours!" he said. Wei smiled back, revealing a set of teeth ruined by 18 years in the Chinese gulag. "I just hope he doesn't suffer like me," said Wei. "That's why we're doing this. It's for the next generation."

In his first two months of freedom, Wei Jingsheng had addressed France's National Assembly, been awarded the Sakharov Prize by the European Parliament, met Bill Clinton and partied with Richard Gere. New York Mayor Rudolph Giuliani assigned him two police officers as bodyguards. They accompanied him to Gere's latest movie, *Red Corner*, about an American lawyer caught in the nightmare of the Chinese legal system.

"Did they really treat you like that?" one bodyguard asked.

"That's just the beginning," Wei told him.

It was Chinese New Year's Eve, so I ordered a whole bottle of Wei's favorite Shaoxing rice wine. Word of the famous dissident's arrival had already spread to the kitchen. The chef, all smiles, came out to shake hands. We asked him to make us his tastiest dishes. As Wei sipped hot wine, we munched on a fiery appetizer of fried green chilies with tiny fermented black soybeans and garlic. Gong Bao Chicken, with red chili peppers and crunchy peanuts, was next. That was followed by a golden consommé garnished with a cloud of minced squab, served in a bamboo cup. Sautéed shrimp, home-style bean curd, then honeyed ham sandwiches on soft white bread, an authentic Yunnan dish, followed. "I'm not allowed to eat ham," said Wei, biting into a delectable sandwich. "My American doctor gave me two thick books filled with what I can't eat."

Wei was never one for obeying orders. When his jailers brought the "medical parole" papers, he refused to sign unless they let him take out the $50,000 he had won, as co-recipient with Nelson Mandela, of the Gleitsman International Activist Award. How long had it taken Beijing to cave in? I wondered. "Two hours," he said, lighting up the first of six Marlboros.

He confessed that he was tired of giving interviews. "Everyone always asks the same questions." I felt a twinge of professional mortification. *Fine*, I thought, and took a deep breath. "Considering you've spent most of your adult life in solitary confinement, how's your sex life?"

"Where would I have time for that?" he said, momentarily putting down his tumbler of Shaoxing rice wine.

"Wouldn't a unilingual American girlfriend be the fastest way to learn English?" I persisted.

"Perhaps I'll try it," said Wei Jingsheng, blushing.

It was January 26, 1998. Naturally, we couldn't help talking about Clinton's escapades with a certain White House intern. Wei's first glimpse of democracy both impressed and appalled him. He was amazed that a busy man like Clinton spent so much energy on someone like Monica Lewinsky. "Of course, Chairman Mao had a lot of girlfriends, too," said Wei.

He was living off his Gleitsman award and using it to support a mutual friend, Zhang Lin (Forest Zhang). Wei had introduced me to Forest, who in turn had helped me meet peasant activists in Anhui Province. Forest, who was married with one child, had subsequently spent four years in a labor camp, in part for taking me to Anhui. He, too, was now living in exile in New York. His wife and child were still stuck in China.

I worried about how long the Gleitsman money would last them. Wei Jingsheng told me Columbia University had given him a free dorm room and office. "I don't spend much," he said. "I'll eat this with you. But then I'll go home tonight and have a bowl of instant noodles."

The maître d', a stooped man in his 60s, suddenly appeared in the doorway to our private room. He was crying. "I read about Tiananmen in the newspaper on the subway in New York that day," he said, gulping back his tears. "It was as if our own children were being killed. They were crueler than a foreign enemy."

We stopped eating. Wei Jingsheng nodded gravely. When the maître d' collected himself and left the room, Wei whispered, "That's why I don't usually go to Chinese restaurants."

The fortune cookies arrived. I jokingly urged him to take one to see what the future held. He declined. He already knew what would happen. "The situation is changing rapidly," he said solemnly. "Ordinary people, even Party members, have reached the limits of their tolerance."

We couldn't eat another bite. The waiter packed up two bulging doggy bags. In China, Wei always took home leftovers. "No one else would," he said. "They were afraid to lose face. But I never cared about that." At least for one night in New York, Wei wouldn't be eating instant noodles.

In April, 1998, Beijing sent Wang Dan into exile, too. Again, the pretext was "medical parole." My friend Lena Sun, the former Beijing correspondent for the *Washington Post*, snagged the first interview with Wang Dan and let me tag along. We met him at the Harvard Club in New York, where he was juggling a number of offers from Ivy League universities.

Orville Schell, dean of Berkeley's graduate school of journalism, gave us all a brief tour of the Harvard Club's stuffed rhino and warthog trophies. "That was shot by Teddy Roosevelt," said Schell, pointing at the stuffed head of an African elephant.

"Beijing University should have a club like this," said Wang Dan, suitably awed.

After seven years in jail, he had arrived in the United States with only the clothes on his back. He didn't even have an overcoat. When the stuffy Harvard Club wouldn't allow any photos inside, Wang Dan had to stand on the street for our photographer. It was a chilly spring morning, so I lent him my London Fog trench-coat, which was two sizes too small. Both the *Post* and the *Globe* ran photos of Wang Dan, wearing my tight trenchcoat over his shapeless gray Chinese cotton jacket.

Wang was getting feelers from Harvard, Yale, Columbia, Brown and Berkeley. "It's a bit like the first-draft choice in professional sports," said Schell wryly. "It's very difficult for him. What is Berkeley? What is Harvard? What is Yale? What is Democrat? What is Republican? What is Oldsmobile? What is Buick? It's sort of pluralism gone mad."

The great leap from the gulag to the West was exhilarating. After all, at 29, he was "still a virgin," he acknowledged with a shy laugh. "I really like the freedom here in America, the chances for individuals to make their own choices, to make the most of opportunities," he said. He was most impressed by the respect for the individual, citing the sidewalk curb-cuts in New York that made it easier for handicapped people to cross a street.

In prison in Jinzhou, in northeast China, Wang Dan's jailers had even dictated his wake-up time. Because of his prominence, he had been exempted from producing electrical switches with the other inmates. Instead, he spent his days reading and tending a vegetable plot.

He cried only once, he said, when his mother, a researcher at Beijing's Museum of Revolutionary History, was jailed for 50 days for speaking out on his behalf. He said he had accepted "medical parole" because he couldn't bear to see his aging parents make the ten-hour trip on jammed trains each month to visit him.

On Friday, April 17, 1998, the prison warden told Wang Dan he would be sent into exile in eight hours. His parents, there on their monthly visit, found out at the same time. Wang Dan was driven through the night to Beijing in an 11-car convoy. Cruelly, the authorities made him travel in a separate vehicle from his parents. "They had to treat me badly one last time," he said quietly.

The convoy reached the Beijing airport at dawn, three hours before his flight. His older sister met the family there. There had been no time for anyone to prepare any parting gifts, not even money. Wang Dan didn't have the watch his parents had given him the first time he was released from prison. So his father slipped off his own watch and gave it to his son. As his parents embraced him for the last time, they urged him to study hard.

Wang Dan kept his promise to his parents. He studied intensive English that first summer, then enrolled at Harvard to finish his Chinese history degree. But his studies were only a temporary priority. He would always fight for democracy, he said, because he felt so guilty about those who died at Tiananmen Square.

In 1998, as autumn stiffened the last rosebushes in Niagara-on-the-Lake, about 60 Chinese dissidents converged on that sleepy Ontario town, a short drive from Niagara Falls. Wei Jingsheng had summoned them, and they flew in from the United States, the Netherlands, Germany, France, Britain, Japan and Hong Kong. He had also invited me along as an observer, the only Western journalist present.

The retreat was supposed to hammer out a new long-term strategy. This was a precarious time for Chinese activists. Donations were drying up. The pro-democracy movement was riven by competing egos, splinter factions and mutual suspicions. The dissidents yearned for a Nelson Mandela, a Dalai Lama, a symbolic leader who could unite them to continue the struggle. Some hoped that leader might be Wei Jingsheng, who had been nominated several times for the Nobel Peace Prize.

The weekend of soul-searching at the luxurious Prince of Wales Hotel coincided with the first anniversary of Wei's expulsion from China. Each dissident had paid his or her own airfare, but the rooms, meals and a side trip to Niagara Falls had been donated by Si Wai Lai, the hotel's owner. She herself had escaped from Communist China years earlier by swimming through the sharks to Hong Kong and now swanned around Niagara-on-the-Lake in a Rolls Royce.

In a chintz-draped conference room, the delegates sucked on hard candies and listened to speech after droning speech. Everyone sat sedately at rows of white-draped narrow tables, supplied with pots of hot tea and notepads and pencils. Wei Jingsheng, naturally, ignored the hotel's smoking ban.

Fax, phone and e-mail now linked dissidents on the outside with dissidents on the inside. Everyone gasped when Wei suddenly announced that Wang Ce, a democracy activist, had just been arrested for sneaking back into China. He had been trying to bring $1,000 in cash to the China Democratic Party, a fledgling group trying to register as the country's first opposition party.

That sparked a flurry of faxed press releases announcing the arrest. The dissidents cut their planned speeches and debated whether or not it was worthwhile to risk returning to China. Most agreed that it was.

The delegates reflected the dissident diaspora. They were mostly male, middle-aged, battle-scarred veterans of the pro-Democracy struggle. Liu Qing, who wore a dark suit and striped tie, had spent ten years in prison for publishing the secret transcript to Wei's 1979 trial. I hadn't seen Liu Qing since 1978, when I had watched him surreptitiously mimeographing underground journals in his bedroom to sell at Democracy Wall. He now lived in New York and was an executive of Human Rights in China, a dissident group. During a break, we talked about his brother, Liu Nianchun, a friend of Forest Zhang's and a labor activist who was still in a labor camp, partly for giving interviews in China to Lena Sun and me. (Liu Nianchun was subsequently exiled on "medical parole," two months later, with his family, to the United States.)

That weekend in Niagara-on-the-Lake, the delegates acclaimed Wei Jingsheng as chairman of their newly formed group, called Chinese Democracy Movement Overseas. At a gala dinner, in a private room dripping with crystal chandeliers, we sat on slip-covered chairs tied with large gold bows and ate purée of fresh pea soup, mesclun salad and smoked loin of Ontario pork. One dissident from Britain brought a large duty-free bottle of 12-year-old single malt Glenlivet. As Wei Jingsheng worked the room like a seasoned politician, everyone toasted the first anniversary of his freedom.

I wondered why Forest Zhang, our mutual dissident friend, wasn't there. It turned out he had secretly slipped back into China. Forest was arrested within days, apparently at a barber shop. Authorities claimed it was actually a brothel. It charged him with evading the border police and "hiring prostitutes." Maybe the government thought it could sully Forest's image that way. But then they made the mistake of arresting several other activists that month and laying the same charge of "hiring prostitutes." Like "medical parole," it rang a bit hollow after a while.

Forest Zhang got three more years in a labor camp. The leaders of the China Democratic Party were sentenced to terms of 11 to 13 years. Wang Ce, the other activist who had also sneaked back, got four years in jail.

Within hours of his sentencing, other activists announced the establishment of five more branches of the China Democratic Party. Then, on April 5, 1999, another exiled activist, Wang Xizhe, flew back to Beijing. At least, he tried to. Chinese authorities got wind in time and pressured the South Korean airliner he was on to divert him to Bangkok, and it did.

What was a dictatorship to do? It could toss dissidents into the gulag, but it had to free them when their terms were up. When it freed them, they wouldn't shut up. So it arrested them again. Then international condemnation grew too loud. So it exiled them. But then they just sneaked back in for another round of the gulag.

In 1999, I decided I had to sneak back in myself for another round. I wanted to see what was *really* going on.

2

Waterdown Village

Top: Root Shen with his second child, Sprout, whom he bought for $50 at the vegetable market in Waterdown Village. Photo: Jan Wong

It seemed apt that the first stop on my return journey in 1999 should be Waterdown, the village I visited on my very first reporting trip in 1988. Back then, I had set the pattern for my China reporting by evading government handlers and finding the village on my own. Authorities preferred controlled, quickie visits to designated villages. I had wanted a place I could hang around for a week.

A retired friend, Yao Yuexiu (Elegance Yao), had told me about Gaobei, literally, "north of the high land beside the water." Waterdown, as I had translated it, was an up-and-coming village in Zhejiang Province. As a microcosm of the changes sweeping the Chinese countryside, it had sounded promising. No foreigner had ever been there. Better yet, it lacked the government's Good Housekeeping Seal of Approval.

Just before the Autumn Moon Festival in 1988, Elegance and I had flown from Beijing south to Hangzhou, the closest city with an airport. We stayed in Shaoxing, the closest place with a hotel. Back then, Waterdown (population: 12,054) was a bucolic land of lush paddy fields, mirror-like ponds and graceful bamboo groves. Its sweet, unpolluted ponds yielded fish and freshwater pearls. Each year, the local peasants coaxed three crops from its fertile fields, two of rice and one of winter wheat. The site of the Yue Kingdom (fourth century BC), Waterdown still seemed part of China's Iron Age. Peasants hauled water from wells, lit lamps after dark and brewed earthen jugs of Shaoxing's famous yellow rice wine, the kind Wei Jingsheng liked so much.

In 1988, Waterdown was neither the richest nor the poorest village in the region. It had no street lights. Its two telephones were the old-fashioned kind you had to crank by hand. And no one had that 20th-century miracle, running water. But the old way of life was just beginning to change. After years as an agricultural backwater, Waterdown was taking advantage of its proximity to a major highway, a canal and a railway line. A couple of months before I arrived, the village built its first road to the outside world. Then the county government gave Waterdown the right to negotiate directly with foreign investors.

"They picked us because we're small and we have a bright future," said Yan Guanlong (Dragon Yan), the village's ambitious Communist Party Secretary. He had just returned from his first trip to Hong Kong to drum up investment. As he mused about the future, he sounded a bit like Lee Iaccoca. "We're just an average village right now. We want to be the very best."

The future of China's economic reforms hinged on a hundred thousand villages like Waterdown. Parts of it looked like a giant construction site. Peasants who once lazed about after the autumn harvest now earned cash in new village-run factories. But I soon learned that Waterdown also contained the seeds of new problems, including a growing gap between rich and poor.

Dragon Yan was a new-style Communist. He had read *Das Kapital,* not to overthrow capitalism, but to figure out how to make it happen. Class struggle was the last thing on his mind. "We don't care about politics anymore," he said, as we picked our way through a construction site. "We just concentrate on making money."

Waterdown planned to use industrial profits to mechanize agriculture. It already paid a few of its most skilled peasants the equivalent of a factory salary to handle all the fields. Except during the busy planting and harvesting seasons when everyone trooped out to the fields, its peasants had been transformed into industrial workers. Their ultimate dream was to let others do backbreaking labor.

"One day we'll hire people to farm our land," predicted one peasant.

China's new generation had new expectations. When I asked a 14-year-old named Zhang Weiqiang what he wanted to be when he grew up, he knew only what he didn't want to do.

"I don't want to farm," he said.

But who will plant his family's land?

"My little brother," he said promptly.

Prosperity was already at Waterdown's door. Young peasant women wore velvet skirts, pearls and high heels. The men smoked imported cigarettes. On the main street, peddlers sold previously unheard-of luxuries – expensive bananas shipped from the south and apples from the north. In the two years since Dragon Yan began running the village, average annual per capita income had risen 58 percent. When he gazed out his office window, he didn't see the paddy fields. He envisioned a shopping mall, several restaurants, a hotel, a theater and a billiards hall.

At 35, Dragon Yan was slim, almost skinny, with high cheek-bones and an open, honest face. He was on the Communist fast track, the youngest among the 63 village Party Secretaries in the county. Waterdown already was his third posting. He lived alone in a tiny room next to his office. His room was furnished with a narrow bed, a small desk and a bamboo bookshelf crammed with economic texts. The year before, his annual bonus had been 80 yuan ($10), a pittance compared to the 1,000-yuan bonus the peasants got working at the village manganese factory.

"As a cadre, I don't look for money," he said. "I look for satis-faction." As I wrote that down in my notebook, I wondered: Was Dragon Yan really a selfless Communist at heart, straight out of a Chinese propaganda magazine? Or was he too good to be true?

While prosperous villagers built new homes, his wife and seven-year-old son lived in Shaoxing, a 40-minute bike ride away. Dragon Yan's goal was to earn a college degree, by correspondence, in eco-nomics. To keep up, he rose at 5:30 a.m. to study. He took only one day off every six months. Days would go by before he had a moment to see his family. His wife, a typist and a former district volleyball champion, complained that their son scarcely recognized him. "It's difficult," Dragon Yan said. "But between my family and my work, my work is the main thing."

He wasn't above flirting, though. During one break, he cajoled his attractive young female assistant into singing a southern-style aria. She agreed, on condition he sing after her. When she finished, he grinned, pulled rank and declared it was time to get back to work.

For my 1988 trip to Waterdown, I budgeted 500 yuan in cash. Alas, I hadn't realized how much inflation had devalued the People's Money. Five hundred yuan was more than Chairman Mao's monthly salary in the 1970s, but by 1988, it wasn't enough to pay for more than two days in the renovated wing of the Shaoxing Hotel. Not if my friend and I wanted to eat, too. Nor was my American Express card any use. Credit cards weren't widely accepted until a few years later.

Apologizing to my retired friend, I took a mildewed room in the hotel's unrenovated wing, which came infested with creepy-crawly critters. But Elegance, who was physically frail with a long history of ailments, never complained. Until her husband wired us some emergency cash from Beijing, we subsisted on pickle soup and rice. Luckily, we could bulk up at lunch. Journalists aren't supposed to take freebies, but my ethics quickly dissolved each day at noon when village officials at Waterdown invited us to dine on freshwater crabs, braised fish and tiny sweet shrimp.

The other freebie gave me nightmares. Each afternoon, Dragon Yan's pretty assistant would peel me an apple when I sat down in the village meeting hall to interview someone. An apple, trucked all the way from the north of China, was a luxury in Waterdown. In rural China, polite hosts, no matter how poor, always gave guests the best that they had. And polite guests, especially reporters who wanted to keep coming back day after day, always accepted.

The problem was, for hygienic reasons, Chinese always peeled fruit. But with no running water in Waterdown, peeled fruit just compounded the risk of death by apples. The beautiful young assistant, who had glamorously long, none-too-clean nails, rarely washed her hands. (And neither did I under the circumstances, so nothing personal.)

But when she finished peeling the apple, she'd always plunk it down upon a dirt-encrusted, fly-blown coffee table. To refuse was out of the question. Actually, proper Chinese etiquette demanded I *pretend* to refuse it. Polite guests never accepted something the first time it was offered. Or the second. The third time was borderline okay. But you always accepted in the end. The young assistant thought I had exquisite manners when I kept refusing to eat her apples. Eventually, like every good guest, I acquiesced. As I munched away, I closed my eyes, and prayed to the god of the intestinal tract.

An upset tummy would be annoying anytime, but in Waterdown, it would have been disastrous, or at least, seriously gross. After a visit to the village's pitch-black, windowless latrines, oozing with maggots and slime, Elegance and I both aimed for complete system shutdown. Each day, we wouldn't drink anything until we could get back to our very own creepy-crawly toilet at the hotel. At least it flushed.

Shen Aying (Noble Shen) had heard Elegance and I were there. We spotted her peeking at us from the narrow doorway of her adobe home. When we stopped to chat, she invited us into her windowless two-room house. At 62, Noble Shen was a tiny woman with short gray hair and a sad smile. She was one of Waterdown's poorer residents. Her neighbors were all building new houses, but she expected to live in hers until she died. She had raised her six children there. Even on a warm autumn day, its stone floors felt cold and damp. A slit in the roof let in the only light. Her "toilet" was a covered wooden bucket beside the bed. Each morning, she lugged it across a bridge to empty into a putrid stone holding tank, to be used later for fertilizer. The more prosperous denizens of Waterdown had gas stoves, but Noble Shen burned wood and rice straw. Above her primitive oven, she had pasted a paper slogan: "Get richer every day."

A five-minute walk away, her neighbor, Wang Chunrong (Springtime Wang), was getting richer. He was once so poor that when he married, he had moved in with his in-laws, a significant loss of face for a man. His two children had even taken his wife's surname. But fortune was smiling on Springtime now. He was part of Waterdown's new up-and-coming middle class. At 42, he had swapped his plow for a salaried job. With the 100 yuan he earned as village administrator and the income his wife and daughter got from working in the factories during the slack season, the family's monthly income was 300 yuan, triple that of Noble Shen's.

A lean man with a salt-and-pepper brush cut, he grinned broadly as he showed off his new six-room home. He had spent every penny of his savings to build it. Some rooms were still empty. "I can't afford furniture yet," he said, apologetically. He dreamed of buying a rug and a sofa. He also planned to lay a stone patio in his front yard. "After that," he said, "I'll be satisfied."

In Waterdown, the economic reforms enabled the young and the strong to prosper, but locked older peasants like Noble Shen into poverty. China's push for profits was splintering its peasants into new classes – the new rich and the newly dispossessed. In a tightly knit village like Waterdown, this income gap had far greater resonance than in the cities. If someone here bought a shiny new bike, the whole village knew. If someone cooked meat, the neighbors could smell it.

Noble Shen could afford meat only every third day. So when her neighbor, Shen Agen (Root Shen), had a fancy meal, her mouth watered. Root Shen felt no obligation toward Noble Shen. Although they shared the same surname, they weren't related. He was a brash, mustachioed man of 32, with a hint of a pot belly. As a building contractor, he was raking it in during the economic boom. But past persecutions of the rich made him cautious. He admitted to an income of 500 yuan a month, more than Deng Xiaoping earned. When I ran that figure by Springtime Wang, he laughed. "He's afraid of showing his wealth. Why, he has at least 50,000 yuan in the bank."

Root Shen wasn't shy, though, about conspicuous consumption. When Elegance and I asked if we could see his house, he even let Springtime Wang tag along. "I have *two* houses," Root boasted, waving me into his courtyard. He didn't mean that he had two houses in different places. He meant he had two houses, back to back. "We eat in one and sleep in the other," he said, proudly.

Somehow we all ended up in his cavernous pink master bedroom. Springtime Wang, whose house was still bare, stared enviously at the chandelier, parquet floors, color television, tape recorder and white lacquered bedroom furniture. An array of fancy perfume bottles decorated the top of the mirrored vanity. There was even an ensuite bathroom. Elegance and I checked it out, naturally. Compared to the slug-infested communal latrines, it looked heavenly – even without plumbing. Until Waterdown installed running water, Root Shen had to carry a bucket upstairs each time he wanted to flush. Still, we were impressed, perhaps too impressed. Root Shen grew defensive. "I'm not the only one who's rich," he said. "More than ten homes here have toilets."

He and his tall, striking wife, Tang Jufen (Chrysanthemum Tang), had one son. "I'd like to have a daughter, too," she said. She hinted they wouldn't mind violating the one-child policy. A fine of several thousand yuan was insignificant to a couple like them. Unlike other village women her age, Chrysanthemum didn't work in the factories. Root Shen could support her in style. Instead, she spent her time cooking fragrant six-course meals that drove the neighbors crazy. At lunch that day, Root Shen had dined on two kinds of fish, sautéed shrimp, boiled fresh crabs and stir-fried pork, all washed down with warm Shaoxing wine.

He was a third-grade dropout who had balked at working in the collectivized fields. At 16, he became a migrant bricklayer. Officials turned a blind eye as long as he turned over half his income. As the economy prospered, so did Root Shen. Three years earlier, he began hiring others. Now his construction team of 50 was building a 10,000-square-foot factory near Shanghai.

Root dreamed of retiring early. In the meantime, he said, "I want to make more and more money." He had just opened a convenience store. He'd figured it all out: while he was away at a site, Chrysanthemum would run it. And their six-year-old son, his teeth already blackened, could help himself to all the free candy he could eat.

What did the next generation of peasants believe in? At Waterdown Junior High, its 324 students could gaze through the school's airy windows and see ducks splashing in pristine ponds – and the new factory smokestacks beckoning them. With so much exciting economic development going on right under the students' noses, it was hard keeping them in school. Zhu Shenggen, who had been teaching Chinese literature for 19 years, was worried. "Now all we stress is money," he said. "So they think, why bother to study?"

In one class, a 14-year-old student told me he couldn't wait to get out of high school. Zhang Jianchang's greatest ambition, he said, was a factory job. He already had a shopping list typical of a young Chinese man about to get married. "I want to buy furniture, cupboards, beds …" He broke off in embarrassment as his classmates tittered.

Many students were dropping out. "The factories keep coming to us, asking for workers," said Chen Xingqi (Chen Sing-chee), the school's affable principal. Reluctantly, Waterdown Junior High was cooperating. To meet the demand of industry, the school was sacrificing a cherished Communist ideal: equality. In 1989, it planned to start streaming its graduating class. The brighter students would concentrate on passing the entrance exams to senior high school. The slower ones would learn technical skills and go straight into the factories.

"I hope I can go to senior high," said Shi Yamei, a shy 16-year-old who loved learning English. Perhaps she would, but the odds were not good. Many would not even complete three years of junior high. Only half would be accepted into senior high. Perhaps only one in the whole village would attend university.

Education had never been much of a priority in Waterdown. The local leaders were mostly illiterate. Before the boom, peasants had chafed at paying 80 yuan a year in tuition, roughly two-thirds of one month's income. After all, when their children graduated, their only prospect had been farm labor. Now, the burgeoning economy created new opportunities and new problems. The previous year, Waterdown had plowed some of its profits into education. It had constructed a brand new two-storey building, but it didn't have enough for a library or lab equipment. Nor did it pay the teachers very well. Morale was becoming a problem at Waterdown High.

In the rest of China, 40 million school-age children had already dropped out of school to work by the late 1980s. To encourage Waterdown students to stay in school, the village was using its new wealth to waive tuition. It fined dropouts 200 yuan, and it rewarded 20 yuan each to those who managed to graduate.

Waterdown had wined and dined me for a week. It would have been the height of rudeness to ask for a bill at the end, after the emergency loan finally arrived from Elegance's husband. But I could repay them another way. On the last day, we hit the New China Book Store in Shaoxing, scooping up armloads of novels, dictionaries, and history, geography, English and science texts. We piled them in the trunk of a taxi and delivered them in the pouring rain. With a library at Waterdown Junior High, maybe one more kid might stay in school.

I never did get sick from the peeled apples, but Elegance succumbed the day we left. By then we were already ensconced in a nice Hangzhou hotel – with an insect-free flush toilet – awaiting our flight back to Beijing.

On my trip back to Waterdown in 1999, I no longer had to stay in a mildewed hotel room in Shaoxing. A new superhighway had shrunk the drive from Hangzhou to Waterdown to a mere 90 minutes compared with four hours a decade earlier. Along the way, I gaped at peasant castles – I'm not sure what else to call them – in pastel shades of strawberry, pistachio and aqua. Surrounded by fields of bok choy and spring onions, they rose three or four storeys high, with arched windows of tinted blue glass. Each peasant castle was topped by a post-medieval turret and a huge TV antenna.

In 1999, Waterdown could no longer be described as bucolic. It was an unrecognizable jumble of shops, nouveau-riche homes and imposing factories. I couldn't remember where anyone lived, so I headed straight for Waterdown Junior High. Alas, perhaps too many kids had dropped out; it was now the village clinic.

Someone there directed me to Springtime Wang's home. I found his door padlocked. (Peasants often used padlocks, which were cheap and, of course, didn't require a locksmith to install.) His next-door neighbor told me Springtime was out, working at Waterdown's medical gauze factory. By chance, the neighbor also happened to be Waterdown's current Communist Party Secretary. Wang Xinyou, who was lunching with three friends, was slightly startled, especially by my tall and hairy film-crew entourage.

Robin Benger and Alister Bell were consummate professionals who had worked in the Ukraine, Nicaragua, Beirut, Iran and Iraq. But on this day they looked like a couple of bumbling tourists. (I nicknamed them Tweedledum and Tweedledumber because I had to help them with everything, including finding the public latrines. They dubbed me the Wongster, because I wasn't too gracious about it.)

To allay the Party Secretary's suspicions, I babbled an explanation about visiting Waterdown 11 years earlier. He relaxed when the village accountant, part of a curious crowd that trailed us into the Party Secretary's dining room, remembered my earlier visit and vouched for me. The Party Secretary then invited me to join him and his buddies at lunch. I declined, as befits an insignificant female in rural China. Instead, I sat slightly off to one side, which further reassured the Party Secretary.

As he ate, I asked about the latest developments in Waterdown. Between bites of fish and fresh bamboo shoots, he told me that the village now owned 190 enterprises. The new superhighway had changed the economics of the region. Instead of an isolated hamlet, it was now just a few hours drive from the great metropolis of Shanghai. Running water was installed in the entire village in 1993; 90 percent of households had flush toilets; one-third of the families had telephones and by 2000, about 70 percent of the village would be wired. Most impressive of all, that far-out dream of Waterdown's peasants had actually come true. They no longer tilled their own fields. Instead, they hired peasants from poorer villages to do the work.

After lunch, the Party Secretary directed me to Root Shen's home, or rather, his back-to-back homes. They no longer seemed so grand compared to the peasant castles on the superhighway. Nor was Root Shen still one of the richest men in Waterdown. His net worth was probably 100,000 yuan, a fortune back in 1988. But it was nothing now compared to Waterdown's richest, some of whom had assets of 15 million yuan ($1.9 million).

Root Shen was still in construction, but his team had shrunk to a dozen workers. "I'm falling behind. There's too much competition," he sighed. "Everybody's undercutting everybody. If I bid 800 yuan (for a job), someone else will bid 700 yuan. I'm already losing money." Nor had his convenience store idea worked out. "Chrysanthemum is illiterate," he explained. "When I wasn't here, she couldn't manage the place."

Root Shen was dressed in a soiled Western suit which still bore the label on the outside of one sleeve, to prove it was store-bought and not homemade. In the next room, friends played mahjong while his wife, Chrysanthemum, served tea. As Alister filmed him, Root Shen bowed to a poster of the Kitchen God pasted above his stove, and lit offerings of candles and incense, hoping that his fortunes might improve.

I was a bit out of practice with visits to the Chinese countryside, and had forgotten to implement total system shutdown, so Chrysanthemum showed me to the main-floor bathroom. Robin and Alister couldn't understand why I came out gushing over the plumbing.

The Shens' only son, now 18, worked as a mechanic. I asked them if they had ever had that second child. "We adopted a daughter," said Root Shen. "I bought her at the vegetable market."

Six months after my 1988 visit, he had encountered two peasant women in their 40s, standing at the market, holding a week-old infant. On impulse, Root Shen peeked at the baby. He was instantly smitten. He gave them 400 yuan and told the women he never wanted to see them again. If they came back, he said, he would deny ever meeting them.

When he brought the baby home, Chrysanthemum was angry at first. "She wanted to have her own," Root Shen explained. Waterdown authorities weren't happy, either. They fined the Shens 2,000 yuan for having a second child. Root grudgingly paid up. But he balked when the village ordered Chrysanthemum to have her tubes tied. Eventually, the authorities backed down. "I wouldn't agree to the operation," said Root. "We didn't have our *own* second child. I adopted her because I felt sorry for her. I knew she wasn't wanted."

But Chrysanthemum soon fell in love with the baby, too. They named her Miao, which means "sprout." Root proudly showed me photos of her. I asked if I could meet Miao. We strolled down the lane to the village elementary school, where she was in music class. Miao came out into the schoolyard in a powder-blue track suit. At ten, she had shiny dark eyes and two fat glossy braids bobbing out from the sides of her head. She was terribly shy and kept looking at the ground. "She's so obedient and smart," Root gushed. "Every year she wins awards at school." I thought of the Ten Minute Baby, and felt very happy for Miao and her father.

Root Shen later walked me over to Noble Shen's. Her door was padlocked. "She must be out playing mahjong or praying at the temple," he said. I noticed she finally had windows. I peered inside and could tell that even she now had running water and electricity.

Before leaving Waterdown, I stopped by the medical gauze factory to look for Springtime Wang. He came running out of a workshop, wiping his hands on a rag. He and his wife, who also worked at the factory, insisted I go back to his home for tea. Springtime's dreams had come true, too, I noticed. He had paved his courtyard, and his home was no longer empty. There was a green velvet sofa, two outsized matching armchairs and a bedroom set, including a red velvet headboard.

I asked how Dragon Yan, the dynamic Party Secretary, was doing. I figured he would be 46 by now. Springtime Wang told me Dragon Yan had been transferred to the municipality of Shaoxing. Then he lowered his voice. "He made a *jingji cuowu* (an economic mistake)," said Springtime, using a euphemism for corruption. How much money? I asked. Springtime shook his head. "He's still under investigation."

So even someone as selfless, as upright, as pure as Dragon Yan had succumbed to the new money culture. Springtime himself looked much older and heavier than I remembered. At 55, his hair had turned white and he seemed sad. I remembered he had been the top administrator in 1988. Perhaps he had made his own "economic mistake." Why else would he be slaving away in a factory at the end of his career? Looking at his white hair, I couldn't bring myself to ask.

By 1999, corruption had seeped down to the grassroots level. As I left Waterdown, I recalled something Root Shen had said when we saw the current village Party Secretary cycling past us, taking calls on his cellphone. "All he does is gamble," said Root. "He has two grown sons who don't work. They gamble, too. The Party Secretary is very corrupt."

3

Big Mound Village

Top: With schoolchildren in 1989 in Gansu, one of China's poorest provinces.
Photo: Private collection

Bottom: Shopping for Zhejiang-tailored clothes in 1999 in Big Red Door, an enclave of migrant workers in Beijing.
Photo: Jan Wong

Seven hundred miles to the north, another village was prospering, deep in rural Hubei Province. But unlike Waterdown, this one resembled a middle-class Vancouver suburb. It had two-storey homes of glassed-in breakfast nooks and lush rose gardens. But it also had armed guards, barred windows and German Shepherds on the prowl.

I'd come to Da Qiu Zhuang (Big Mound Village) in 1989, intrigued, after Chinese friends told me its half-starved peasants had invested wisely and were now living better than cabinet ministers in Beijing. But was it really that simple? In my Maoist student days, I'd plowed through all three volumes of *Das Kapital*. The workers of Big Mound Village had studied Marx, too. "Our situation is no different from capitalists exploiting workers," said Zhao Guanghai, a skinny, 21-year-old migrant worker in the dingy auto-body shop.

This was Big Mound's dirty secret. About 5,000 badly paid migrant workers kept the village's 226 enterprises humming, 24 hours a day, 7 days a week. This was the unspoken side of China's economic reform, where the rich got really rich and the poor got a bit less poor.

A historian stumbling onto Big Mound would be reminded of our own Industrial Revolution, compressed in time. There was the same unbridled greed, the same emerging new-rich class and the same miserable mass of impoverished workers. Yet this was fledgling capitalism with a twist, "socialist capitalism," as Yu Guangyuan, an eminent Chinese economist, called it. Villagers owned all the factories collectively and hired others to toil for them.

Migrant Worker Zhao wiped his grimy hands. "We have no future here. They don't let outsiders get rich," he said. Although he was from a neighboring county, he had no hope of marrying a local girl. To prevent ownership dilution, Big Mound informally banned intermarriage between villagers and outsiders. The 600 village families monopolized management jobs, paid themselves comfortable salaries and bestowed full university scholarships on each of their children. Outsiders like Migrant Worker Zhao were paid for piece-work and lived in segregated housing.

Big Mound needed outside labor, but also feared it. After a rash of burglaries, it hired a private 108-member "economic militia," or 1 armed guard for every 33 villagers. "People know we're rich," explained Li Fengzhuang, the village deputy manager, when I asked about the German Shepherds. "There's a lot of migrants. They come here to steal."

Like gated communities in Florida or South Africa or the Bahamas, managers like him barricaded themselves behind high brick walls. But instead of being surrounded by golf courses and country clubs, Big Mound's executive homes were in the midst of farm fields. Ordinary Big Mounders lived well, too, in centrally heated apartments with telephones, closed-circuit television and bathtubs. They even had hot running water, something the late Deng Xiaoping could count on just a couple of times a week. Almost every service was free, including electricity, hot water, heat, cooking gas, medical care and public school tuition. All Big Mounders got a rent-free apartment when they married.

Migrant workers, however, slept separately. Zhao Binghui, a 22-year-old newlywed from Inner Mongolia, lived in a dorm apart from his bride, who was also a migrant worker. Indeed, the village's only eyesores were the ramshackle dormitories of the 5,000 *waidi gongren* or "outside workers." In contrast to the villagers, the migrants lived 16 to a shack, sleeping on rough-hewn bunk beds

with only a small coal stove for heat in winter. Yellowing newspapers served as window curtains, and running water was an outdoor
tap, jutting straight up from the dirt.

Ten years ago, Big Mound was a desolate, low-lying alkaline
patch, 30 miles from the Bohai Sea. The place was so poor that
men had trouble finding brides. "I'd rather eat three years of chaff
than marry my daughter to Big Mound Village," went a local song.

In 1978, as economic reforms swept China, Big Mounders
pooled their savings to start a tiny sheet-metal factory. A decade
later they had 150 companies and marketing agents in 38 Chinese
cities. Then they invested $2.3 million to mechanize agriculture.
Where once everyone toiled in the fields, now nine peasants grew
enough wheat to feed the whole village.

Nearly half the women of Big Mound had become housewives.
Mao had once proclaimed, "Women hold up half of heaven." By
that, he meant that women should play an equally important role
in society. But the village was so prosperous, many of the women
spent their afternoons playing mahjong or having tea parties. "We're
rich," laughed Li Zhenge, a 38-year-old housewife.

Big Mound had unusually wide, paved streets, edged with brand
new lampposts and poplar saplings. The village was so proud of its
achievements that it built a huge reception center, with a giant
skylight and circular dance floor, to receive visitors. More than a
thousand had come in the past year, including Zhao Ziyang, then
Communist Party chief. But no one had ever asked to talk to the
outside workers.

In furtive conversations, the migrants told me that the village
foremen cursed and slapped them. They said they had to work
for three months on unpaid probation. Many grew discouraged
and quit before earning a cent. When the pay finally kicked in,
they said, it was at half the rate Big Mounders were paid for
similar work. Naturally there were no pension or health bene-
fits. If they lost a hand or a foot in a work-related accident, the
village gave them two and a half months pay and sent them on
their way.

Migrant Worker Zhao said he found it hard to save. Just as company stores squeezed workers all over the world, migrants here

spent nearly all their pay at the village-run canteens. "Rice and vegetables are really expensive here," said Migrant Worker Zhao.

When I began nosing around the wretched dormitories, Big Mound officials were first nervous, then furious. The village deputy manager abruptly ordered me to leave. "The visit is over," he announced grimly. As I got into my car, he reminded me that the migrants were much better off than at home. "If they don't like it," he said, "they can leave." He didn't have to say what everyone knew. Other Chinese were always ready to take their place.

The village deputy manager was right, of course. In the late 1980s and throughout the 1990s, more than 100 million peasants were pouring into China's cities in search of work. It was one of the biggest demographic changes in history. Outside workers built Beijing's skyscrapers and expressways. In the golden triangle around Shanghai, Hangzhou and Nanking, 10 million migrants worked in manufacturing and construction. In Guangdong Province, 10 million of its 60 million residents were outsiders.

Beijing, which had 12.7 million permanent legal residents, had an additional 3 million migrants who did all the dirty, dangerous and demeaning jobs. They worked as maids, cooks and garbage collectors. As "outside workers," they weren't allowed to rent housing within the city limits. As a result, separate communities, clustered by provincial dialect, sprang up on the edge of Beijing. There was one for maids from Anhui, another for construction workers from Henan, yet another for tailors from Zhejiang. The overcrowded enclaves of crude brick shacks, with mortar so weak you could chip away at it with your fingernail, reminded me of old-style ramshackle Chinatowns – except that we were already in China.

In the 1980s, Da Hong Men (Big Red Door), on the southern edge of Beijing's city limits, had been farm fields. In 1994 it was a little piece of Zhejiang Province. About 100,000 Zhejiangers lived here, speaking the distinctive southern dialect, drinking warm Shaoxing rice wine and churning out dresses, coats, suits and curtains for the residents of Beijing. It was a self-contained community that operated its own nurseries, clinics, garbage pickup and, for a time, its own militia.

One sweltering June day in 1994, I visited Big Red Door. Its main drag was chaotic with cars and swerving pedicabs. Restaurants offered seafood air-freighted from the coast. Peddlers sold lichees, pineapples, cigarettes and beer. In the heat of the afternoon, the air was rank with rotting watermelon rinds.

At a roadside stall, a young man leaped up from his bowl of noodles, grabbed a bottle of soy sauce from the table and screamed, "I'm going to kill you!" A peasant in a Mao jacket retreated a few steps. Then, like in the Wild West, five young toughs swaggered over, hands on hips. I had no idea what the dispute was over, but as they approached the peasant, a waitress managed to hustle him away. The young toughs hung around for a moment, then sauntered off to help themselves to dripping chunks of watermelon.

Across the street, police swarmed a minivan crammed with finished garments. Someone said the driver had been blocking traffic. In all, I counted six cops plus two squad cars full of more policemen nearby. Suddenly, a pot-bellied officer waded into the gawking crowd and began slapping and pushing everyone. I took a hit to my shoulders, and backed off to one side.

The Zhejiangers lived off their renowned talent with a needle and thread. Down one alley, I dropped into the tiny workshop of Zhang Xian. A spare man in his 40s, he was making burgundy leather bomber jackets with his wife, their 20-year-old daughter and three hired seamstresses. He and his daughter hammered on the snaps, his wife sewed buttons and two seamstresses pedaled shiny black Butterfly-brand sewing machines. A third hunched under a fluorescent light, hand-stitching on fake fur collars.

All six gulped meals together. At night, they slept in the same room, two to a bed, hired hands included. Their cooking pots were on the floor, next to bottles of dye, bags of buttons and an uncut watermelon. Finished leather jackets hung in bunches from an indoor clothesline.

The little sweatshop produced about 30 jackets a day, for a profit of tens of thousands of yuan a year. But Tailor Zhang dismissed that amount. He needed 50,000 yuan just to marry off his 17-year-old son back home. "You have to buy the bride a whole set of electrical appliances, like an imported color television, an imported fridge. It's really expensive."

Like the parents of the Ten Minute Baby, the residents of Big Red Door were beyond the reach of family-planning authorities. Birth records were kept in their home villages. Tailor Zhang, for instance, went back just once a year. He already had four children. But if he had a fifth, chances are no one would have noticed.

China tried to control where its 1.3 billion people lived with a system of residency permits. Those lucky enough to live legally in the cities despised the migrant workers. Even as they hired them to cook and clean and wash, they blamed them for the packed city buses and the rising crime rate. They especially blamed them for the disappearing manhole covers. In China, the down-and-out stole them for scrap iron, just as Miami's homeless stripped power lines for copper. In 1992 alone, nearly 10,000 manhole covers disappeared from the streets of China. The press was full of stories about people falling into them and breaking their legs, or worse.

In Guangdong, a sign under a new elevated expressway admonished: "No sleeping under the bridge." In Beijing, about 20,000 *yao fan*, literally, "those asking for rice," moved into the capital. In Shanghai, beggars worked the richest shopping districts.

In 1999, three little children homed in on me as I walked down a neon-lit street in Shanghai one misty spring evening. They waved grimy paper cups, scavenged from a nearby Kentucky Fried Chicken outlet. Their parents, dressed in rags, sat in a nearby doorway, smiling benignly. The father of one said the children were four, six and nine. They were from Hubei Province, he said, and had arrived in Shanghai three nights earlier, after floods had destroyed their village. They were sleeping on the street.

Just then, a shopkeeper emerged from her shoe store. "Why don't you work!" she screamed, wrapping her camel-wool coat around her. "Why don't you go back to the countryside and do a decent day's work!" The children scattered. The man moved away, unembarrassed. The shopkeeper harrumphed, and said to me, "They come here every day!" Then she went back into her shoe store.

In Beijing, I stopped to talk to a man in a park who was scrubbing a battered pot with a bit of grayish water. Tang Jichun, who was in his 60s and had pure white hair, had deeply bronzed skin from living on a concrete park bench. His possessions, piled beside him, included an enamel bowl, a grimy quilt and a well-thumbed copy of Mao's *Selected Works*.

"You still read that?" asked a young man, who stopped to scrounge a match from him.

"Of course," said Tang, looking pained. "I read Marx and Lenin, too. How else will you understand the political situation today? You young people!"

The younger man shrugged and went on his way. Tang told me his troubles began in 1962 when Party zealots labeled him a "rightist," the Communist kiss of death. After the Cultural Revolution, he was told it had all been a mistake. But officials in his native Northeast refused to assign him a job. In the years before capitalism took hold, there had been no other way to get work.

After years of fighting red tape, Tang came to Beijing seeking justice. Just as those who had been wronged in imperial China petitioned officials in the capital, so Tang had come to petition the highest levels of the Communist Party. That was the theory, anyway. He occasionally got in to see a government official. The rest of the time he sat on his park bench, perusing his books of Mao Thought. All he wanted, he said, was a job. I left him as he began preparing his evening meal on a tiny portable stove.

Many of the homeless congregated across town in Kiln Pit, Beijing's poorest neighborhood. This was a claustrophobic rabbit warren of twisting lanes and crumbling shacks, home to more than two million Beijingers, or one in every six. Kiln Pit was a ghetto, Beijing's Harlem – and the world's original Chinatown.

When the Mongol and Manchu dynasties established their capitals in Beijing in the 13th and 17th centuries respectively, they inhabited the elegant Tartar City. This was the area within the city walls, surrounding the imperial palace. The subjugated Han, or ethnic Chinese, were relegated to the southwest area outside the walls, loosely known as the Chinese City. Coolies, peddlers and despised shopkeepers all lived here. Theaters and brothels moved here too, after the Mongol and Manchu rulers banned them as decadent and forbade them to operate within the city walls.

"The ethnic-minority emperors felt their people must not be contaminated by the depravity of the Chinese," said Ying Ruocheng, a Manchu friend of mine who was a vice minister of culture.

Within the city walls, *hutongs*, or alleys, had to be wide enough for an official's palanquin to pass. In Kiln Pit, where officials rarely ventured in the old imperial days (or even now, under Communist rule), the *hutongs* were sometimes so narrow two people could barely squeeze by. While the Tartar City had prettily named streets, such as "Sandalwood Buddha Temple," those in Kiln Pit, such as "Midwife Alley," reflected its vulgar past.

The neighborhood derived its own name from a former brick kiln whose operators dug up clay at random, leaving scars that collected pools of stagnant water. The imperial rulers chose the local produce market, Vegetable Market Crossroads, for public executions. A nearby vacant lot became a potter's field. The homeless were wrapped in straw matting and dumped in shallow graves. "There were no pretensions to a gravestone," said Ying Ruocheng.

By the time I visited it in 1988, the ancient city wall had been replaced by a subway and an expressway, the potter's field had become a public park and Vegetable Market Crossroads was just another bustling intersection. But while high-rises sprouted in the rest of the city, Kiln Pit remained Beijing's underbelly. It was home to the capital's only prison, its only venereal disease clinic and the notorious Beijing Lockup, an unmarked compound for prisoners on death row.

The closest railway station was the disreputable Yongding Gate Terminus. Here, soldiers in combat helmets, armed with pistols, kept watch over the ragged crowds of peasants who had come to the capital to seek redress for their grievances. A weathered bulletin board held a few hand-scrawled messages, often in ungrammatical Chinese. "Uncle, I waited for you two days. I've now gone to look for a place to sleep," said one pathetic note.

The Supreme Court, the State Council and the National People's Congress had all opened branch offices here. The idea was to keep unsightly petitioners and the homeless away from the city center. The Supreme Court's office, for instance, was a convenient five-minute walk away from Yongding Gate Terminus.

For many, though, justice was elusive. On the day I visited the dusty courtyard of the Supreme Court Reception Office, old women with wicker baskets under their arms, a man with a burned, deformed right hand and gaunt peasants jostled for a moment at a small wicket to thrust in their handwritten petitions. Periodically, the police rounded up the petitioners and forced them onto trains back to their villages. Many later drifted back to the capital. No life in Beijing was still better than no life at home.

Some of the homeless had set up makeshift tents of plastic sheeting along the city moat. I dropped by one dreary winter day and found an old man named Wang Shengxiang sitting on a mound of dun-colored earth. He stirred a battered enamel mug of steaming slops, cadged from a restaurant table after the customers had left.

"Have some?" he said, gallantly offering me a taste. By day, he and a dozen other hobos warmed scraps over tiny fires and idled away the short daylight hours. At night they braced themselves against the icy northwest wind. So far that winter, two of his neighbors had died from exposure.

Wang wrapped himself in a motheaten blue coat with a fake fur collar. At 72, his goatee was gray, his eyes narrow slits in a face darkened by sun and dirt. He told me he had arrived in Beijing 13 years ago after losing his state job — wrongly, he believed — as a railway worker in Henan Province. After exhausting all avenues of redress with his local government, he had come to the capital.

His "neighbor," a peasant in a grimy Mao jacket, was also from Henan province. Cai Linglin, 64, told me he had been severely beaten in a dispute over a donkey. Each morning for the past nine years, he had hobbled on his crutches to the petition station. "If I'm wrong, put a bullet through me. If I'm right, settle my case," he would scream at the officials there, over and over again. At night, he slept on a straw mat by the canal. A nearby tree served as his coat rack.

Perhaps it was because they themselves had been down-and-out for so long, but the residents of Kiln Pit were mostly unsympathetic. Many even refused to give the homeless water, forcing them to drink from the stagnant moat. It didn't occur to Wang Shengxiang, the ex-railway worker, to beg for spare change. His expectations were so low he actually thought most Kiln Pit people were nice. How so? I asked.

"They leave me alone," he said.

And the bad ones?

"The bad people deliberately spoil their garbage. They stick their cigarette butts in the leftovers."

While a hundred million people streamed into the cities, seven or eight hundred million more continued to work the land. Much of rural China was as poor as it had been for a thousand years. Average per capita grain production was unchanged from the 18th century. Steady improvements in fertilizer and seed were wiped out by steady population growth.

Many Chinese peasants ate meat just once every 30 or 40 meals, sometimes not even that. Now that public schools charged tuition, many rural parents put their children to work instead. By the 1990s, 145 million Chinese over the age of 15 were illiterate. And after 50 years of Communist rule, one in every ten Chinese still struggled to survive, according to the United Nations. Even the Chinese, who drew the poverty line at starvation levels, put the number at one in fifteen.

A seventh-century Tang Dynasty poet once described Gansu Province as "the poorest place under heaven." By the end of the 20th century, little had changed. Gansu was still China's poorest province. It was a blighted wasteland where peasants blanketed their fields with stones to retain moisture when drought hit, which was nine years out of ten. The tenth year the floods came.

The poorest villages in China's poorest province were closed to foreigners. But the Canadian Embassy had special access through a grassroots aid program. In late 1989, an embassy official invited me along, and I leaped at the chance. Only midway through the trip did I discover I was there illegally – the provincial Foreign Affairs Office had never been informed. But I kept my mouth shut, and so did everybody else. That was how I traveled to China's Appalachia, to see places few foreigners had ever seen.

More than 40 percent of Gansu's 22 million people did not have enough to eat or wear, according to a World Bank study. Gansu was plagued by all the diseases of poverty – leprosy, dysentery and tuberculosis. Its infant mortality rate was 50 percent higher than the national average. But the most horrific sight was the extraordinary numbers of retarded people.

Bouncing along Gansu's dusty back roads in an embassy van, I saw mentally handicapped people wandering, dazed and in rags. This was the terrible face of Chinese poverty. China had 10.2 million retarded people. Of these, 270,000 were in Gansu, a rate 60 percent above the national average. In some villages, one-third or more of the population was mentally handicapped. Poor hygiene, intermarriage, malnutrition, iodine deficiency and polluted water were all to blame.

In Gansu, about 2,000 retarded babies were born each year, many to retarded parents. In a place without a single children's hospital, where one in five children didn't attend school, there were zero services for these children. In the late 1980s, Gansu passed China's first eugenics law. Mentally retarded people were prohibited from bearing children, retarded women were forced to have abortions and mentally handicapped people couldn't marry until they had been sterilized.

To the outside world, the law reeked of the Third Reich. The Chinese have never been very tolerant of mental retardation. Even the official press called mentally handicapped people, *dai sha* – "slow-witted" or "stupid." But when I saw the poverty and suffering in Gansu, forcible sterilization seemed more humane than doing nothing. Children of mentally retarded parents in Gansu sometimes starved to death from neglect.

The Canadian embassy had a fixed itinerary of aid-project villages, but I managed to persuade the Chinese officials with us to stop our minibus a couple of times at random. At a muddy hellhole called Luo Family Mill, the village head told me there were 76 mentally retarded people among the 48 families. One major culprit was cretinism, a kind of mental retardation that develops in a fetus, caused by a lack of iodine in the mother's diet. In Li Shulan's case, cretinism had been passed from one iodine-deficient generation to the next. At 42, she was a cretin who stood less than four feet tall. Two of her three children were also cretins. Li, who was mildly retarded, told me she was also worried about her ten-year-old daughter. The child persisted in eating dirt, an indication of a mineral deficiency.

The solution to cretinism was, of course, stunningly simple: iodize the salt. But in 1989 one frustrated county official told me, "We just don't have enough medicine or personnel or resources."

Li Shulan's neighbor, Kang Running, was also four feet tall. Her three children were all retarded. She herself had Kashin-Beck's disease, a deforming type of arthritis, possibly caused by eating cereal grains infected with a fungus, or by a lack of selenium, a trace element in water essential for growth. At 46, she was a widow; her husband had been killed in a tractor accident.

We stopped at another village, where I found a woman named Ma Shi preparing a meal of rancid gluten cakes for her 27-year-old retarded daughter. The daughter was naked below the waist, her twisted legs filthy and blue with cold. She was crouched on all fours on the icy dirt floor of their crumbling mud hut. "She tears off all her clothes if I try to put pants on her," said Ma Shi helplessly. "She's been like that ever since she was born."

Of the 83 households in this village, a dozen had at least one family member who was mentally handicapped. Ma Shi could barely feed herself and her three other children, but the government gave her no help for her handicapped daughter. Although she was 48, a lifetime of poverty and hardship made her look more like 70.

In the 1930s, when the Communists were trying to stave off annihilation by Chiang Kai-shek's KMT forces, Chairman Mao led his epic 10,000-kilometer Long March through here. Mao was so grateful to the local peasants for aiding his guerrilla fighters that he wrote a poem in commemoration. But now Gansu's people were the have-nots the revolution forgot. Ma Shi's aging father-in-law, who had joined Mao's original Red Army, received a veteran's pension of just 15 cents a day, not even enough for food.

In many ways, life had worsened for these people since Deng Xiaoping launched his economic reforms. The expected trickle-down effect had not happened. Instead, inflation had sent the cost of fertilizer, seed and pesticide soaring. A visit to the village paramedic, once free, now cost one-fifth of a day's pay.

Gansu was so poor that even though the Canadian diplomats and I stayed in the best available lodgings, they were often primitive hostels without heat or plumbing. Each day, the local officials banqueted us as lavishly as they could, partly to be polite, partly so they could get a good meal themselves. "Eat meat, eat meat," they'd urge, while swallowing mouthfuls themselves. At one lunch, they plied us with so much stewed beef that we ended up wasting several bowls. I couldn't understand the local obsession with animal protein. But right after that lunch, I found out why, and it made me sick.

At a village called Dragon Pool, a pigtailed young woman told me she and her family last tasted meat three years earlier. Three *years*. How could government officials waste meat, when they knew that just down the road people were going without? In the 1970s, when I toiled with my Chinese classmates at Big Joy Farm, I was also protein-starved and dreamed of steaks and lemon meringue pie. But I spent only eight months being deprived. I couldn't imagine the kind of hunger this young woman was talking about. At 26, Liu Xiufang raised laying hens. But neither she nor her two children had ever tasted an egg. Every precious one went to pay the electricity bill on her single 15-watt lightbulb.

Her overriding concern, however, was water, not meat. Drought had withered her cabbages and her primitive cistern was dry. When she wanted to wash her children, she gathered snow in a basket, scraping a thin layer off the ground. When there wasn't even snow, she had to hike more than two hours to the nearest well.

Her elderly neighbor, Zhao Jinhua, had ten days supply of water left in her cistern. When that ran out, her adult sons would have to rise at 3 a.m. and lead their two cows to find water. "We go at night because we have to farm during the day," she said. When the drought was really severe, the government sent in tanker trucks. Each person got one liter of water a day – for cooking, washing and drinking. There was nothing for livestock.

It was hard to imagine, but there were families even worse off in Gansu than the ones I saw. In more remote villages, a day or two from the nearest road, some families had no blankets, even though the climate was like Minnesota's. Some couples shared a pair of trousers between husband and wife, so only one could go outside at a time. And because the government emergency water trucks could not reach them, Gansu officials said, they sometimes drank their own urine.

In the mid–1990s China pledged to iodize its salt by 2000, with the help of a World Bank loan. UNICEF, which estimated that two million Chinese suffered from Kashin-Beck's disease, proposed spending $18 million to improve conditions in 300 of China's poorest counties.

After passing through Gansu Province on the Long March, Mao Zedong's tattered troops ended up in Shaanxi Province, in Yanan, near Sunshine Village. As in Gansu, sympathetic peasants there sheltered the guerrillas and gave them grain. But after Mao won control of China, he traded in his loess cave for an imperial palace in Beijing – and never returned.

No wonder people here cared little about national events. Six months after the Tiananmen Massacre, few seemed to know much about it. They'd heard that Chairman Mao had died – it was, after all, 13 years later – but few could name the current chief of the Chinese Communist Party.

As prosperity mantled the coast of China, the peasants in the heart of the Red Army's old base area were left behind. Here, in the cradle of Chinese civilization, progress was also measured by how often a peasant ate meat. Sunshine Village still had no running water. Its peasants still lived in caves scooped out of the soft loess hills. And they tilled the soil with plows much like the 2,000-year-old artifacts displayed in the nearby Shaanxi Provincial Museum of History. The only difference was that those in Sunshine were iron, not bronze, and lacked the pale green patina of age.

China's leaders once expressed guilt over the region's unremitting poverty. "The Yanan people sustained us. Now we've been liberated so many years, but you still don't have enough to eat or wear. We have failed you," the late premier Chou En-lai told them, shedding tears during a 1970s inspection tour.

Chinese civilization first took root here 6,000 years before Christ. In early spring when I visited, fragments of ice still fringed the river. Wild apricot trees were in bloom, clouds of delicate pink dotting the wheat fields. Calling them "fields," though, was a euphemism. The slices of land were carved from eroded slopes so steep the peasants joked they had to lash their oxen together to keep them from tumbling down the mountainside.

In this impoverished village of 130 families, the richest man was a weatherbeaten peasant named, appropriately, Yang Fugui or Riches Yang. Wealth in Sunshine Village was relative. The arched windows of his cave had real glass, not mere rice paper. And for his eldest daughter's marriage, he had been able to afford a dowry of some plastic flowers, a coffee table, a suitcase and some clothes. He was also the proud owner of a television set, not that it broadened his horizons much. The surrounding mountains limited reception to one station. It broadcast no news, but it did air Western soaps. Riches Yang, 47, said he couldn't understand *Dynasty*, not even when it was dubbed into Chinese. What *were* all those fancy people talking about?

Like his neighbors, he headed for the hills at dawn on an empty stomach. Breakfast, much later, was a steamed wheat bun, chewed as he squatted in his fields of soybean and millet. I dropped in at lunchtime. We chatted as he helped his wife prepare a meal of plain buckwheat noodles. As she fed a lump of dough into what looked like a giant garlic press, he leaned on a lever, extruding the pasta into a large wok of boiling water. The peasants of Sunshine Village ate meat only one in 20 or so meals, and Riches Yang was no different.

When I asked what the revolution had done for him lately, he became tongue-tied. "It's difficult for me to talk. There's many things I don't know." Then he said simply, "We want a better life."

Migrant Worker Zhao back in Big Mound Village also wanted a better life. He was badly exploited, but the village official who terminated my visit there was right: most peasants in Gansu or Shaanxi would have traded places with Migrant Worker Zhao in a flash. This same rural-urban migration happened in our own

Industrial Revolution and, slowly, everyone's standard of living went up. But not before Dickens wrote some great novels about poverty, cruelty and despair.

Big Mound Village was the capitalist process in microcosm. Development inevitably meant some got rich first. Mao had tried it the other way. Everyone was supposed to get rich in lockstep. Instead, everyone stayed poor in lockstep. The very fact that Migrant Worker Zhao felt exploited was progress. He'd come to Big Mound because he knew it was better than what he had back home. Yet, already he was discontented. He'd seen the world. And he, too, wanted a rose garden and a glassed-in breakfast nook.

For so many Chinese, life wasn't getting better fast enough. In 1978, the peasants were among the first to benefit from Deng's economic reforms. But as the cost of fertilizer, machinery and transportation soared, rural growth stagnated. In 1985, average per capita income in rural areas was 62 percent of that in the cities. By 1990, it had fallen to 50 percent. And in 1994, it was 43 percent.

The first few years of economic reform had been easy. Letting peasants decide what to plant had been a no-brainer. So was opening the country to foreign investment and giving free rein to private enterprise. But China never reformed the existing state economy so much as allowed a parallel economy to grow up. By the 1990s, the clash between the two economies was unavoidable. Fixed prices for grain pleased the urban proletariat, but sparked unrest among peasants. Soaring grain prices pleased the peasants, but sparked unrest among workers.

Throughout the 1990s, protests erupted across rural China. In 1994 in Renshou County, thousands of Sichuan peasants, angry at excessive levies, blockaded traffic, held police hostage and attacked officials with bricks and clubs. In 1999, 10,000 peasants surrounded a government office in Daolin, in Hunan Province, demanding an end to corruption and exorbitant taxes. As riot police waded in, one peasant was killed by an exploding tear-gas canister and dozens more were injured. The ringleaders escaped arrest. The government put up wanted posters offering rewards, but angry peasants just tore them down. No one turned the leaders in.

■

China's first private boarding school was a tiny window into grassroots corruption. Like a mirage, Bright Asia Private Primary School, a walled compound of red, white and blue tepee-shaped pavilions, rose from the paddy fields of Du Jiang Yan in Sichuan Province. "I'm running a school for aristocrats. No, make that a school for little emperors," said Qing Guangya, the principal and owner, who named the school after himself. (Guangya means Bright Asia.)

The one-time enrolment fee was about 12 years pay for a worker. Annual tuition was extra. The equivalent in Western terms would be Eton charging $360,000 on acceptance plus $88,000 a year for tuition. In its first year, Bright Asia had already enrolled 200 pupils, aged five to eight. Originally the school planned to offer only first grade. But so many parents lied about their child's real level that it decided to start kindergarten, second and third grades as well.

The principal's own education had been terminated in third grade when the Cultural Revolution erupted. When Qing (pronounced Ching) looked at the options facing his six-year-old son, he decided to open a school. He raised money from family and friends, but authorities in Beijing balked at the notion of a *private* school. Finally, the local Communist Party Secretary gave his blessing, and sent his own child. "He said, 'We have dance halls and karaoke bars. Why not have something good like a school?'" Principal Qing recalled.

He quit his television job that May, broke ground in July, and opened for business in September. Bright Asia's pupil-staff ratio was an amazing two to one, including five American teachers. Each air-conditioned classroom had a computer, a piano, a Japanese television, a VCR, a compact-disc player and five kid-size flush toilets. A swimming pool and tennis courts were under construction.

Bright Asia sparked nationwide interest. Several other private schools opened in its wake. Hardly a week went by without visitors taking photos, taping classes and copying his construction blueprints. To deflect criticism that it was catering to the elite, Bright Asia provided scholarships to five orphans.

I watched Elizabeth Conachy of Portland, Oregon, teach a circle of first-graders to sing and dance *The Hokey Pokey*. Kimberly Lays of Rochester, New York, drilled another class in English. "Dennis, run to something green," she ordered. Each child had been given a Western name. One eight-year-old handed me a business card that said, simply, "Gordon." Six or seven pupils even had the ultimate nouveau-riche Chinese accessory, a foreign passport, from countries such as Thailand, Singapore, Hungary, Japan and the United States. A first-grader named Adam said, "The school told us, if our English is good we can go to America."

"Are we serving the bourgeoisie?" said Principal Qing. "Hmm, we're serving a special class. They're not privileged. They just have more money."

A few students were children of newly rich entrepreneurs. But most were the offspring of senior government officials, who seemed to have no trouble paying the exorbitant tuition. Some had grown wealthy from bribes. Others bought scarce commodities at low state prices and resold them at a huge profit. The bolder parents donated contraband directly to the school. One dad sent tons of government cement. A grandfather, general manager of the Chengdu Seamless Steel Pipe Factory, presented a flagpole.

"It's stuff that belongs to their companies. If they give something worth more than 36,000 yuan, we waive the enrolment fee," said Principal Qing. The previous month, one Party official pulled his daughter out. "Too many people gossiped. He was worried about an investigation."

That's why Bright Asia was as confidential as a Swiss bank. "I don't ask any questions. I just tell them to give me a mailing address." But Principal Qing, a 37-year-old former television producer, was not averse to a little parental name-dropping. Among them were the Deputy Governor of Sichuan, the Communist Party Secretary of Chengdu and several PLA generals.

4

Going Postal

With Lena Sun, Washington Post *correspondent in Tiananmen Square in 1994.*   Photo: Jerome Mindes

If corruption was a huge problem in the Chinese countryside, *guanxi* (pronounced gwaan-see) was also part of the problem. *Guanxi* meant "connections." But it was really about contacts, networking, influence-peddling, the old-boys network, cronyism and nepotism – all woven into one critical web. *Guanxi* got you running water, tax waivers, business deals and insider information.

You needed *guanxi* to cut through China's fabled bureaucracy. One of my classmates from Beijing University ended up running the Municipal Department of Antiquities. Anyone wanting to film a commercial at, say, the Forbidden City, needed her permission. She always assured me she'd smooth the way if I ever felt the urge to sell shampoo at the Great Wall.

Guanxi was good as gold. In Beijing, I was lunching with two young entrepreneurs when one of them suddenly jumped up to pump the hand of a middle-aged man in the restaurant. "He's the local emperor," whispered Chen Yi, who was in business with his twin sister, Chen Mei. The man, he explained, was chief of the local law courts. Through their father, a Communist Party Secretary, they also had *guanxi* in the bureaus of taxation, industry and commerce.

At 25, the twins owned Di Chen Electronics Co. and six other companies. They themselves were Communist Youth League members. In 1990, they'd fallen in love with capitalism when their mother took them to Hong Kong to visit relatives. "I felt that, every second, people were trying to figure out how to get ahead. It was a real inspiration," said Chen Yi, who dressed the part of a young capitalist in a double-breasted suit and flowered silk tie.

The day after their return to Beijing, the twins biked over to apply for a business license. They opened a small typesetting company and plowed the profits into computers. Chen Yi was in charge of finance and Chen Mei handled marketing. Within a few years, net profits exceeded $200,000. Their goal: $2 million profit a year.

A few days later, I paid a visit to their air-conditioned headquarters, in Beijing's high-tech district, dubbed Silicon Alley. Chen Mei, a plump woman in a calf-length black velvet dress, was fielding two calls at once. To hedge her bets, she had furnished her office with both a statue of Buddha and a fax. In the next room, her employees were wolfing down the lunch Chen Mei had delivered free every day. It wasn't because she was generous. She figured that way the break would last just ten minutes.

"We believe in ourselves," she said. She supported the Communist Party because it brought stability. Both she and her brother had found the Tiananmen demonstrations annoying.

"You couldn't get any business done. Society was paralyzed," said Chen Yi, taking a call on his cell phone.

Yet for pragmatic reasons, they wanted democracy and freedom. "We need fast information to make decisions," Chen Mei said. Unlike her father, she had no desire to join the Communist Party. "The way we measure people is by their ability to make money," she said. She paused. "But if it would help my enterprise, I would join the Party."

In Changsha, the capital of Hunan Province, I met another savvy young entrepreneur named Cheng Xingguo, who treated me to an expensive lunch of exotic turtle soup and deep-fried pigeons. At 30, he was a lanky, workaholic ex-reporter who thrived on three hours sleep. His venture was foolproof, he chortled. His company produced videos elucidating government policies. In return for a cut of the profits, each ministry forced the state companies under its aegis to buy Cheng's videos – at exorbitant rates.

Cheng had wisely invited the head of the provincial tax bureau to be his honorary chairman. The first video, naturally, explained China's new tax law. Under the honorary chairman's influence, the tax bureau forced every state-owned enterprise in Hunan Province to buy a copy, at $300 a pop. Cheng (and his honorary chairman) kept 90 percent of the profits. The tax bureau got 10 percent. Other projects included a riveting video on boiler safety, distributed by the labor ministry. That ministry, naturally, just happened to be in charge of shutting down unsafe boilers.

"In China, the most important thing is *guanxi*," said Cheng, flashing a heavy gold ring embossed with *fu*, the ideogram for prosperity.

Bribes, *guanxi*, kickbacks. It all began to blur, especially when Communist Party Secretaries began selling job appointments. China launched a national campaign against corruption. Actually, it launched one every two months. In 1993, in what might be the biggest bust in history, authorities in Anhui arrested 300,000 cadres – or 1 in every 5 officials in the province – on charges of corruption.

Many ordinary citizens felt the campaigns were cosmetic. Authorities would find some poor sap whose *guanxi* had dried up, execute him with a bullet to the back of the head and heavily publicize the incident. At any rate, the graft and greed didn't stop. Jane Su, an American friend of mine in Beijing, told me in 1999 that her new apartment had sub-par wiring and thinner walls than the plans had specified because of corruption in the construction industry. That same spring, a new bridge in Sichuan collapsed, killing several dozen people. Everyone whispered corners had been cut. The bridge's chief engineer was tried, and summarily executed.

Singapore dictator Lee Kuan Yew, a friend of China's leaders, warned that public dissatisfaction with corruption had a "tinderbox" quality. "The biggest single fear they (the leaders) have," he told *New York Times* columnist William Safire, "is the corrosive effect of graft and the revulsion that it evokes in people. They're never quite sure when it will blow up."

Anti-corruption campaigns snared the former mayor of Beijing, the former head of the Guizhou provincial police and the son of the former head of the biggest steelworks in Beijing. Note the emphasis on "former." These officials once had *guanxi*. Now they didn't, and so they were toast.

In January, 1999, authorities fingered Chu Shijian as culprit-of-the-week. My files showed that five years earlier Chu, the chief of China's largest and most lucrative tobacco company, had been a "national model worker" and winner of something called the "May 1 Model and Gold Global Award." But his fate was sealed when his main *guanxi*, the Yunnan Provincial Party Secretary, was himself fired in 1996. In 1999, Chu was convicted of embezzling $3.5 million. The cigarette king's career went up in smoke. Luckily for him, he was only sentenced to life in prison. He must have still had some *guanxi*.

As a reporter, *guanxi* was particularly invaluable. I soon learned to rely on the network of friends and contacts I had developed during my earlier years in China. Doing things officially was basically a complete waste of time.

While most foreigners could travel freely through most of China, journalists had to apply for permission to go *anywhere*. Every Chinese organization, every province, city, county and town had a Foreign Affairs Office. They handled interview requests and, indignity of indignities, sometimes even charged for their "service."

I once requested to go to Canton, mecca of China's open-door economy. Its Foreign Affairs Office telexed me that everyone, all six million residents, were too busy to handle a visit. When I applied to go to Tibet, its Foreign Affairs Office turned me down. Lhasa, it explained, didn't have "enough oxygen."

The Foreign Ministry Information Department was the mother of all Foreign Affairs Offices. It accredited journalists, held weekly press briefings and summoned us for scoldings and glasses of warm Coke whenever we produced stories they didn't like. The Foreign Ministry also organized regular press trips to the provinces. Interviews consisted of a nervous peasant or factory manager reciting a pre-approved speech. Translations ate up half the allotted time. After my first trip – with 50 other foreign correspondents to watch a satellite launch in Sichuan Province – I never went on a press junket again.

At the weekly Foreign Ministry briefings in Beijing, the questions my colleagues asked were fabulous, but the answers were unusable. I soon stopped going to those, too. I knew from my earlier years in China that the best stories were out there, among the people.

Other journalists had the same idea. So authorities kept us under constant surveillance. Our Chinese staff filed reports on us. Our apartments elevators were monitored by hidden video cameras. State Security agents tapped our phones, bugged our homes and offices and opened our mail. Sometimes they tailed us. Sometimes they roughed us up. Sometimes they slashed our tires and smashed our windshields.

As I recounted in *Red China Blues*, the Chinese police even stole the *Globe's* Toyota and used it as a squad car, complete with red flashing lights strapped across the roof. (A year later, I caught them with it, and made them give it back.) Police also detained BBC correspondent James Miles for interviewing European labor activists who had shouted democracy slogans in Tiananmen Square. During a five-hour interrogation, the police told James it was "not normal journalistic practice to cover illegal demonstrations."

All this was nothing compared to what they did to our Chinese sources. A Hangzhou student named Zhang Weiping was sentenced to nine years in jail after telling a Voice of America reporter that students had forced the city government to fly a flag at half-mast after the Tiananmen Massacre. As I mentioned earlier, two dissidents, Forest Zhang and Liu Nianchun, spent several years each in the gulag, in part for speaking to me and a colleague, Lena Sun of the *Washington Post*.

Authorities also harassed Lena and me during a trip to Fujian Province. But they were much worse to our sources. State Security officials subsequently interrogated friends we had met for a meal. They even hauled in a taxi driver we had hired for a day. One young friend's salary was subsequently slashed, and a prostitute we interviewed was later arrested.

We knew about the reprisals in Fujian because some of our sources kept talking to us. And if dissidents like Forest Zhang were determined to take the risk of contacting me, I felt duty-bound to meet them. Still, when I noticed I was being followed, I aborted appointments. And since Fat Paycheck always refused to go shopping, I didn't really mind having the secret police spend the afternoon with me, browsing for silk blouses. I did learn not to phone sources from my home or office, and I warned them not to give their names when they called.

"Keep talking. I'll figure out who you are." So they'd say, "It's me," and I would wonder which "me" it was. By prior agreement with various sources, "3 p.m." sometimes meant 5 p.m. With others, it meant 10 a.m. "Monday" sometimes meant Tuesday. Or was it Wednesday? When they didn't show up, I wondered whether they had been arrested, or if I had just gotten the day wrong.

Every now and then, a correspondent got expelled. To use a Chinese aphorism, Beijing killed a chicken to frighten the monkeys. No one wanted to be banned. Many of us had invested years learning the language and studying the country. Gradually, though, I understood that fear was paralyzing. Like the dissidents, I couldn't worry about what the government might do if I wanted to do my job as a reporter.

Covering China dispassionately was beyond me. I kind of liked human rights. And I kind of hated dictatorships. Any reporter who claimed not to feel the strain of working in this environment was either lying or stupid. It wore you down. I remember the relief of flying into Hong Kong in the pre-1997 era, before the British colony was handed back to Beijing. I also remember the feeling of landing in Beijing, feeling the pressure in my skull, as though I had just donned an iron helmet. The residual paranoia was strong. For months after I moved back to Canada and Lena moved back to Washington, we talked in code when we discussed China on the telephone.

To cope with unruly journalists, the Foreign Ministry authored a kind of secret Michelin guide to hated correspondents. Besides biographical data and a photo, there was a category for *taidu* or "attitude." *Taidu* was a litmus test. Were you a friend or an enemy? For them or against them? Nice or not nice? The Foreign Ministry distributed these guides to authorities in all 30 Chinese provinces.

That way, the local Foreign Affairs Office knew in advance who was a troublemaker.

The worst troublemakers were foreign correspondents who looked Chinese and spoke Chinese. We were dangerous in a police state because we could observe daily life unnoticed. We also could, and did, slip into forbidden places. There were a handful of us, mostly female: Lena Sun of the *Washington Post*, Kathy Chen of the *Wall Street Journal*, Mary Wong of the CBC, Charlene Fu of the Associated Press and Sheryl WuDunn of the *New York Times*. As a joke, we formed a club, the Macho Sino Girls Club. Like all proper clubs, the MSG Club (motto: "we give you a headache") was designed to exclude everyone else and make them feel bad. In fact, all we did was have lunch and gossip. We were much too competitive to bond.

The Chinese held us MSG types to different standards. In summarizing our *taidu*, the Foreign Ministry accused both Lena and me of being "traitors." *Traitors?* My motherland was Canada. Lena's was the United States.

To be a not-so-foreign correspondent was to live between two worlds. In 1989, after the Tiananmen Massacre, plainclothes police tried to kidnap me off the street in broad daylight, another tale I recounted in *Red China Blues*. I am convinced they mistook me for a Chinese student because as soon as I yelled "Help!" in English, they stopped trying to stuff me into the back seat of their Volkswagen Santana.

Another time, State Security agents nabbed Lena as she and her family were returning from a Sunday outing. Two agents confined her husband and their two-year-old son to their apartment. Five other agents videotaped an interrogation of her in her office. For three hours, they searched her files, forced her to open her safe and confiscated several items, including a two-page list of telephone numbers of prominent Chinese dissidents.

China accused Lena of engaging "in activities incompatible with her status as a foreign journalist." They also arrested one of her sources. We all expected Lena to be expelled. She wasn't. Both the *Washington Post* and the U.S. Congress took up her cause. Lena was spared, I believe, in part because her mother was Yu Lihua, a famous Taiwanese novelist on friendly terms with Beijing. Kicking out her daughter would have generated bad publicity among Overseas Chinese.

Gag me with a chopstick. There, in the *Chinese Women's Journal* (circulation 500,000), was a story about my life headlined, "Native Yellow Banana." Who wrote this garbage? The answer was a shock. *I* did. Which just goes to show, don't believe everything you read in the official Chinese press.

No, I didn't write the article. But I did submit to an interview by a 25-year-old reporter named Yao Dan. I expected to be misquoted. I didn't expect an entire fabrication. But there I was, rattling on for 2,000 words in the first person, under *my* byline. I got the most basic details about myself wrong. And I had even called myself a "native yellow banana."

I should have known better than to agree to an interview. In 1989 the *People's Daily* reported that the BBC's James Miles had "apologized" for violating martial law. Absolutely untrue, James told me later. Then the *Chinese Women's Journal* described Lena Sun as having "tears in her eyes" when she said she'd like to interview Deng Xiaoping. "Who wouldn't want to interview Deng?" Lena told me. "But I most certainly did not have tears in my eyes."

I'd often quoted the Chinese media in my stories, giving them a weightiness perhaps undeserved by calling them "official." I thought an interview with a Chinese reporter would give me firsthand knowledge of the gap between what was said and what was printed. When Yao Dan arrived at my office, I set one ground rule: only depict me in tears if I actually cried. She said she'd try, but added ominously, "Our editors force us to make up stuff."

After the story appeared, I took a deep breath, then phoned Yao Dan to ask what had happened. "The last time I wrote a story in the third person," she explained, "the editor changed it all to the first person. So I thought I might as well save them the trouble. I guess I should have warned you."

There were also a few mistakes, I said carefully. I didn't want to hurt her feelings. But why did she write that Ben and Sam were born in China when they were born in Hong Kong? "Oh," she said, "I didn't mean literally *born* in China. I meant you were *raising* them in China."

Then I came to my key complaint. Why did she have me saying "I'm a banana." Or worse, "I think when I'm old, my son Ben can become the second generation of native yellow bananas." Didn't she know that was an Uncle Tom-ish insult, what you'd call a skin-deep Asian, someone who was yellow on the outside, white on the inside?

She was appalled and deeply apologetic. "You never said 'banana,'" she immediately agreed, "but when I was trying to conceptualize the story, I picked that as my theme." Yao Dan thought she was paying me the ultimate compliment: Although I was a third-generation Canadian, she thought I blended in so well I was practically one of them, as opposed to your average round-eyed barbarian.

Indeed, the story verged on sycophantic. Maybe it would open doors. Its publication in an official newspaper would be seen as a symbolic stamp of approval. And since the Chinese government was always warning its citizens that foreign journalists were really spies, a little image-building never hurt.

Some foreigners thought Chinese had no sense of humor. Tell me a Chinese joke, they'd demand. That was hard. Most were untranslatable, based on puns or parsing. Western humor was equally impenetrable for Chinese.

At Bob Hope's first and only monologue in Beijing in 1979, he made a joke about how the Great Wall was "built like Raquel Welch." I held my breath, wondering how Ying Ruocheng, my friend who became vice minister of culture, would translate it.

"I didn't understand that. Who's Raquel Welch?" Ying said to the audience in Chinese, instead of translating the joke. That cracked them up. Hearing the laughter, Bob Hope beamed happily, which further cracked everyone up. (Incidentally, Norman, who had been in China too long, didn't know who Raquel Welch was, either.)

What many Westerners didn't realize was the whole country was a joke. The Chinese themselves chuckled at the absurdities of life in a capitalist country run by hard-line Communists. That is, when they weren't crying.

Take the Chinese Post Office. Delivery was police-state efficient, but mailing anything was police-state inefficient. A large sign "absolutely banned the mailing of radioactive substances, perishable goods, reactionary books and propaganda, obscene or immoral articles and live animals." (Dead ones presumably fell into the perishable category.)

"You have to show them everything," said a man, who was sending a calendar to a friend. "If they say it's okay, then you can wrap it."

That is why, in addition to stamps, the post office helpfully sold plywood boxes, nails, cardboard, brown paper, needles, thread and unbleached cotton bags in various sizes. My local post office always resembled an adults' remedial arts and crafts course. Some people painstakingly crayoned addresses on cotton bags. Others sewed or wrapped. A sticky table provided troughs of free fluffy white paste because Chinese stamps came without glue. Staplers and hammers were also provided for free, apparently because no one there had heard about going postal.

Early on, I decided I was ill-suited to the rigors of a socialist post office. Mailing letters became a key responsibility of Liu Xinyong, the *Globe*'s energetic, street-smart driver. Gradually he trained me in the arcane rules of Chinese postal proprieties. Destination addresses had to begin 15 millimeters from the side. Return addresses must be on the bottom, front, for domestic mail. For international mail, return addresses had to be on the *top left*. Destination countries must be printed in a foreign language, in capital letters, and only in black or blue ink.

So much for the East is Red. The Chinese Post Office was the only place in China that banned the color red among the masses. Just as China's emperors demanded exclusive use of imperial yellow in clothing and ceramic roof tiles, top Communist organizations, such as the All-China Women's Federation, monopolized red ink on envelopes. Alfred Peng, a Canadian-Chinese architect who owned a design firm in Beijing, discovered that the hard way. He had to junk thousands of envelopes after printing his corporate logo in red.

The Great Wall Sheraton made a similar mistake. It engraved its envelopes in forbidden gold and silver, with its return address incorrectly printed in the top left corner. Each time the Sheraton sent a letter, some poor sap in the back office had to glue a white strip of paper over the offending upper-left address and rewrite it by hand – in blue ink – on the bottom.

Size mattered. Driver Liu tried to teach me that envelopes couldn't be smaller than 140 mm by 90 mm, or bigger than 235 mm by 120 mm, nor could the length be smaller than 1.4 times the width. Got that? I still have no idea what size he was talking about. I do know it was some crazed Communist bureaucrat's creation. It certainly wasn't standard office size. Because Chinese envelopes, like Chinese stamps, came glue-free, I stupidly ordered a thousand normal envelopes from Hong Kong. Mindful of the Draconian return-address rules, I had our return address printed, in proper black ink, in *both* Chinese and English, in the correct spots.

No, no and no. First, the envelopes exceeded China's permissible dimensions by one centimeter. Clerks at the Central Post Office were world-class experts at rooting out subversive stationery. They'd take one glance at our envelopes, then whip out metal rulers. Then they'd fling the letters back at Driver Liu and send him out the door.

Even without that extra centimeter, we were already in trouble, return-address-wise. It didn't matter if one return address was in the right place. What mattered was that one return address was in the *wrong* place. So for years, Driver Liu carefully whited out whichever address offended. Then, like a guerrilla fighter planting car bombs, he made the rounds of unsuspecting neighborhood post offices to drop off our illegal-sized envelopes, never frequenting the same one too often.

Living in China taught me the importance of feudal hierarchy. For the *Globe*'s operations to function smoothly, I realized I needed a grand title. I briefly considered "Duchess," but settled on "Beijing bureau chief." Sometimes, even that wasn't grandiose enough. Major transactions, such as installing a phone, required letters of approval from my managing editor, 13 time zones away. So I did what any savvy Chinese would do. I stocked up on a supply of head-office stationery and churned out suitably florid letters as needed. The bureau operations hummed along nicely.

An absentee boss was actually an advantage when it came to negotiating rent increases. The Diplomatic Housing Bureau, which controlled housing for most journalists and diplomats, sent me a notice one day of a huge rent increase. And, the notice added, all rents would henceforth be calculated in U.S. dollars.

Most foreign tenants acquiesced. I phoned to thank the Housing Bureau for their "precious notice" and explained I would forthwith petition my "leaders." Weeks passed. The Bureau called. *Haven't heard a thing*, I said. *You know how it is with leaders.*

A few more weeks passed. The Housing Bureau cadres said they wanted to talk things over. *Great*, I said, setting a date for them to come see me. At the last minute, naturally, I had to run out. I left my news assistant to apologize profusely on my behalf. We rescheduled the appointment. Again, I missed it. *You know how it is with journalism*, I said. *So unpredictable.*

I knew I was making progress when Madame Xie, the head of the Housing Bureau, personally called the third time to fix a third appointment *and* brought a gift, a chartreuse stuffed rabbit, for Ben. *Aha!* I thought. She was trying to make *guanxi* with me.

This time, I stuck around, poured tea and smiled. But I never mentioned the rent hike. Instead, I zeroed in on the ideological problem. *My editor in Canada is so confused*, I told Madame Xie. *Isn't China a sovereign nation? Doesn't it have its own currency? What was wrong with the People's Currency? Didn't they know Canadians also hated American imperialism?* (When we weren't madly shopping for bargains across the border, that is.)

It had been years since I'd said "American imperialism" in Chinese, but it rolled effortlessly off my tongue. Madame Xie looked discomfited. It didn't really matter to the *Globe* if our rent was denominated in U.S. dollars. Complaining about it was a diversionary tactic. After a year of discussion, I finally agreed to pay the rent in American money. By then, the Housing Bureau was so worn down it had already abandoned the rent increase.

Even unhiked, our rent was still exorbitant – about $7,000 per month for a whitewashed office and a three-bedroom apartment. For that, you got those aforementioned surveillance cameras, cockroaches, elevators that trapped you between floors and smoke detectors that sounded, not in your burning apartment, but in a distant management office.

Hot water was quirky. Our toilet once transformed itself into a bum sauna, flushing only scalding water. A more annoying problem was the annual hot-water shutdown. "Dear Tenant," read the annual notice. "The Beijing Housing Service Corp. for Diplomatic Missions presents its compliments to its tenants and has the honor to inform (you) … that the hot water shall be temporarily cut off during June 1 and July 1." For one summer month each year, when the pipes were being cleaned, diplomats and foreign correspondents joined the great unwashed. "I boil two pots of water every morning and take one of my son's bath toys, a plastic scooper, and pour the water over myself," said Mike Chinoy, CNN's Beijing correspondent. "I'm just barely presentable enough that my audience doesn't know I haven't had a proper shower in three weeks."

Most diplomats cut back on social engagements, but the British soldiered on. Its embassy always threw a garden party in honor of the Queen's birthday. One year, I called a British diplomat to ask how it, uh, smelled. "Most of us had showered and washed and were scrubbed and clean," said Peter Davies, a first secretary. "Being cunning and perfidious Brits, we have installed electric hot-water heaters in most of our apartments."

Many Chinese also installed tiny water heaters. Others showered communally at work. But millions of Beijingers had to use public bathhouses, which looked like gas chambers. Segregated by sex, everyone soaped en masse in dimly lit concrete rooms, then vied for a moment under a collective nozzle.

In Beijing, Flourishing Garden Bathhouse began offering a dozen scented baths, from jasmine tea to Shaoxing rice wine to Nescafe. "People don't want to just get clean," said Cao Baocai, its Mao-suited general manager. "They want to have a good time."

But instant-coffee baths? "I've never thought of using coffee to wash, but the more consumed, the better," chortled Peter Wu, chief representative for Nestle China Ltd. Nescafe suggested one heaping teaspoon a cup, he said, but didn't have a recommendation for tubs.

Founded in 1921 in Beijing, Flourishing Garden reflected the upheavals of modern Chinese history. Silk-robed merchants used to come for a cup of tea, a game of *wei qi* and a hot soak. After the Communist victory in 1949, back scrubs were denounced as "exploitative" and Flourishing Garden was ordered to "serve the people." Ticket prices were kept so low that it lost 37 yuan for every 100 yuan it took in.

In 1992, when state enterprises were ordered to sink or swim, Flourishing Garden remade itself into a spa. It doubled the price of a shower and charged a day's pay for a flavored bath. Attendants in white pantsuits padded around in cloth slippers, pouring tea, running baths and giving massages.

"We're so embarrassed by the service," said Zhang Ming, 40, after emerging from a perfumed bath. "They keep coming in and doing things for us. We're not used to this." A worker at a state-run watch factory, she had brought her 14-year-old daughter to celebrate the start of the school winter break. "We can't come all the time, but once in a while we can afford it. Next time, we're going to try the milk bath."

Inside a sauna, five women sweated on pink towels. "I used to go to another bathhouse, but I hated waiting in line," said Zheng Yanjian, 27, a restaurateur, thumbing through a pulp magazine. Huang Yanxia, a plump hotel worker, had spent five and half hours that day switching between the shower and the sauna. "I'm addicted," she said, dabbing her pink skin with lotion. "I can wash at work, but it's not the same."

In a suite with twin enamel bathtubs, I slipped into an aqua terry robe. A uniformed female attendant swabbed one tub with disinfectant and filled it with steaming water. After I soaked for 20 minutes, another well-muscled female gave me an exploitative-style back scrub. A disgusting shower of dirt fell on the white tub. "It's just old skin," she said diplomatically.

After I had rested for 15 minutes on a red chaise longue in the adjoining room, it was time to choose my bath. The menu claimed that jasmine tea was good for wrinkles, herbs soothed aches and pains and vinegar relaxed muscles. Shaoxing rice wine improved circulation, sea water treated inflammations and milk baths, a favorite of imperial concubines, whitened skin. I decided I needed Nescafe to "alleviate fatigue."

The attendant returned with a pot of concentrated instant coffee. She poured it into the tub, then filled it full of hot water. I climbed in and felt like I was sitting in a giant cup of weak coffee.

"How is it?" she asked. "Feeling perky?"

"Any cream and sugar?" I replied. In fact, she didn't actually say "perky," but I really did ask for cream and sugar. She told me they had experimented with sugar, with sticky results. Well, what about café-au-lait? I asked. This being China, such flexibility was not possible. The attendant came back with a pitcher of milk. She dumped it into the other tub and turned on the hot water.

For years, you couldn't buy decent office furniture in China. Filing cabinets were especially problematic. Then, one day in 1994, word spread among the foreign correspondents that some were available at the Eastern Peace Iron Cabinet Co. Driver Liu and I dashed through the swinging front doors of the dusty state-run store. Five surly clerks in navy-blue lab coats pretended that we, the only customers, weren't there.

The filing cabinets were stacked to the ceiling. Some were hidden behind huge steel safes. I buttonholed a clerk to ask about the differences among the various filing cabinets. She stared at me from behind round tortoiseshell glasses. "*Dou cha bu duo*" (All more or less the same), she said, too bored to utter a pronoun.

"But this one is taller than the others," I insisted, pointing to one model.

"*Dou cha bu duo*," she repeated, this time in a tone that implied, "*moron.*"

"Obviously, there's a difference," I insisted, in my best *Consumer Reports* shopping mode. "And there must be a reason. What is it?"

She wordlessly thrust a tape measure at me. If I couldn't remember the size of regulation envelopes, I certainly didn't know the dimensions of standard file folders. Helplessly, I continued to poke around the inventory. Some cabinets had deep drawers. Others had individual locks. I spied a sorry-looking yellow cabinet. It was a third cheaper than the others.

"Why?" I asked.

The clerk gave me a withering glance. "It's scratched," she snorted.

"How am I supposed to know that's a sale item," I retorted. "Half the goods in your store look like garbage. Besides, I'm the customer."

She seemed astonished. After I recovered my equilibrium, I told her I would take the cheapest undamaged filing cabinet. Driver Liu, who had drifted away during my face-losing outburst, sidled back. "Bargain a bit," he whispered.

Bargain? When I've just bitten off the clerk's head? I looked beseechingly at him. He stepped into the breach, and bravely asked for a discount — in vain. Clerks in state stores couldn't care less if you bought anything. They preferred that you went away empty-handed and didn't make them utter pronouns. Accepting defeat, I took out a wad of cash. The clerk passed each bill under a purple light bulb that supposedly detected counterfeit money. When my People's Money passed muster, she asked if I wanted tan or gray.

A choice! What went best with whitewash? After dithering for a moment, I chose the gray. "We only have tan," said the clerk, triumphantly adjusting her tortoiseshell glasses.

Driver Liu and I discussed how to load the heavy filing cabinet into the Jeep. Could the roof could handle it? What about flattening the back seat? When we decided the roof could handle it, the clerk sneered, "We don't have any filing cabinets *here*. You have to pick it up from our warehouse."

As I was digesting that latest scrap of customer-service information, another bored clerk ambled over. "*Ni shi nar de?*" (Where are you from?) I exploded again. "What difference does it make where I'm from," I shouted. "It's none of your business."

"Well," he said, "I just wanted to know. Because we have free delivery."

I crawled out of the Eastern Peace Iron Cabinet Co. Again, Driver Liu stepped into the breach. Later, outside, he said mildly, "You know, the service isn't really bad. It's a state store. That's normal for them. They weren't being mean to you. I tried to explain to them that foreigners want service when they buy things, and that they also hate being asked a lot of questions."

We barely got back to the office when the doorbell rang. I opened the door. "Filing cabinet," said the young man. Driver Liu rushed over, afraid I would also sabotage the delivery. But I was so astonished at the speed of delivery, that I just beamed in silence. In Toronto or New York, I thought to myself, this would have taken at least a week.

Driver Liu went down to help the delivery man. He returned, dragging the filing cabinet all by himself.

"What happened?" I asked.

"He would only deliver it to the ground floor," said Driver Liu. "If I wanted him to bring it to the third floor, even in the elevator, he said it would cost extra."

"Too bad he didn't ask to use our toilet," I snapped. "I would have charged him, too."

Driver Liu ignored my outburst and tore off the cardboard wrapping. "Look," he said, glumly. I looked. I saw a beautiful, brand new filing cabinet. "It's gray," he pointed out. So it was, and a lovely shade, too.

"It's because you asked for tan," he said. "So they gave you gray."

No, actually, I'd asked for gray. Which is when they said they only had tan. So I said tan was fine. Which is why they gave me gray.

5

State Sloth

Worker in a state-owned steel factory in Wuhan in 1972. Photo: Jan Wong

By the 1990s, China had McDonald's, *Cosmopolitan* and Ikea, but it still hadn't given up the ghost of central planning. Authorities decreed, for instance, that only 36 people should drown in the capital in 1993. Alas, 47 did. That was tough for Sun Zhanpo, the hapless official in charge of drownings in Beijing. "We've exceeded the quota," he sighed, when I phoned him that December. "We're going to be criticized."

December was the cruelest month for quota counters. Had it been a good year for executions? (It had.) How about carbon-monoxide asphyxiation? (So-so.) Studying Deng Xiaoping's *Selected Works*? (Not great.)

"Who's asking that? Who are you talking to?" I heard a woman demanding in the background. "It's a foreigner, it's a foreigner," Sun whispered. Then he continued explaining the system over the phone. There were quotas for everything from pneumonia cases to house fires, he said. Take drownings. A Beijing vice-mayor in charge of drownings and five other kinds of unnatural deaths would issue the annual drowning quota. That number was then divvied up among Beijing's 18 districts and counties, depending on the number of people, swimming pools, canals and lakes each had.

Too many drownings in one district meant reduced bonuses, not to mention a couple of criticism sessions, for the officials in charge.

To ensure the following year's quota wasn't exceeded, Sun was pushing through stiffer safety rules and new fines. Fine the *victim*? I asked. No, no, he said, the swimming-pool administrators.

China's fixation with baby and steel quotas was famous. But few outsiders knew about its attempts to fetter the intangible, the accidental and the serendipitous. Stalinist-style quota fever infected virtually every aspect of life in China. What other country had three different ways to say "quota"? China's cultural obsession with numbers stemmed from a 4,000-year-old bureaucratic urge to quantify, combined with a Communist zeal to override Nature. Other philosophers tried to understand the world, says the epitaph on Karl Marx's tomb. "The point, however, is to change it." Mao Zedong agreed, saying, "Battling the heavens brings unlimited pleasure."

As a history student at Beijing University, this other Mao slogan was also seared into my brain: "People, and only people, are the motive force creating world history." Communists believed human beings can alter the course of history. So you needed plans, goals and targets. It was the opposite of fate or destiny.

The adherence to Communist-style quotas, even as China raced down the capitalist path, revealed how much the country was changing, and not changing. In the 1950s, anti-pest campaigns set quotas for dead flies and rat tails, which you actually brought into an office to be counted. In the 1990s, austerity campaigns set quotas for corporate bank loans.

While Western companies sometimes have affirmative-action quotas for minorities, China had quotas for drug dealers. During the 1957 Anti-Rightist Campaign, Mao estimated that China had 4,000 "bourgeois rightists." But enthusiasm for over-fulfilling the political-pariah quota sent more than 500,000 people to the gulag, some for as long as 20 years.

Quotas could be a matter of life and death. In 1988, when Deng Xiaoping launched an anti-crime campaign, authorities in Changping county, north of Beijing, fulfilled their quota by summarily executing several dozen locals. "They rounded up a bunch of people and shot them, just like that," said Joan Hinton, an American who worked on a dairy farm there. "We knew because they posted the names afterward, with a red check mark, meaning the executions had been carried out."

Quotas fixed the number of migrants allowed in Beijing. It set the number of cars an organization could own. It also established the number of primary students who would flunk each year. For budgetary reasons in 1994, the province of Anhui set its failure quota at zero. That meant no child repeated a grade there that year.

The system was confusing. Some quotas had to be filled. Others couldn't be exceeded. Prisoners had to produce a daily quota of bricks, or face beatings and reduced rations. Village governments had to supply an annual quota of new soldiers, or face fines. Traffic-fatality quotas were another matter.

"We don't try to fulfill the quota for dead people," said Zhao Jiaying, as other officials in the room tittered. "We try to reduce the number."

Zhao, deputy director of Beijing's traffic management bureau, parceled out carnage quotas to 18 counties and districts. Just like drowning quotas, they were based on a brain-numbing formula of each district's population, bikes, vehicles, roads, police force and previous fatalities.

To keep Beijing's death toll below a pre-determined total of 476, Deputy Director Zhao ordered shameful yellow signs nailed at the entrances of organizations with bad safety records. He urged newspapers to print the names of officials in districts with too many fatalities and he forced reckless drivers to attend remedial classes. But despite his best efforts, there had been 55 traffic deaths too many the previous year. So he ordered a traffic-ticket blitz. Police handed out so many fines that some Beijingers assumed there was a quota for that, too. (Not true, said Deputy Director Zhao.)

The doctor in charge of Beijing's disease quotas had headaches, too. "We have too many quotas," complained Yao Hong, waving a thick white book of specifications. "We have quotas for 28 illnesses. Each one has 42 sub-quotas. You need a computer to figure it out."

His colleague, Wang Yi, grew rattled as he tried to clarify the quota on food poisonings. In 1990, he said, it was two deaths for Beijing, but no one died. "We didn't fulfill our quota."

"You mean people have to die?" Dr. Yao teased. Wang Yi glared at him, then continued, "And in 1991, we had a quota of two deaths, and we fulfilled it exactly."

In 1992, the quota for food-poisoning deaths in Beijing fell to one per year. "I'm most afraid of getting a call from him," said Dr. Yao, pointing to Wang Yi. "He calls me and we have to send a rescue team immediately to the hospital. The whole city's resources are poured into saving this one person."

In 1988, when a hepatitis epidemic swept Shanghai, health officials in Beijing checked every traveler arriving from there. "We took blood samples and requested every hotel to report any sickness," said Wang Yi. The massive effort worked. Beijing didn't exceed its hepatitis quota that year.

But try as they might, there was still one quota that they always had trouble fulfilling. "Autopsies," sighed Dr. Yao. "We're supposed to perform autopsies in 20 percent of deaths, but hardly any family gives us permission."

As a foreign correspondent, I had a driver, a cook, a nanny and a housekeeper. But they didn't really work for me. They were state workers belonging to the Foreign Ministry's Diplomatic Service Bureau (DSB).

Rent-A-Serf Inc., as I preferred to call the DSB, shamelessly grabbed the bulk of my staff's salaries. That eliminated the carrot. As state workers, they also ate from the proverbial "iron rice bowl," the Chinese term for cradle-to-grave security. Even if I fired them, the DSB would always find them a job elsewhere. That eliminated the stick. With no carrot and no stick, I simply paid them secret bonuses to do the job I was paying them to do in the first place.

If only state-owned enterprises could have done the same. They had no carrots or sticks, either. And they certainly had no slush fund. State enterprises were drowning in red ink. The smartest, fastest, toughest workers had quit for the private sector. That left behind the elderly, the timid, the stupid and the losers, or the free-loaders who collected state paychecks while moonlighting in the private sector. In the 1990s, Beijing declared that one-third of

China's 100 million state workers were surplus – the size of the entire population of Canada.

For years, Beijing kept announcing it would "reform" state enterprises. In the 1980s, it even passed a bankruptcy law. But firing the proletariat cut to the very heart of Communism. Who dared put workers out on the street, especially with more than 100 million peasants already crowding those same streets?

Industrial workers weren't the only ones facing a bleak future by the end of the millennium. In 1999, I looked up my old friend, Elegance, who had taken me to Waterdown 11 years earlier. She was sick that day and couldn't see me. But her husband, who had been Norman's boss at the Institute of Computing Technology, poured me tea. He told me that the once-prestigious Chinese Academy of Sciences was downsizing its researchers. "It chooses 25 percent of the researchers and throws money and resources at them. The rest, it freezes their salaries, gives them no research funds and tells them to go out on their own."

In Beijing, my old classmate, Gu Weiming (Future Gu), had finally moved out of his shabby turn-of-the-century housing and into a new apartment. In our entire class, he was the last to get indoor plumbing and central heating. I was so pleased for him. But his appearance shocked me deeply. His once-bristling black brushcut had gone grey, and was falling out in patches. It looked motheaten. His face was deeply lined.

"Stress," said Future. "I have so much stress at work." Over a dinner of takeout Chinese food, he told me that half the staff at the History Institute where he worked would be dismissed over the next few years. His own job as deputy librarian was in jeopardy. The chief librarian wanted to promote a young woman he fancied. The boss insinuated that Future, who was in charge of book purchases, was embezzling.

"It used to be they'd accuse you of political problems," he said sadly. "Then it was improper relations with the opposite sex. Now it's always corruption."

I was incensed. Future would never do anything dishonest, which is probably why he was the last in our class to get indoor plumbing. When we toiled on Big Joy Farm, he had always worked the hardest. If a straight-arrow like Future was in trouble, the whole system was crumbling.

In 1998 alone, state-owned enterprises lost $8 billion and four million state workers were dismissed. The total ranks of the unemployed numbered at least 30 million. That did not include six million workers "in transition," a euphemism for those on a temporary dole.

In Sichuan, China's largest province, with a population of more than 120 million, one-third of its factories were losing money. "They have their hands outstretched to me," Governor Xiao Yang told me. "But I also have to pay attention to what peasants want. The price of fertilizer can't be too high."

In 1999, an illegal labor market sprang up in Beijing, a one-minute drive from Chairman Mao's mausoleum. Like wallflowers at a high-school dance, about 200 migrant workers milled around, hoping someone would hire them. Instead of carnations, they pinned torn pieces of cardboard on their jackets and scrawled on them: "bricklayer," "carpenter," "painter." One man's said, "Cook: can prepare all kinds of dishes."

Dalian, in China's rust belt, was reeling from an unemployment rate close to 20 percent. Even in the booming south, the rate was 10 percent in many places. Laid-off workers in Hangzhou squeezed by on stipends of 270 yuan ($34) a month, enough to sustain a sparse diet and nothing more.

When the proletariat had nothing to lose but its chains, massive unemployment meant massive unrest. At the Wuhan Iron and Steel Works, unpaid workers began stealing steel. After the factory called in the army, clashes left one soldier dead and several workers injured. "China relied on the workers to take power. Then it betrayed them," said Han Dongfang, a labor activist in exile in Hong Kong.

Even in remote Tibet, hundreds of Chinese retirees staged a sit-in at the Transport Department after inflation eroded their pensions. "All the Communist officials went out and persuaded them to go home," said one senior cadre in Lhasa. "They promised to take care of them. But it's all lies. There is no money."

■

The average Chinese state worker spent about 2,440 hours on the job a year, compared with 1,900 for Canadian workers and 2,100 for the famously workaholic Japanese. Aside from Chinese New Year's, China had just three public holidays a year: New Year's Day, May 1 International Labor Day and October 1st National Day. One Wall Street analyst took one look and recommended his clients invest in Chinese stocks.

He didn't know that the Chinese word for goldbricking was *mo yang gong*, or "faking work for the foreigner." Holidays were a fluid concept. Take Chinese New Year, or Spring Festival, which in the 1970s consisted of three days in February. But the more the state sector disintegrated, the more the holiday grew. By the 1980s, Spring Festival had become five days. By the 1990s, it had expanded to 30 or 40 days for many workers. During that time, one-fifth of the world's population did little but eat, sleep and visit relatives.

The rest of the year, it was hard to tell the difference. Everyone shopped, napped and visited relatives during working hours. An out-of-town guest was good for three days paid leave. Donating blood got you a month off to recuperate. In Ningxia, the capital of Qinghai Province, it was 100 days before any of the courthouse workers noticed that the flag out front was upside down.

Chinese weren't inherently slothful. It was the Communist system. State workers who straddled both worlds saved all their energies for moonlighting. In Sichuan, an investigation caught 108 senior provincial officials with second jobs in private industry. In Chengdu, the provincial capital, I met a 29-year-old auto worker named Huang Caijian who had persuaded a doctor to diagnose him with an ulcer. Huang never showed up at his factory again – except to collect his paycheck. While on this open-ended "sick leave," he doubled his income by working at a privately owned restaurant.

Keeping down unemployment meant absurd over-employment. Gas-meter readers always came in pairs. So did telex repairmen. At the People's Bank, a routine withdrawal required five employees and most of a morning. The first teller checked your identification card. The second ensured the forms had been correctly filled out.

A third okayed your signature. A fourth counted the money. And a fifth recounted the money – before finally flinging the bills in your direction.

When I ordered room service in Chengdu, two waitresses delivered the two bowls of noodles and two pairs of chopsticks. What if I had ordered noodles for ten? At a summer barbeque at Beijing's Great Wall Sheraton, I once counted 23 waiters, chefs and maître d's for 20 guests. "We tried to reduce, but it was too big a hassle," said Max Wilhelm, the general manager, unhappily alluding to the "full-employment policy" China imposed on foreign companies.

At the Shanghai Hotel, a comely young woman in a red silk cheongsam stood all day long on the ground floor by the elevators. Her sole task: pushing the "up" button whenever a guest approached. In the adjacent seafood restaurant, four similarly clad young women, clutching menus, stood in formation at the entrance. Their job: shouting a chorus of greetings to customers.

Dare I say how many Chinese it took to change a light bulb? Five. When a bulb burned out in the *Globe*'s office, Driver Liu would phone the dispatcher at the Diplomatic Housing Bureau. The dispatcher would send over two workers. They would show up empty-handed. So a fifth person had to be summoned to fetch a ladder – and a light bulb.

The noon siesta, once enshrined in the Chinese Constitution, was abolished in the 1980s. But lots of siesta-style jobs remained. One was standing beside escalators, apparently to pick up anybody who fell down. I'm being serious; in a developing country of 1.3 billion, there was always someone who had never been on an escalator.

In the Shanghai subway, uniformed attendants blew warning whistles every time trains approached. That one didn't make sense to me. If the attendant could hear the train coming, so could everyone else. Then the Shanghai subway introduced "smart cards," which were pretty dumb, considering. Instead of saving labor, attendants were stationed at every turnstile – coming *and* going – to show passengers how to slip the magnetic fare cards into the slot.

Another siesta-style job was operating automatic elevators. Unlike the young lady at the Shanghai Hotel, these operators went right inside the elevator with you. Actually, you went inside *their* elevators. I always felt like I was intruding in their personal space because they usually furnished the elevators with chairs, small desks, tea thermoses, magazines, books and electric space heaters. At Radio Beijing, one operator actually moved a bed into the elevator. The operator, who didn't bother pushing the buttons – it was, after all, an *automatic* elevator – was believed to be a man. "You only see this huddled mass in one of those army coats," said Michael D'Souza, a Torontonian who worked the early-morning shift there for a few years.

One time, I arrived at a Beijing high-rise to find the operator gone AWOL. "Where's the attendant?" I asked a middle-aged woman, who was visibly annoyed by the delay. "No idea," she snapped. I noticed that the key was still in the control panel, locked on manual. I fantasized about taking the elevator up myself. What if I turned the key one notch to automatic and stormed the elevator? Would the Communist Party fall? Would democracy come to China? Would I take the crabby woman along, too? I must have been in China too long because I didn't make a move.

My reverie was disturbed by footfalls, a clearing of the throat and the unmistakable thwack of spit hitting the concrete floor. The attendant, a young man in a western suit, removed the key and stepped inside the elevator. We followed meekly. The woman smiled warmly at him and exchanged pleasantries. I marveled at how magically she had buried her annoyance. Suppressing emotions like that must be the glue that held Chinese society together, I mused. I was so caught up in these thoughts that I forgot to ask for my floor. Finally, the attendant turned to me. "Ten," I said. And I smiled, too.

China's military-industrial complex was the dregs of the state sector. Its problem: location, location, location. Fifty thousand factories had been deliberately built in the worst possible places, part of Chairman Mao's 1950s plan to shelter China's defense industry from nuclear war. In the 1990s, their remote locations – and their Maoist mindset – became insurmountable handicaps.

"Military products remain our priority," said Zheng Peiying, deputy general manager of astronautics in the Ministry of Aerospace and Astronautics Industry. That was brave talk. As government subsidies dried up, military factories desperately diversified into civilian products. The target for 1999 was 80 percent civilian output.

Easier said than done. At the New Prosperity Instrument Factory in Chengdu, Fang Xiliang unlocked a door to the Product Display Room. A better name might have been the Museum of Rusting Plowshares. Under red velvet dust covers was an array of all its failed products: electric etching pens, negative-ion generators, steel frying-pan handles, clunky ultrasound monitors and golf-club heads. New Prosperity, which once made missile-guidance systems, could not make golf-club heads to meet U.S. import standards.

"This one was obsolete before we finished," said Fang, the factory's administrative director, unhappily pointing to a record player. He motioned to a set of stereo headphones pinned to a board like an insect specimen. "That was too primitive. We stopped production after a few hundred sets." He showed me a personal computer made of Pakistani components. That proved substandard, and importing the parts cost more than a finished one sold for domestically. "We were duped," he said.

Built in 1957 with Soviet aid and obsolete technology, New Prosperity was once the exclusive supplier of compasses to Chinese air force transport planes. Now, after a series of failed products, it was trying to make a stove that burned sugar-cane waste.

The factory longed for a white knight from abroad. Despite visitors from Canada, Taiwan and the United States, no one had signed up for a joint venture. No wonder. Still under Cold-War security measures, the factory wouldn't allow any photographs, not even of its workers making horse-bridle bits for export to the United States.

Like many state factories, New Prosperity was huge and rambling, with dozens of workshops, leafy trees and its own nursery, clinic, canteens and repair shops. I'd heard rumors that two-thirds of capacity at the average military factory was idle. I asked Director Fang if I could visit a workshop, any workshop. He twitched with embarrassment. "None are operating today," he said. "We hardly ever work during the first week of the month. After that, it depends on whether there are any orders."

Dinosaurs that had never uttered the word "profit" tried to transform themselves into earners of hard currency. One military factory adapted trigger-making technology to automatic garage-door openers. Others churned out coffee mugs, snake wine and lingerie. Norinco, China's largest arms conglomerate, accounted for half the country's annual motorcycle production and one-third of its minivans. It also opened for-profit shooting arcades. One Sunday morning, I decided to visit one to see if it was a hit.

Norinco's shooting range was in the heart of a secret military zone, midway between the Great Wall and the Ming Tombs. To keep you on the straight and narrow, each side street posted big, unfriendly signs in Chinese, Russian and English, "Foreigners forbidden from this road."

Miniature golf, it wasn't. Soldiers with fixed bayonets guarded the parking lot. You could choose from 20 different types of military weapons, everything from mortars to anti-aircraft machine guns. I arrived just as three busloads of Chinese factory workers and their families rushed into a nondescript yellow building. "Ooh," squealed one middle-aged woman, running up to a display of Chinese-made AK-47s. "Where do we start?"

We all crowded into a reception room to watch a six-minute video about guns. "Don't point the gun at other people," it advised. Then we hurried through an exhibit of Chinese-made M-16s, pistols that doubled as daggers, semi-automatic sniper rifles and anti-tank rockets. "This is fun," said Liu Guiping, 23, a worker at a locomotive-repair factory. She was dressed to kill, in high-heeled sandals, a white silk dress and pale pink sparkling nail polish.

The shooting range was an open-air area that overlooked a large field. We adults, apparently defined as anyone over age 12, took turns going into the firing booths. Each was separated by steel walls from its neighbors and manned by experienced marksmen. I donned ear protectors, squeezed off a round and completely missed a distant paper target. That was not surprising, considering I had shut my eyes.

Deng Yue, a worker from an electrical cable factory, brought her 14-year-old son. He managed to hit the target twice. "Not bad," she said, with maternal pride. Then it was her turn. She donned a shoulder pad and ear muffs before hunching over a submachine gun. Like me, she closed her eyes when she squeezed the trigger and missed the target.

The workers' outing was subsidized by their factories. AK-47s rented for $20, plus 60 cents per bullet. A 40-millimeter anti-tank rocket cost $186, a bargain considering the price included the right to demolish a cement-and-brick guardhouse.

Against the backdrop of artillery fire, children caught dragonflies and scavenged for spent shells. A five-year-old who tried to sneak into the gallery and was shooed away responded with a ground-flailing tantrum. The shooting range had hoped for 1,000 customers in the first year, but 7,000 came. Even so, the range hadn't been able to pay back its initial $2.6-million investment.

A lone Chinese tourist took a bus to the nearby town, then walked the last few kilometers to the range. But when he found out the cost, he wanted to fire just one bullet. The shooting range refused. "How would we make money that way?" sniffed Wang Guiyang, a weapons designer doing double duty as a hostess.

Tourism, Chinese-style, was not for the romantic or the faint of heart. In Beijing, I met a Shanghai couple on their first package tour. "We're on our honeymoon," explained Wu Jianxin, discreetly holding hands with his bride on their tour bus. The only problem was they weren't, uh, sharing a room – the hotel was packing them four to a room, segregated by sex.

"Our people can handle tough conditions," said Zhou Fuhui, an official of the Shanghai Travel Service. "They're crazy about tourism. Before, we considered it a bourgeois luxury. But now we call it 'seeing the sights of the motherland.'"

China always had state-organized tours of revolutionary sites. Student Red Guards, however, were more interested in site-destroying than sightseeing. But in the late 1980s, Chinese began indulging in leisure travel for the first time in 40 years. Some peasant tycoons even chartered planes to go touring.

"We peasants love to travel," said Jiang Liangshen. He, however, was not a tycoon. With his wife and 13-year-old son, he had endured a 17-hour overnight ride from Shanghai in a third-class train compartment. "We never had the chance before. I told my family, 'You must see Beijing.'"

They were on the same eight-day tour as the newlyweds. On arrival at the Beijing Train Station, they were whisked — in the pouring rain — to the Temple of Heaven. Four days later, it was still raining when they breakfasted on rice gruel and steamed buns. At 7:45 a.m., they picked their way through the mud and boarded their bus.

At the Ming Tombs, the guide shouted through a bullhorn, "Everybody stay together." Then he barreled ahead, waving a small blue flag. Down in the underground mausoleum, the group gawked at solid gold wash basins and tossed coins onto the coffin of the Yong Le Emperor. At lunch, we squeezed ten to a table, sharing platters of scrambled eggs and tomatoes, stir-fried pork, braised cabbage and all the rice we could eat. Aside from a big bowl of egg-drop soup, there was nothing to drink — not even water. After spending the equivalent of six weeks wages on the tour, no one wanted to pay one more yuan for a Coke.

In remote Qinghai Province, China's most bizarre hotel struggled to transform itself from a secret military installation into a tourist hot spot. The Qinghai Lake Guest House was located in a ghost town called Jiangxigou, 10,400 feet above sea level. Call it Club Dead. Built on the shores of China's largest saltwater lake, it overlooked, not the lake, but a dozen abandoned buildings. The lake itself was devoid of pleasure craft. And instead of tanned waiters bearing exotic drinks, scrawny pigs roamed at will.

Mention the place to ordinary Chinese, and they shuddered. Qinghai (pronounced Ching-High) was the heart of China's notorious gulag. For centuries, Chinese emperors exiled disgraced officials to a living death in this landlocked, sparsely populated province of snowcapped mountains. Every Chinese province had its share of labor camps and prisons, but Qinghai was China's Siberia, its dumping ground for surplus convicts.

The gulag permeated Qinghai more than any other province. Truckloads of condemned criminals, in tattered black-and-blue prison garb, were sentenced to death before huge crowds in Xining, the provincial capital. "When I was in middle school, we had to attend every single execution rally," said a television producer who grew up in Qinghai. "It was revolting."

One-fourth of Qinghai's 4.3 million people were prisoners, ex-prisoners and their families. All convicts, except the very ill, had to work. They also had to pay for their own food. Few escaped. As in Qing Dynasty times, prisoners had shaved heads. Thus marked, fugitives had little chance of finding food or shelter. The windswept Qinghai-Tibet Plateau, romantically called the Roof of the World, was in fact a barren death trap. Altitude sickness – Qinghai averaged 9,800 feet above sea level – affected even long-time residents. "It's as if we're always carrying more than 10 catties (11 pounds) on our backs," complained one local official.

Chairman Mao considered the remote location ideal for China's defense industry. During the Cold War, he uprooted thousands of people and dozens of factories from the industrial heartland and plunked them down in the middle of pastureland. By the 1990s, Qinghai was an uneasy blend of loyal Communist cadres who had heeded the party's call and residents of the gulag who had not. Added to this were Tibetans, Mongolians and Muslims who were less than thrilled about having the gulag in their backyard.

For years, the province was closed to all but a handful of foreigners. When I went in 1992, vast parts of its windswept plains remained off-limits. Air travel was still so exotic that when my plane landed in the provincial capital of Xining, dozens of herdsmen gathered to watch. (Cows, yaks and sheep outnumbered people there five to one.)

I'd gone to Qinghai to report on the gulag. But I couldn't say that, of course. I told the provincial Foreign Affairs Office I wanted to write about tourism. They were so happy they allowed me invite a colleague. I brought along Caroline Straathof of *De Volkskrant*, which, she never tired of telling the Chinese, meant the *People's Daily* in Dutch.

To keep up appearances, Caroline and I agreed to visit the Qinghai Lake Guest House, a day's high-altitude drive from Xining. And that is how we ended up as Club Dead's only guests. The hostile staff told us the site was a former textile factory. We picked our way through the ruins, which included a vast auditorium and, yes, a shooting range. We encountered some young men playing basketball on an abandoned concrete court. They told us the real story. Until 1987, Club Dead had been Factory No. 151, a secret military installation for manufacturing torpedoes.

Suddenly, it clicked. We were at Koko Nor, the Mongolian name for Qinghai Lake. And this was the famous torpedo test site of the Chinese Navy. Braving April winds so cold we got earaches, Caroline and I stumbled down to the pebbled shores of the huge ice-blue lake. We discovered a well-built, abandoned pier. Presumably, this was where freshly made torpedoes had been loaded onto ships for military exercises.

The only thing still in the lake now was Qinghai's unjustly famous Naked Carp, a scaleless, bony, primordial-looking fish that grew one pound every ten years, metabolically slowed by the water's icy temperature. At dinner each night, the hotel served us Naked Carp cooked eight different ways, including candied. After the third course, we gave up trying to pick our way through the needle-like bones, and stuck to the gray, wizened rice.

The Qinghai Lake Guest House was two stars below Spartan. Considering parts were once actual barracks, no wonder we didn't have a seat on our toilet or towels in the room, not to mention amenities like heat and hot water. But the staff had thoughtfully provided thermometers so we'd know when the temperature in our room plunged to a knuckle-numbing 50°F at night.

Recycling a torpedo factory into a hotel was only a small part of Qinghai's grand design to develop tourism for the tough. Provincial authorities were mulling whether to let foreigners sightsee at prison factories, too. And brochures promoted bus tours so arduous that whole days were listed as "recuperation."

On our last day, the Foreign Affairs Office feted us with a banquet of sautéed yak penis (terrible and spongy) and chili-fried camel's footpads (so-so and spongy). "Everybody says we are barren, that we have no people and lots of criminals," said Liu Wenxiang, deputy director of Qinghai's Planning Commission, as he politely deposited another slice of yak penis on my plate. "But we have lots of electricity, minerals and potash fertilizer."

When I seemed unimpressed – by the potash, not the penis – he added, hopefully, "In summer, you don't need air conditioning."

6

Serve the People

Lin Shutao, a 90-year-old gourmet and cookbook author who received me weekly in his home in 1980 to talk about Chinese cuisine.   Photo: Jan Wong

Decades of socialist sloth had transformed Mao's famous slogan, "Serve the People," into "Screw the People." When consumers initially shunned Coke in favor of Sprite, some Tianjin shops forced anyone wanting Sprite to buy a bottle of Coke, too. The Chinese eventually learned to love Coke.

That's a pity, considering half the country's 1.3 billion people don't brush their teeth. A survey in northern Shanxi province found that 95 percent of peasants lacked toothbrushes and toothpaste. Dental care mostly consisted of sidewalk barbers yanking out rotting molars.

Like many Chinese, Nanny Ma had terrible teeth, a legacy of growing up in dentist-free rural China. But as a state worker, her perks included free visits to a state-run dental clinic. Or maybe it wasn't a perk.

"Look at your filthy shoes!" the dentist screamed, as Nanny Ma climbed into the chair. "You're soiling the footrest! Keep your feet off it." Nanny Ma, then in her 40s, flushed deeply. But she dutifully kept her legs splayed.

"I felt like I was at the gynecologist's," she huffed later.

I'd accompanied her there, and I don't mean to the waiting room. Privacy was a foreign concept. I stood right beside her and the dentist, who was in turn shadowed by her assistant.

The dentist, a rotund battleaxe in her 50s named Ren Geli, wore a white lab coat and gauze mask, revealing only a pair of angry eyes. "Take out your false tooth," she growled. "How do you expect me to work on your mouth?" Nanny Ma put her dental plate on the table beside her. Dr. Ren glared. "Don't put your tooth there!" She rapped a metal container with one of her picks. Nanny Ma meekly put her dental plate in the container.

She was in terrible pain. A large filling had fallen out just before Chinese New Year. With the entire country in month-long siesta mode, Nanny Ma's tooth had become infected. Dr. Ren peered inside. "Look at this mess," she told her assistant. "The dental pulp is all black. I have no guarantee I can fill this tooth without splitting it." Dr. Ren swabbed the affected tooth with medicine and inserted some cotton pads. "I'm not going to fill it today," she told Nanny Ma. "Don't eat on that side. Don't brush it."

"Please," said Nanny Ma, adopting the obsequious tone Chinese use when dealing with authority, "when will you be able to fill it?"

"Next week," Dr. Ren snapped.

What about a cleaning? Nanny Ma pleaded. The government had cut that perk, but she had brought her own money. Dr. Ren glared again. "I can't do it today. How can I have time to clean teeth! Look how many people I have waiting."

I looked. We were her second patients of the day. There were three others, and that was it. The registration desk out front had already closed. Nanny Ma asked when Dr. Ren might have a spare moment to clean teeth. "When there's fewer people," the dentist snarled.

When we left, Nanny Ma was shaking with rage, near tears and still in pain. I passed her a tissue. After she calmed down, she waxed philosophical. "That's the way things are done here. Getting mad accomplishes nothing."

I always got mad. On a three-hour flight from Chengdu to Beijing, I had a showdown with a flight attendant who refused to remove the dinner trays. "Later," she snapped, when I managed to flag her down. Then she ducked into First Class for a siesta and yanked the curtain divider closed. Soon, the other passengers began dumping their trays, gravy and all, into the seat pockets in front. I set mine down on the aisle floor. My row-mates passed theirs over for good measure.

Just before landing, the flight attendant reappeared, smiling and refreshed, to retrieve the dripping trays from the seat pockets. When she came to my row, she couldn't push her cart past the three trays blocking the aisle. Then she remembered.

"Pick up your tray," she ordered.

"You pick it up," I said, not at all obsequiously.

"Pick up your tray," she repeated.

"You pick it up."

That was how Chinese argued. Everyone repeated the same phrase, over and over again. I, however, had the advantage: we were landing. Besides, I was way more stubborn. Another passenger finally ended the air-rage impasse by getting up and retrieving the trays.

"Who do you think you are?" the flight attendant snapped at me, knowing she'd lost the battle. "A foreigner?"

What did it matter? Even though foreigners until recently were charged more for their airline tickets, the service was equally bad. These were the unfriendly skies of the Civil Aviation Administration of China, or CAAC, which some wag insisted stood for China Airlines Always Canceled. Its unofficial motto: Service with a snarl.

It's not that they weren't selective about flight attendants. You had to be a tall, slender, pretty virgin. Fan Luqi, a tall, slender, pretty flight attendant-in-training, confirmed to me that she had had to undergo a gynecological exam.

The training itself was perfunctory. At China's only flight-attendant school, I watched applicants being spun around four times on a swivel chair. If they didn't get dizzy, they were in. Once accepted, they spent 72 classroom hours on emergency procedures – and 78 hours on makeup, aviation history and "the psychological effect of colors on passengers."

After complaints about surly service, China sent some staff to Singapore Airlines for smiling practice. Norman must have got one of those the day fog closed down the Beijing airport. Worried that he would miss a computer conference in San Francisco the next morning, he approached a CAAC clerk. She examined his ticket.

"Don't worry," she said with a wide smile. "Your ticket is good for a year."

In the early 1990s, China's safety record plummeted as pilots, many of them newly trained, smashed into mountainsides, over-ran runways and wrestled with hijackers. Nor did flight attendants care whether you buckled your seat belt or stood with your suitcase in the aisle during a landing. China's safety record has since improved, but authorities weren't taking chances with Year 2000 computer bugs. As an incentive to be prepared, airline chiefs were ordered to board their own flights on New Year's Day. "All the heads of the airlines have got to be in the air on January 1, 2000," said Zhao Bo, the official in charge of handling China's Y2K problem.

The food matched the bad service and dubious safety practices. In-flight meals often consisted of hard-boiled eggs and packets of dried squid. On one flight from Beijing to San Francisco, the crew moved into business class, spat watermelon seeds on the carpet and enjoyed a hot breakfast while serving cold ones to passengers, according to a complaint by John Rumrich, a teacher from Austin, Texas. In a response printed in the English-language *China Daily*, CAAC agreed that spitting seeds was "unsightly." But it said crews were always entitled to first-class food. And business class seats were reserved for crews on long-haul flights. "Actually, passengers sat in the crew members' compartment," the airline said.

A Dutch businessman told me that he once had the feeling something was missing from his lunch tray on a flight from Xian to Shanghai. "There was rice. There were vegetables. There was a smudge of brown gravy." Later, he spied the crew in the galley, wolfing down stacks of meat. "They had opened each and every box and taken out the meat and were sitting there eating it." Their reaction when they saw him? "They just closed the curtain."

I have Chinese food in my genes. At one time, my father owned five restaurants in Montreal, including the House of Wong, Hong Kong House and a huge one on Decarie Boulevard called Bill Wong's. So when I first arrived in China in 1972, the restaurants shocked me. First, there were hardly any. New York City had more

Chinese restaurants than the capital of China. Beijing's were so few and far between that every single one was impossibly crowded.

You had to plant yourself behind a diner to grab the seat the moment it was vacant. Then you gingerly brushed off the table – and sometimes the seat – and ate with your feet on the accumulated spit and spat-out bones. You also fetched your own chopsticks and paid in advance. Napkins, tea, even drinking water, weren't available. Nor did restaurants open at lunch or dinner. That's when the staff ate. Customers lunched before noon and dined in the late afternoon. Everything shut down by 6:30 p.m.

Yet socialist sloth never diminished the glory of Chinese food. Even in the austere 1970s, you could always get juicy morsels of Peking Duck tucked into paper-thin steamed crepes. From November 15 to March 15, exactly the dates that state-run furnaces switched on each winter, you could share a Mongolian Hotpot, swishing thin sliced raw mutton in a simmering broth. And every man, woman and child knew how to make *jiaozi*, the ravioli stuffed with minced pork, tender cabbage, ginger and garlic. I inhaled them by the dozens, dipped in dark rice vinegar.

In 1980, I befriended a 90-year-old widower named Lin Shutao. The grandson of a Qing Dynasty general, Lin had grown up in luxury, spoiled by four chefs and an army of nursemaids and servants. In 1951, newly dispossessed after the Communist revolution, Lin opened the Kang Le, a restaurant that would become one of the most famous in Beijing. Premier Chou En-lai patronized it. Madame Sun Yat-sen sent two of her cooks there to learn the restaurant's secrets.

Lin retired in 1961, and lived alone in a tiny room in a traditional courtyard home. Once a week, I bicycled over with gifts of crisp Tianjin pears or warm roasted chestnuts and sat, literally at his knee, to chat about Chinese history, culture and above all, cuisine. With Gourmet Lin as my guide, I learned about such gastronomic delights as Peach Blossom Rice, Jadeite Custard and Crossing-the-Bridge Noodles.

A stooped man with a wispy white beard, Lin was a little hard of hearing and sometimes hazy about dates. Every now and then, he had to ask what year we were in. But I was embarrassed more than once when I asked a question, only to be told I had asked it two weeks earlier.

In the 1990s, Chinese dining underwent a cultural revolution. Profit-hungry restaurateurs served tea, opened at mealtimes and trusted customers to pay afterwards. At the Tipsy Restaurant, men were entitled to unlimited beer. Women, who had never quite caught up with men in the Maoist era and were now falling rapidly behind, were offered all the Sprite they wanted.

At Red Hibiscus, waitresses distributed condoms with the crispy chicken. Dubbed the "Safe Sex Diner" by the *China Daily*, it was partly owned by the State Family Planning Commission. Prospective parents could start the evening at the family-planning bar, which provided cocktails along with one-child propaganda and baby-care leaflets.

With China's divorce rate hitting 24 percent, up from zero in 1978, the Divorce Diner in Beijing claimed to ease the trauma of splitting up. Its theme menu included Lovebird Soup, Happy Family Reunion – and Going-Your-Own-Way Shrimp. The manager, himself divorced, claimed that in its first few weeks of operation, more than 100 such couples had come in for a last supper.

Nostalgia restaurants recreated the gulag for Chinese boomers. At Black Earth, middle-aged survivors of the Cultural Revolution met to munch on turnips and reminisce about their mass migration to the countryside.

Yi Ku Si Tian, another nostalgia eatery, titillated jaded palates with an array of famine-era food. Its name literally meant "Remembering the Bitterness of the Past to Savor the Sweetness of the Present." I took part in a few of these *yi ku si tian* consciousness-raising rituals during the Cultural Revolution. Usually, a tearful peasant would recite tales of woe. The audience would cry, too. Then we'd all share an inedible meal of weeds. In lieu of dessert, everyone would clench their fists and chant, "Down with landlords and all reactionaries!"

The restaurant's courtyard was festooned, like a peasant's cottage, with dried ears of corn and ropes of chili peppers. A trio of blind musicians serenaded diners with Chinese versions of *Red River Valley* and *Jingle Bells*. After the meal, a "beggar" offered a free shoeshine. A "coolie" pulled a rickshaw, now banned in China, provided you only wanted to go as far as the corner. The menu included steamed unseasoned cornmeal buns, braised weeds and deep-fried silkworm chrysalis. Scorpions, served on a bed of crispy vermicelli, were an expensive update on the twitching grasshoppers starving Chinese peasants once consumed. The food was surprisingly expensive and surprisingly tasty. "We can't really expect people to eat tree bark," said Duan Yunsong, the manager.

Several restaurants cashed in on the Mao-memorabilia craze. The Mao Family Restaurant even had a small red shrine to the Great Helmsman, always with a fresh offering of Mao's favorite dish, Soy-Braised Fatty Pork with Whole Garlic Cloves. Each diner got a free Mao button. Customers who collected 24 buttons got a free dish of Fatty Pork, the same idea as those little punch-hole cards that get you a free tenth cup of coffee at Starbucks.

Perhaps some Mao Family frequent eaters ended up at Fatty's. This restaurant sold "slimming teas," positioned a bathroom scale at the entrance and offered a 5 percent discount for fat people, good for their entire party. Males exceeding 207 pounds and females exceeding 183 pounds qualified. "There are too many restaurants and competition is fierce. You have to do something special to attract customers," said Zhang Yan, the restaurant's pot-bellied owner, who said he wanted to create a place where overweight people felt welcome. As he stepped onto the scale to prove he weighed 209 pounds, I asked why all his waitresses were slim. "Fat people are lazy." As I jotted that in my notebook, he hastily added, "Just kidding."

Nudge. The man in seat 22B woke me up. It was midafternoon and we had been airborne for an hour. I didn't know my row-mate, but while I dozed, he had tucked a sugary orange drink into my seat pocket. Now he was handing me the straw. "No thanks," I said, smiling weakly. "Take it anyway," he urged. I took it, thanked him, and drifted back to sleep.

Nudge. Here's your lunch box. Nudge. Do you want fizzy lichee juice? Mercifully, he didn't wake me a fourth or fifth time for the fresh mandarin orange and the packet of herbal cough drops. Instead, he left them on my tray table, which he had thoughtfully lowered for me.

For Chinese, food was a consuming passion. After thousands of years of famine, they seem to have developed a special anti-starvation gene. Or was it merely because two hours later, you were hungry again?

Our Boeing 737 landed just in time for supper in Chengdu, the capital of Sichuan Province. Known in the West as Szechwan, people here were even more obsessed with food than the average Chinese. The Sichuanese were so passionate about spices that some packed their own while traveling. And they rarely ate anything au naturel. Even a snack of peanuts came dosed with chili peppers and sea salt.

Like France, China had great regional cuisines. Gastronomes argued ferociously, over a banquet, of course, about which region was best. Three cuisines were coastal: Guangdong, in the south, which specialized in delicate dishes using the freshest ingredients; Jiangsu, in the middle, famous for its succulent Shanghainese soy-based cooking; and Shandong, in the north, birthplace of Confucius and home of leek-studded flatbreads and vinegar-pepper poached fish.

Only Sichuan, in the southwest, was landlocked. But fast-running waterways – its name means "Four Rivers" – traversed its bamboo-fringed mountains and fed into its fertile alluvial plain. Bigger than France, the province produced more rice than any other, enough to sustain its 120 million people, or nearly one in ten Chinese. In springtime, its fields glowed with the buttercup-yellow flowers of the canola crop.

Sichuan's humid subtropical climate made food preservation crucial. Smoking, drying, pickling and above all, a wanton use of spices, especially chili peppers, became the hallmark of its earthy, voluptuous cuisine. So-called Sichuan restaurants in the West were mostly phony. I knew of only two exceptions, one in New York and one near San Mateo, California, and even they couldn't make proper *dan dan* noodles. Most restaurants in the West cheated by hiring Cantonese chefs and pouring commercial chili sauce in everything. Sichuanese gagged when I told them restaurants in North America made Hot and Sour Soup with chili oil instead of the requisite jolt of ground white pepper.

Sichuan's earliest recipes, according to Chengdu's culinary historian Xiong Sizhi, were tonics for the emperor, created to invigorate him and ensure that he spawned many sons. In 1992, Chengdu's renowned Hall of Harmony and Benevolence was both a restaurant and a pharmacy. It served three-snake wine for numbness, bisque of dried sea horses for indigestion and tonic of caterpillar fungus for anemia.

At the city's sprawling Green Stone Bridge Market, vendors sold Pekinese puppies, puffy-cheeked goldfish and lime-green parrots – not for the pot, but as pets. Amateur gardeners, with only a windowsill to their names, lusted over potted orchids, azaleas, grapevines, freesias and lilies. Weary shoppers reclined on bamboo chairs and ordered tiny earthen pots of espresso-strength oolong tea in teahouses that opened onto the street.

Market stalls overflowed with produce: stubby orange-red carrots, fat white turnips, wicker baskets of pearl onions, bamboo shoots still swathed in dry golden leaves, firm ivory cakes of fresh bean curd and mounds of dewy leeks, cabbages, shelled peas and lima beans. At mid-morning, vendors slurped steaming bowls of chili-laced noodles while urging shoppers to buy an extra lacquered duck, another bunch of homemade smoked sausages or a fresh-killed rabbit.

Spices spilled out of burlap sacks: blood-red chili peppers, whole white peppercorns and dark green knots of *zha cai*, aromatic preserved mustard tubers. To understand spice was to know the secret of the Sichuan sizzle. Its explosive chilies detonated on the palate, aromatic "flower peppercorns" numbed the mouth, and *dou ban* chili paste set the tongue dancing for relief. A spoonful of sliced *zha cai*, tossed into a pot of boiling water with a few slivers of lean pork made a fragrant clear consommé. And flower peppercorns weren't really peppercorns at all, but the pleasantly numbing aromatic buds of the prickly ash tree. Called "flower" because their outer skins unfurled like a tiny brown peony, the best ones came from Hanyuan, a mountain town on the Dadu River.

Chengdu was home to the Sichuan Culinary Institute, which trained about 200 Chinese students a year. When I heard the school was planning to offer classes to foreign tourists, I quickly persuaded an editor that we needed the story. Chinese students at the Institute spent three years learning to cook. I had one day.

As the first foreign guinea pig, I was given a chef named Lu Maoguo who had worked in Toronto's Fon San Jin Jiang Restaurant a few years earlier. He greeted me that winter's day in a spotless white toque and jacket, and handed me a matching set. The school, situated in a crumbling compound in the original walled city, was freezing in the winter of 1992, so I pulled the white jacket over my down jacket. I looked just like the Pilsbury Doughboy.

At 39, Chef Lu was the Martha Stewart of Sichuan cooking, without the silly smile. A shy perfectionist, he could carve lotuses out of turnips and prepare still-lifes of carrot boats sailing on a lake of jellied bean paste. But I was more interested in something I could eat.

So Chef Lu grabbed a handful of dried chili peppers and a cleaver and began chopping. He sliced garlic so white and glossy they looked like South Sea pearls. Then he minced a knot of fresh ginger root with sand still clinging to its pale-gold parchment skin. He'd found it difficult cooking Sichuan food in Canada, he said. The chilies were hot enough, but lacked perfume, and the vinegars had no zip. After the first frustrating month, he air-freighted a supply of his own spices from Chengdu to Toronto.

Our classrom was huge, an empty amphitheater fitted with three powerful gas burners and a blackboard. It felt like we were in an operating theater. Sichuan cuisine, I would learn, did require surgical precision. Like our classroom, Chinese kitchens were minimalist, with concrete floors, cold water, bad lighting and no decent counter space. But in these conditions, with only a wok, a cleaver and a chopping board, people had created one of the most wondrous cuisines in the world.

Wielding his menacing knife, Chef Lu could slice pork as thin as prosciutto, chop through a ham bone or, using its flat side, whack a thrashing fish unconscious. Once a day, he sharpened his cleaver on a smooth stone. "In Canada, you have a machine for slicing meat," said Chef Lu. "But you can cut your fingers off. It's dangerous."

The cleaver wasn't? He conceded most students cut themselves once. "Then, it doesn't happen again." Looking at the lethal knife, I expressed skepticism. Well, he agreed, the clumsier ones wound themselves half a dozen times or more. He showed me how he held the blade with his right thumb and forefinger. His left hand, curled into a tight claw, held the food, the knuckles forming a shield against fingertip loss.

Alas, I am left-handed. Because all Chinese were coerced into right-handedness from birth, Chef Lu had never taught a lefty before. I wondered if the Institute was insured against dismemberment and, if so, whether there was a policy exclusion for lefties. Very carefully, I tried out Chef Lu's cleaver. It was sharp as a razor. With each slice, the blade sank into the hunk of tree trunk we used as a chopping board. That was a culinary no-no. Real chefs practiced slicing meat on swatches of silk. If they managed not to cut the fabric, they graduated to using someone's bare back. Chef Lu didn't offer to disrobe for me.

Like karate experts, Chinese chefs had nine levels of achievement, depending on training, skill and seniority. Promotions depended on regular examinations. Chef Lu was a first-grade chef. The highest rank was a "special first," usually attained after 20 years.

While I sliced away, he began arranging the raw ingredients in the order he planned to fling them into the wok. There was lean pork, stiff garlic shoots that looked like green drinking straws, tendrils of emerald pea sprouts, glossy red pickled peppers, soft bean curd the color of goat cheese and crunchy black wood-ear fungus.

The lightning speed of wok cooking required that sauces be premixed. Using no written recipes and without measuring anything, Chef Lu dipped his ladle here and there into a set of 11 stainless-steel spice bowls arranged like a painter's palette, next to his wok. I frantically tried to estimate amounts and jot down notes. There was dull red chili powder, flame-red clear chili oil, cornstarch, yellow rice wine, soy sauce, dark rice vinegar, sesame oil, salt, sugar and *dou ban* chili paste, a pungent mix of garlic, fermented soybeans and chilies.

The last stainless-steel dish contained a dull white powder, monosodium glutamate, or MSG. Chef Lu, who had never heard of Chinese Restaurant Syndrome, couldn't understand why anyone would object to it. "Some customers in Toronto said no MSG, or no salt or garlic," he recalled, wrinkling his nose at the bad memory. In Canada, MSG was a crystalline chemical substance that caused headaches, he said. But in China, MSG was a wheat extract with no side effects.

Chef Lu dumped ginger peel, vegetable trimmings, bones, anything he couldn't use, into a soup pot. Centuries of famine had created the original lean cuisine. By the end of a day of cooking, we had a handful of garbage: one eggshell and a few chili seeds.

Around 11 a.m., Chef Lu lit the gas burners. So did Chengdu's 9.8 million other residents. Chinese cooking required intense heat, but as everyone in the city turned on their gas stoves, the flame on ours flickered frustratingly low. Chef Lu compensated by heating the empty wok a long time.

To make a classic Ma Po Bean Curd, he simmered cubed tofu in salted water. In a separate wok, he stir-fried some minced beef in peanut oil until it changed color, then tossed in yellow rice wine and soy sauce. After a moment, he scooped the beef onto a plate. Then he sautéed a dollop of *dou ban* chili paste in the wok and added a ladleful of broth, some ground chili powder and chopped fermented soybeans. When it boiled down a bit, he added the hot, drained bean curd, and splashed in a bit more broth, some soy sauce, salt, MSG and cornstarch. He added the warm minced beef and some bright green garlic shoots, flipped the mixture in the wok a few times as if it were an omelet, and poured it into a dish. The final touch was a liberal sprinkling of fresh-ground Sichuan flower peppercorns. It smelled heavenly. We ate it standing up, in the classroom.

All morning, he cooked and lectured while I scribbled notes and ate. After a brief break, it was my turn to replicate everything he had done. For the next two hours, I sliced and chopped until my hands ached. My slices of pork were lumpy and ragged, but I escaped with fingertips intact. To my shame, I discovered I could hardly lift his wok. Sichuan woks, it turned out, were solid cast iron with no handles – and I hadn't thought to bring over oven mitts. Chef Lu proffered a crumpled dishcloth.

When it was time for me to stir-fry, Chef Lu lit the stove, then stood on the other side, ready to intervene if I faltered. As smoke rose from the hot, oiled wok, I felt a growing sense of panic. I consulted my notes and steeled myself. I started with Yu Xiang Pork, throwing in the raw meat and jumping back, startled, when it spattered. Then I swirled in the minced red peppers, *dou ban* chili paste, ginger, garlic and minced green onions. With Chef Lu urging me to go faster, I dumped in black wood-ear fungus, slivered bamboo shoots and a ladle of broth. I finished it off with my bowl of premixed sauce: sugar, vinegar, soy sauce, rice wine, sesame oil, MSG and cornstarch.

Amazingly, it looked, smelled and tasted wonderful, a complex blend of sweet, spicy and garlicky flavors. By late afternoon, my six dishes were cooked. Chef Lu tasted them and critiqued them. My Gong Bao Chili Pork with Peanuts was too sweet, he said. The Ma Po Spicy Bean Curd was fiery on impact, but faded on the palate. My Hot and Sour Soup lacked zest. Too little vinegar, Chef Lu diagnosed. And my Dan Dan Noodles were boring. But my Yu Xiang Pork and my Pickled Mustard Tuber Consommé passed muster. "Not bad for the first time," he said.

We both beamed. To celebrate that evening, I went out for a 20-course banquet with Chef Lu and his wife, also a first-grade chef. At Chengdu's Dragon Dumpling House, the food was excellent, and for a change, so was the service.

7

Foreign Devils

In 1973, state workers at Beijing No. 1 machine tool factory took a break underneath a Maoist slogan: "Long live the great unity of the peoples of the whole world!" The billboard beside it exhorts: "Proletariat of the world unite."

Photo: Jan Wong

For Chinese New Year's, Nanny Ma took Ben home for the holiday and taught him to kowtow before her aging father. As Ben, then two, knelt down, gently knocking his forehead on the ground before the Chinese patriarch, all her relatives erupted in peals of laughter. Ben was just the latest in a string of dumb foreigners to pay homage to the Middle Kingdom.

In the 18th century, the Qianlong Emperor demanded in vain that European envoys kowtow, too. The British and French responded with two opium wars. Then they followed up with signs on parks in Tianjin and Shanghai that said: "No Chinese or dogs allowed."

Under Maoism, apartheid continued, this time imposed by Chinese. Authorities banned intermarriage. In the 1970s, when Kippy Ye, who was half-Chinese and half white, wanted to marry a Chinese woman, Premier Chou En-lai himself had to consent. Authorities also called foreigners "Honored Friends," and gave them colonial-style privileges. They never waited in lines. They always got seats on crowded buses. And when a tour group was late for a night at the revolutionary opera, performers and the rest of the audience patiently waited.

"It makes our people feel inferior," groused Hu Qiaomu, then secretary of the powerful Central Committee. "Just think, many ordinary Chinese people also have been to other countries. Have they ever been called 'Friend' there? Is this not a means of lowering our national dignity?"

With China's opening to the West, the Honored Friend policy faded. Chinese on buses no longer sprang from their seats at the sight of a hairy arm. In 1988, Beijing legalized intermarriage. In 1993 alone, 30,000 Chinese married foreigners.

As the barbarians stormed the gates, China appeared to take the hordes in stride. It began charging them more for everything from phone lines to museum tours. That policy faded only in the late 1990s, with Beijing's attempts to gain entry into the World Trade Organization. But xenophobia remained strong.

In 1992, a secret 15-point document warned Chinese to "be on the alert for foreign nationals who try to pry out and spy on our restricted information." Citizens should not divulge their names. Nor should they hint that they or their children would like to go abroad. Photo ops were optional. Each citizen could decide, "as a friendly gesture," whether to agree to have a picture taken with a foreigner, according to the document, which was issued by the Inner Mongolian Autonomous Region.

If a foreigner attempted to locate "old acquaintances of pre-Liberation (pre-1949) days," citizens should promptly inform their government. If authorities deemed the acquaintance "unfit for foreign dealings, the communications should be ignored. Generally speaking, foreign nationals should not be invited to one's house," the document said.

In 1989, the Chinese partner of AB Electrolux, the Swedish consumer-products giant, distributed a Miss Manners guide to barbarian relations. "Act naturally when meeting foreign guests," it advised its Beijing employees. But "don't get into conversations of any depth with people you don't know well. Sidestep any question for which you are unsure of the answer." The confidential booklet also recommended parroting the Party line. "If the foreign guest asks any questions touching on politics, you should give an answer in line with publicly issued documents of the Party and state."

Despite China's apparent openness, citizens were still getting into trouble in the 1990s for having contacts with foreigners. A friend of mine named Zhou Yue (Great Leap Zhou) once helped direct a lost Pakistani tourist to an airline office in her building. Her Chinese boss later criticized her. But Great Leap, a secretary in a joint-venture firm, ignored him. She was happy to practice English. And the tourist was happy to find someone who understood what he was saying. She saw him several times more that week.

One evening, a dozen plainclothes militiamen accosted them on the street. At the local police station, the tourist was offered slices of watermelon. Great Leap was interrogated as if she were a prostitute. The police searched her purse. They demanded to know who had paid for the meals. (With traditional Chinese hospitality, she had.) Then they asked where she worked. Great Leap refused to say – she was afraid she would lose her job. The police promised that wouldn't happen. After four hours of questioning, she broke down and told them. A month later, she was fired.

Many Westerners were amazed at how open and friendly the Chinese were in the 1990s. What they didn't realize is that the Chinese have always had a love-hate relationship with the West. Their own history of suffering Western invasion, crossed with a proud 4,000-year-old civilization, meant that emotions could turn on a dime.

The century began with the 1900 Boxer Uprising, which left more than 200 Westerners dead, many of them missionaries. It ended in 1999 with thousands of Chinese heaving eggs, tomatoes and chunks of concrete at the U.S. embassy in Beijing after the North Atlantic Treaty Organization mistakenly bombed the Chinese embassy in Yugoslavia.

In between, China wavered between emulating Westerners and despising them. Mao derided the United States as a "paper tiger." When the West isolated China, he slammed the door shut. After his death, as Deng Xiaoping made overtures to the West, Chinese women – and men – began perming their hair. They bought skin whiteners. And some even got eye jobs, surgically altering their eyes to look rounder. The Tiananmen protests in 1989 were practically a love-in with America. Chinese students erected a copycat Statue of Liberty, wore blue jeans and hung out with Western reporters.

Exactly ten years later, a new generation of Chinese students screamed, "Hang Bill Clinton" and trapped the American ambassador in his office for four days. Many abroad were shocked by the virulence of anti-Western sentiment. After the NATO bombing, which killed three Chinese and injured more than 20, protesters in Beijing and at least nine other cities attacked symbols of the West. Mobs trashed McDonald's restaurants, workers went on strike at a French electronics factory near Beijing and movie theaters across the country stopped showing U.S. films and began screening old anti-American propaganda movies from the Maoist era.

Xenophobia lurked in the breast of every red-blooded Chinese. In May, 1999, authorities helped fan the flames of anti-Western sentiment by initially reporting only the NATO bombing raids on Yugoslavia, without disclosing Belgrade's massacres of its ethnic Albanian minority. When Clinton apologized three days in a row for what he called a "mistake," the Chinese media did not report that until the third day – and buried the news on the inside pages of the *People's Daily*.

The Chinese reaction stemmed from a deep sense of inferiority to whites *and* a deep sense of superiority. It was a combustible combination. The Foreign Ministry demanded an apology to the families of the victims, a thorough investigation and severe punishment of those responsible. Commenting on Canadian television, I remarked that the government demanding this was the same one that unleashed the army on its own citizens. And instead of just three Chinese dead, it had killed hundreds, possibly thousands. Ten years after the Tiananmen Massacre, there has never been an apology to those victims, I noted, nor any investigation or punishment, severe or otherwise, of those responsible.

The next day at work, I was deluged with angry phone calls, letters to the editor and e-mails – all from mainland Chinese now living in Canada. They called me everything from a "traitor," to a person who was "ashamed to be Chinese." One wanted to know if I was Chinese, or if my parents were Chinese, or barring that, whether my grandparents were Chinese. I explained my genealogy, then asked what she thought a Canadian was supposed to look like.

Another woman said I was wrong to link the deaths in Tiananmen with those killed by NATO. "It's like when you kill someone in your family," she said. "Then someone on the outside kills someone in your family. How can you compare the two?"

"How can you not?" I said.

In a scene that would have made Chairman Mao cringe in his crystal coffin, in 1993 three female workers making Timberland hiking boots in Tianjin were ordered to kneel down before their Korean managers. The managers felt the workers were being uppity. When the Chinese workers refused to kneel, the Koreans kicked them in the legs, forcing them down.

In Shanghai, a foreign manager slapped a worker who was chatting in the workshop. The next day, the contrite man gave her a month's extra wages. The worker was delighted. Authorities weren't. "How much is a slap worth?" Shanghai's *Liberation Daily* intoned. "If it's okay to take cash when our country's dignity is damaged, then we may become mere slaves."

In Beijing, a scandal erupted when Chinese waitresses in Japanese restaurants began kneeling to serve customers (as they do in fancy restaurants in Japan). When *Black Sun*, a movie about Japanese wartime atrocities opened in Beijing, theaters sold vomit bags. In Tianjin, four employees of a Japanese software company became heroes for refusing to work on a computer game about World War II.

The 1993 kneeling incident sparked a strike of Chinese workers at Korean-owned Hanbee Shoe Co. Ltd. in Tianjin. Management soon caved in. In the aftermath, I went to the factory, a two-hour drive from Beijing, and waited outside the gate to interview workers coming off shift.

"No matter what you say about us Chinese, our hearts are united," said one still-defiant 21-year-old worker. Conditions were abysmal, she said. Workers earned 80 cents for a 12-hour day. Industrial accidents were so common – one cutter lost three fingers – that Hanbee kept its own room at the local hospital. But what really angered her was the Korean-style disciplinary system. The company imposed fines for talking loudly, going to the toilet without a pass or failing to wear the company badge that said, "Love Hanbee."

Later, I talked my way into the factory manager's office. "It's very, very difficult here," sighed Dong Joon Lee, Hanbee's Korean president. "There are so many problems." Hanbee paid Chinese workers one-twentieth of what it paid Korean workers, but productivity was half and the defect rate was 17 times greater than in its Korean factories. As for the kneeling incident, the president said, the managers involved had been sent home. Hanbee had apologized, but neither the Chinese media nor local officials would let the company forget. "If we're here for 50 years," he sighed, "people will still be bringing it up."

The Chinese had many terms for foreigners. *Waiguoren* ("person from outside countries") was neutral. *Lao Wai* ("Old Foreigner") was mildly insulting. It didn't mean you needed a facelift. It was just overly familiar and thus disrespectful. *Da Bizi* ("Big Nose") and *Yang Guizi* ("Foreign Devil") were scornful.

But the Chinese reserved their most insulting terms for Japanese and blacks. They called Japanese *Riben Guizi*, literally Japanese devils, but more accurately translated as "Japs." Blacks were *Hei Gui*, literally "black devil," but its sting was more accurately rendered as "nigger."

A poll found that 51 percent of Chinese ranked Japanese ventures as the least desirable employer. This was understandable, given Japan's brutal invasion of China during World War II. Unlike Germany, which has paid about $80 billion to survivors and their families, Japan has resisted all demands to compensate war victims. Nor has it ever apologized. While the death toll from Japan's biological warfare in China is in dispute, some scholars estimate that an additional 10,000 prisoners were killed in medical experiments, including vivisections.

If the hatred of Japanese was rooted in ancient enmity and modern atrocities, the attitude toward blacks in China was harder to understand. Many Chinese stereotyped them as stupid, lazy and dishonest. The attitude went back at least to 751 AD when Du Huan, a Tang Dynasty military officer, was captured in battle and ended up on the east coast of Africa.

"Their customs are uncouth," he wrote, in perhaps the

earliest recorded Chinese opinion on blacks. "They are the worst of all the barbarians. When they drink liquor, they carouse all day long."

Chinese opinion hadn't changed much in 1,238 years. "We don't think blacks are very civilized," Shi Tunglan, a student at the Beijing Language Institute told me in early 1989. "If we have contact with foreigners, we do so with whites."

A Christmas Eve brawl ten days earlier at Nanking's Hehai University sparked racial strife in three Chinese cities. In Hangzhou, 56 Africans boycotted classes, complaining that authorities had accused them of transmitting AIDS. In Beijing, Chinese students protested after a black man accosted a Chinese woman in her dormitory. And in Nanking, site of the original brawl, thousands marched in the streets shouting, "Nigger go home."

Nigger? Many Chinese used the word without a second thought. Prejudice against dark skin was engrained in this agrarian nation where water was scarce and people toiled under the sun. Some Chinese wondered aloud if blacks were dark because they didn't wash. The language had no nice word for tan. "You've sunned yourself black," people would comment, with wrinkled nose. As in English, the word "black" was synonymous with bad. A shady deal was a "black trade." A "black gang" referred to the local mafia. *Hei ke*, literally a "black guest," meant a computer hacker.

My own Chinese staff were typical. They blithely stated that all African men made passes at Chinese women. Cook Mu, who had previously worked for diplomats from Mali, opined, "They're dirty and they eat on the floor." DSB officials, who supplied staff to journalists and diplomats, sometimes punished recalcitrant workers by assigning them to African families.

One evening, a cab driver spewed venom when I raised the subject. The previous night, he said, he and a half dozen other taxi drivers had intervened in a fight between two black students and the Chinese doorman at Beijing's Holiday Inn Lido. The black students screamed, "Fuck you!" over and over in Chinese. "Black cunt!" my cab driver said he had yelled back.

He confessed that he hated picking up blacks. "They get in my car, slip their feet out of their sandals and put them up on the seat.

They have a Chinese girl in back and immediately start pawing her. It's disgusting."

The Christmas Eve brawl at Hehai University started when African students brought Chinese girlfriends to a campus dance. In the ensuing melee, two Africans and eleven Chinese were injured, one seriously. Police armed with truncheons and electric cattle prods stormed the tiny hotel where the Africans had taken refuge. Later, thousands of Chinese stoned the African students' dormitory and marched through the streets shouting "Down with niggers." After a week of protests, the Chinese expelled four African students.

The conflict began months earlier. Hehai University, following a rash of thefts in the foreign students' dormitories, built a security wall around them. Some Africans tore a hole in the wall, complaining it forced them to walk farther to their classrooms. When the Africans refused to pay for the damage, the school rebuilt the wall and docked their Chinese scholarships. The students tore down the wall again. For good measure, they also occupied the cashier's office, destroyed furniture and took several workers hostage. They left six hours later, after Liang Ruijiu, the university president, intervened.

He later blamed a minority of African students for the trouble. (At Hehai, 69 of its 79 foreign students were black.) "Some of them are constantly abominable in their behavior," he said, quickly adding, "The Chinese people have always cherished their friendship with the African people."

The next week, 200 Chinese students went on strike at the Beijing Language Institute after a black man confronted a Chinese woman in her dormitory hallway in the middle of the night. She ran into a communal bathroom and locked herself in a stall, according to both Chinese and foreign students, including Africans. The man, whom she didn't know, hid in her room, where her two roommates were asleep. On her return, he tried to grab her. Her screams roused the entire dorm. In the confusion, the man escaped.

"We didn't react right away," a male classmate said. "It was New Year's Eve and we were still up playing poker. We thought other people were still partying." When the screams continued, the male students ran upstairs. "She was hysterical," he said. "She was running around screaming and knocking on doors." Shod in shower flip-flops, the woman slipped and fell on some broken beer bottles, cutting her arms and legs.

In 1974, I'd studied briefly at the Beijing Language Institute, so I knew my way around the campus. I slipped inside to interview as many students as I could – Chinese, African and Western. In the Chinese dormitories, where men lived on the lower floors and women on the upper, the mood was angry. "We're afraid to go out at night," said Huang Qing, 19, who shared a cramped dorm room with five other women. Her roommates agreed.

Africans had been studying on scholarships in China since 1960. But as the country leaped from Maoism to materialism, people no longer felt the need to remain politically correct. The ideal of Third World solidarity was gone. Beijing began selling weapons to the highest bidder, rather than giving them gratis to its brothers in struggle. It also began sending host governments the bill for Chinese medical teams.

But even as China raised tuition rates and rejected thousands of its own qualified university applicants, it continued to give full scholarships to 1,500 Africans a year. Their monthly stipends alone were twice what a Chinese university professor earned. African governments worsened matters by sending rowdy all-male contingents, often the offspring of Africa's ruling kleptocracies.

Calling China racist was too simple. Friendship with Africa had always been abstract, a collective effort rather than a personal commitment. In the 1960s and 1970s, while its own people subsisted on rations, China gave Africa $2.5 billion in aid. More than 140 Chinese died in the construction of the ambitious Tan-Zam railway linking landlocked Zambia to coastal Tanzania. By 1980, Beijing had sent 150,000 experts and technicians on 500 African aid projects.

The altruism was strategic, of course. In 1971, China's grateful African allies tipped the balance of votes at the United Nations, kicking out Taiwan and giving the seat to China. But in the 1990s, as Beijing sought détente with the United States – and as the Soviet Union imploded – it no longer needed its African allies. The scholarships became a philanthropic Maoist leftover.

The racial strife quickly undid the goodwill of three decades of aid. The Organization of African Unity called the situation in China "appalling." Libya dramatically offered to provide scholarships to all "oppressed" African students in China. "If this goes on, our students will not come to China any more. Even in South Africa this would be criminal," said Gobo Bio Mamah, first secretary of the Benin Embassy. "The Chinese think all is possible. They pay the money. Our students are ready to go home rather than be treated as dirty beasts."

In fact, the Chinese treated their own people like dirty beasts. In every facet of life, Beijing divided – and subdivided – people by race and passport. In the Maoist 1970s, guards turned away Chinese citizens from hotels, embassies and the ironically named Friendship Store, which was friendly only to foreigners.

"Overseas Chinese" like myself – people who looked Chinese but weren't – had the next-lowest status. I assume this was based partly on a warped self-hatred: *You look just like me, so why should you get privileges?*

When I first went to China in 1972, I was relegated to crummier hotels than whites, blacks, other Asians and other Canadians. In the mid-1970s, when I worked for a summer as a propaganda polisher at Radio Beijing, the station tried to pay me half what it paid the white Canadian male I was temporarily replacing. (When I insisted on equal pay for equal work and spouted some choice Maoist slogans about women's liberation, Radio Beijing hastily capitulated.)

But the system was stacked against Chinese and ethnic Chinese. Even the money was different. Chinese used *renminbi*, literally the "People's Money." Foreigners used a special scrip, called Foreign Exchange Certificates. That meant that until the 1990s, ordinary people couldn't get taxis even in an emergency. Drivers had to fill hard-currency quotas, so they sailed past Chinese. I'll never forget the humiliation of Zhuang Zedong, who was to Chinese ping-pong what Michael Jordan is to basketball. After a dinner interview at his home, Zhuang Zedong graciously saw me to the sidewalk. Then he watched as I tried in vain to hail a cab. A dozen passed by empty, without stopping. (As a foreigner, I had wads of Foreign Exchange Certificates, but I couldn't quite bring myself to stand there, flapping them at the passing traffic.)

"Let me try," he offered, waving at taxi after taxi. But in the darkness, no cab driver recognized China's most famous athlete. He, too, gave up, deeply embarrassed. I took a trolleybus back to my office.

If Overseas Chinese could be mistaken for Chinese, then the reverse was true, too. And since the Chinese government had consigned its own people to the very bottom of this home-spun apartheid system, it led to the bizarre phenomenon of Chinese pretending *not* to be Chinese in China. Stella Wu, who was briefly my Chinese news assistant, was one such fake foreign devil. When a policeman stopped her for a traffic violation, she babbled away in English. Suitably impressed, he let her go.

Chinese authorities treated their own people, pardon me, like chinks. Stella's father, a retired professor from prestigious Qinghua University, opened his own computer company in California. On a trip back to China, he required five stitches after a security guard assaulted him at Beijing International Airport. (He had tried to retrieve a luggage cart from the wrong side of the Customs line.)

When Chinese Customs discovered the victim was someone who lived abroad, they sent a delegation to his home to apologize. No one realized he was an Overseas Chinese, they murmured. Stella couldn't resist interjecting, "Does that mean if they're Chinese, it's okay to beat them?"

8

Blue China Reds

Top: Fat Paycheck Shulman and his team leader at China Reconstructs, Saiman Hui, during the Cultural Revolution in the early 1970s in Beijing.
Photo: Private collection

Bottom: With Sid Engst and Joan Hinton in their living room in Beijing in 1999.
Photo: Robin Benger

In the 1970s, I made friends with a tiny band of foreign Maoists committed to the Chinese Revolution. The community of Lifers was the world's most bizarre, most exclusive club. In a nation of 1.3 billion, I counted only one Canadian, one New Zealander, five Britons and 15 Americans. Israel Epstein, whom we all called Eppie, was the 23rd member. He was born in Poland in 1915, raised in Tianjin and was stateless until he took out Chinese citizenship.

Decades earlier, the Lifers had abandoned the West to live in China. A disproportionate number were Jewish. Just as Jews supported the Civil Rights movement in the United States, they joined China's struggle to create a new society. My husband, Norman Shulman, was merely the latest in a long line of idealistic Jews to land in Beijing. During the Cultural Revolution, four of six Lifers jailed in the notorious Qincheng Prison were Jewish, including Eppie. Sidney Rittenberg, an American, held the record. He spent 16 years in solitary confinement during *two* prison terms.

Most Lifers had arrived early enough to witness the founding of the People's Republic on October 1, 1949. Almost all had met Mao. Without complaint, they survived the deprivations of the 1950s, the famine of the early 1960s and the ordeals of the Cultural Revolution.

The majority saw themselves as a wing of the Ministry of Propaganda. Indeed, many actually worked for Chinese propaganda organs "polishing" revolutionary rhetoric translated from the Chinese. Eppie, for instance, was editor-in-chief of *China Reconstructs*, later called *China Today*. Even after the Tiananmen Massacre, people like him continued to offer sanitized pictures of China.

Their refusal to doff the blinkers wasn't a moral abdication. Having dedicated their lives to Utopia, it was too late to admit that Emperor Mao had no clothes. The Lifers were too old to start anew in the West and too broken-hearted to admit they had wasted their lives. I had gone to China with the same ideals. But I was still young when the scales fell from my eyes. By 1980, when I left for journalism school in the States, I knew I could never be a Lifer. Maoism was fatally flawed. Under its banner, so many people had suffered, and even died.

But I understood their unwavering loyalty. It was part blind faith, part stubbornness, part fear of rejection by the collective they loved. To me, it illuminated why the Chinese themselves had tolerated the Communist Party for so long. During the Cultural Revolution, half the Lifers had been detained as "imperialist spies." Not one had had a trial. And all were later exonerated. Yet not a single one denounced China.

The xenophobic Chinese quarantined the Lifers, both inside and outside of prison. It was the way they had treated "foreign devils" for a thousand years. As a result, some Lifers never learned to speak Chinese. They dressed in Mao suits, ate Chinese food and drank Chinese rum. But Beijing mostly discouraged them from taking out Chinese citizenship. Only two lifers – Sid Rittenberg and George Hatem – were allowed to join the Chinese Communist Party.

There were other foreigners in China, of course. Several hundred, and at times, several thousand foreign Maoists would spend a year or two polishing propaganda or teaching languages. But they came and went. The Lifers stayed. The Chinese respectfully called the Lifers "foreign experts" or "advisors." Simon Leys, the Belgian sinologist, dubbed them the "pensioners of the revolution."

Their salaries were ten times the norm. Their housing was the best China had. Rationing didn't apply to them: Lifers could buy all the eggs, meat, rice and bikes they wanted. They had maids, access to cars and drivers and enjoyed all-expenses-paid vacations around the country. Every two or three years, China gave them plane tickets home.

Fat Paycheck was an exception. He insisted on drawing a pathetic salary. The thought of a chauffeur made him ill. Nor was he keen on plane tickets back to New York. In the Vietnam War era, he was under indictment for dodging the draft.

He also refused to be classified as a "foreign expert," which was perfectly reasonable considering he couldn't spell to save his life. Norman had been a computer programmer in the States, but for the first eight years of his working life in China, he was assigned to the Foreign Languages Press. There, he lived in a dusty dorm and, because his Chinese was excellent, he worked, not as an editor, but as a translator at *China Reconstructs*, the same propaganda monthly where Eppie worked.

China assigned the Lifers a pecking order, according to each one's seniority and perceived contribution to the Revolution. Ordinary experts lived in spacious Chinese apartments with sunny, southern exposures and, sometimes, an honest-to-goodness closet. Or they took suites in the Friendship Hotel, a vast, Soviet-style compound, with maid service and hot water. Frank Coe and Sol Adler, the two highest-ranking Americans, were assigned exquisite century-old courtyard homes which they filled with museum-quality paintings, porcelain and antique furniture.

Many of the Lifers lived schizophrenic lives. A famous Mao quote went, "We have friends all over the world." But the Lifers knew the bitter reality all too well. They chafed at being shut out of Chinese life.

In 1966, during the Cultural Revolution, four American Lifers posted a Big Character Poster, protesting their exclusion. It was brought to Mao's attention. He scribbled a reply, which had the force of an imperial edict. "I agree with the Big Character Poster. All those who are willing should be treated the same as the Chinese. No differences are allowed."

Thrilled by a blessing from the Great Helmsman himself, the Lifers enthusiastically formed the "Bethune-Yanan Rebel

Regiment." (To cover the bases, they named it after Norman Bethune, the Canadian doctor who died for the Chinese Revolution, *and* Yanan, Mao's post-Long March headquarters.) About 50 other foreign Maoists, short-term "experts" from Europe and the Americas, joined the Lifers. The working languages were English, French and Spanish and everyone delivered fiery speeches through interpreters.

Then one day Madame Mao declared that "not all foreigners are spies." That also had the force of an imperial edict. All Chinese instantly understood that Jiang Qing meant most foreigners *were* spies. One by one, the key members of Bethune-Yanan began to disappear. Some were put under house arrest. A number ended up in Qincheng Prison, a top-security facility near the Ming Tombs.

Two authors of that famous Big Character Poster, Joan Hinton and Sid Engst, became Norman's closest friends. They let him crash on their couch during the Cultural Revolution, after the college where he was studying Chinese forced him out. Sid was a farmer from Gooseville Corners, New York. Joan was an atomic physicist who had worked on the Manhattan Project. They had known one another in the States. At the end of World War II, they took separate slow boats to China, met up in Yanan and married there.

After the Communist victory, the United States labeled Joan "the spy that got away." In fact, the Chinese were much too paranoid to ever let a foreigner near the Bomb. Even as dairy farmers, she and Sid had been briefly stripped of their responsibilities in 1964, merely for being American.

During the Cultural Revolution, however, they were practically the only Lifers who didn't get into trouble. By chance, they had just transferred to Beijing from the provinces. As newcomers, they didn't become entangled in factional fighting. They were simply told not to report for work.

With time on their hands, Joan and Sid took part in an anti-Israeli demonstration after the 1967 Six Day War. Because Beijing and Tel Aviv didn't have diplomatic relations, there was no Israeli Embassy to storm. But Britain's made a fine substitute. After all, Britain had invaded Egypt during the Suez Canal crisis ten years earlier. In China, with its 4,000 years of history, a decade was a nanosecond.

"Miraculously, the gate was left unlocked," said Sid, recalling that everyone swarmed inside the stately red brick mission. One Arab "foreign expert" hurled a flowerpot through a window. Their passion eventually spent, the crowd began to drift away. Then someone remembered the British flag was still flying. Several Arabs started tugging on the ropes. The flagpole began to bend. Nobody thought to untie the knot.

"If it fell over, people would get hit on the head," said Sid. "So I took out my pocket knife and cut the rope. Whoosh! It fell right down!"

With his beak-like nose, long gray hair and bony fingers, Sol Adler looked like Scrooge. He wasn't, however, interested in money, except theoretically. He was an Oxford graduate, a champion bridge player and a chess master who had once been president of the Washington, D.C. Chess Club. He was also a linguist who had mastered half a dozen languages, none of them, alas, Chinese.

Sol first lived in China from 1941 to 1947, as a U.S. Treasury attaché. Back in the States, the McCarthyites accused him and other diplomats of having "lost China." In 1962, Sol defected to Beijing. Unlike Joan and Sid, he had no ambition to go native. His delicate stomach couldn't bear garlic or scallions, two mainstays of Chinese cooking. Instead, his British wife, Pat, taught their Chinese housekeeper to bake potatoes and boil vegetables.

Sol worked at Beijing's Institute of World Economics. There, he helped the Chinese analyze everything from trade conflicts to capitalist inflation. Sol read voraciously and had a photographic memory. On the 40th anniversary of the People's Republic, I needed a quote from Marx about history repeating itself for a story on the gala ceremonies at Tiananmen Square. The fireworks and pirouetting PLA soldiers were a spooky echo of the massacre four months earlier.

"First sentence," Sol replied instantly, when I phoned him from the bleachers at Tiananmen Square. He was then 80 and hard of hearing, but he even knew the exact page number. "Marx's introduction to the Eighteenth Brumaire. He's referring to Napoleon III as the farce." Then he recited the complete quote from memory:

"Hegel remarks somewhere that all facts and personages of great importance in world history occur, as it were, twice. He forgot to add: the first time as tragedy, the second as farce." When I got back to the *Globe* office – and my collection of Marx and Lenin – I checked the quote. Sol was right on.

In 1993, he was 83 and had been ill for more than a year. His rank entitled him to a private room in a wing of the Beijing Hospital reserved for China's top officials. After several operations, he had only half of one lung remaining. He'd always been gaunt. Now he looked like a waxen stick figure. A tracheotomy meant he could no longer speak, but his mind was as sharp as ever.

Sol always loved to hear the latest gossip. I told him that Sid Rittenberg, the man with the record for solitary confinement, had just published his autobiography. As I recounted some of the book's more delicious anecdotes, Sol grabbed a piece of cardboard on which his wife had printed the letters of the alphabet. R-I-T-T-E-N-B-E-R-G-I-S-A-S-C-O-U-N-D-R-E-L, he tapped, punching the cardboard for emphasis. D-O-N-T-B-E-L-I-E-V-E-A-W-O-R-D-H-E-S-A-Y-S-D-O-N-T-T-R-U-S-T-H-I-M. Each time I said something new about Rittenberg, Sol grabbed his alphabet board and tapped out the same message. Finally I told him to save time, and just use 'R' to refer to Rittenberg.

Sid Rittenberg's book was called *The Man Who Stayed Behind*. In fact, he was practically the only Lifer who left. And who could blame him? The wonder was that he didn't hightail it out sooner. After his first six years in solitary, from 1949 to 1955, he surprised everyone by staying on. During the Cultural Revolution, he spent ten more years in solitary, from 1968 to 1977. As always with foreigners, both times the charge was spying.

A bear of a man with bad eyesight, rumpled gray hair and a warm hug, Rittenberg was a gifted raconteur. He spoke flawless Chinese. He knew everyone and everything. For a time, he was even a confidant of Madame Mao.

Norman met Rittenberg after his first prison term. I met him after his second. He seemed amazingly unscarred by his 16 years in solitary. His first wife had dumped him during his first incarceration.

Wang Yulin, his second wife, stuck by him during his second. For ten years, she raised their four children alone, and spent some time of her own at labor camp.

Rittenberg was the only son of a prominent Jewish lawyer in Charleston, South Carolina. He arrived in China in 1945, a 24-year-old GI with a few months of Chinese lessons under his belt. He was also a Communist. At 19, when his college classmates were joining fraternities, he had joined the American Communist Party. Rittenberg soon made his way to Yanan. There, as he wrote in his book, he "argued dogma with Mao, mused philosophy with Chou En-lai, danced with Mao's wife, Jiang Qing." Eventually, he was allowed to join the Chinese Communist Party.

Rittenberg was the only Lifer in China to attain political power. During the Cultural Revolution, he shot through the ranks at the Broadcast Administration, a central government organization important enough to merit guards with fixed bayonets. He became a senior cadre and director of foreign-language broadcasts. His Party membership and high-level security clearance gave him access to secret documents. That made him the envy of the other Lifers.

So Sol's vehemence surprised me. Weren't they all comrades? His wife, Pat, spoke up on his behalf. "He opposed Sol's coming to China," she said mysteriously.

Rittenberg had betrayed others, too, it turned out. During the 1957 Anti-Rightist Campaign, the Broadcast Administration was ordered to produce a quota of rightists. Rittenberg's boss told him that the English section had to have at least one. So Rittenberg chose a Chinese-Canadian from Toronto. When Gerald Chen protested that he was not a rightist, Rittenberg took him for a walk. If Gerald confessed, Rittenberg told him, he would be sent to an ordinary farm. If he didn't, he would end up in a prison camp, with no right to see his family. Gerald "confessed," and was sent to a farm in Hebei Province.

In 1993, I met Rittenberg for dinner in Beijing. Over scallion-oil chicken, I broached the subject of betrayal. As someone who, in my misguided Maoist days, had snitched on others, I couldn't think of an indirect way to begin. So I asked about Gerald Chen.

"How do I feel now?" said Rittenberg, who had seen Gerald several years earlier in Hong Kong. "Horrible. Some of the worst things done in the world are done by ideologues who are doing something for some lofty aim."

He told me the Broadcast Administration had never had a specific quota to fill of "rightists," but the pressure had been there all the same. "If Chairman Mao said 2 percent of intellectuals are rightists, you can't have none. If you didn't turn up rightists in your place, you might be suspected yourself of being right-leaning."

Rittenberg himself came to grief in 1968. He ended up in a cell in Qincheng Prison. Nine years later he heard a familiar voice: His one-time confidant, Mao's widow, had also been chucked into Qincheng.

In 1980, Rittenberg and Yulin left China for good. After 35 years there, he was 59 and virtually penniless. To pay their rent in Queens, New York, Yulin knitted fancy sweaters and sold them to Bloomingdale's. Sid tried writing his memoirs. But within a decade, they caught the wave of China's economic reforms. Yulin, herself a Communist Party member, ended up as a super-saleswoman for Computerland. Sid consulted for corporations from Levi Strauss & Co. to Intel. He and Yulin obtained driver's licenses and bought a comfortable home in Seattle next door to a Boeing executive. Each winter, he lectured on Chinese politics at his alma mater, Chapel Hill University in North Carolina.

I once asked Rittenberg what the other Lifers thought of him for leaving. "They do not approve of my starting a new life. Most of them are very loyal. When I pulled out and went back to the States, and began thinking and talking independently, they found it very hard to accept."

Mixed couples like Rittenberg and Yulin were politically vulnerable. It was better to be all Chinese or all foreign. That way, the lines were clearer. Mixing it up just confused the issue of who was a spy and who wasn't.

In the 1970s, our downstairs neighbors at the Foreign Languages Press were another mixed couple. Yang Xianyi (sian-yee) was the scion of a wealthy Chinese family from Tianjin. He combed his silky white hair back from his forehead, spoke upper-crust English and had the wicked wit to match. He was slender and walked with a gentle bounce, but when he sat in his book-filled living room, he resembled a traditional scholar, straight out of a classical Chinese painting.

His wife, Gladys, was the daughter of British missionaries in China. She was tall and striking, with large blue eyes and a clipped accent. Even in her 70s, she cycled everywhere on her old Raleigh. The Yangs had met at Oxford University in the 1930s, when he was studying the classics and she was the first undergraduate to major in Chinese. In the 1940s, they moved to Beijing and became China's top literary translation team.

Power blackouts in the 1970s were so common that Norman and I often spent candlelit evenings at the Yangs'. Their home was a literary salon, with famous artists, writers and poets dropping by for a drink. By the end of an evening, Gladys would have polished off an entire bottle of Chinese rum. Xianyi did the same with something even stronger. Gradually, I understood why they needed to anesthetize themselves every day.

In the 1950s, Xianyi had been criticized for helping "rightist" friends. "You are a man who attracts flies," the Party Secretary at the Foreign Languages Press told him. During the 1958 Great Leap Forward, Gladys came under attack, too.

"I watched cynically as our colleagues attempted to smelt steel in the yard, took no part in the massacre of sparrows (believed to eat precious grain), and did not help to dig the Ming Tombs Reservoirs," she wrote, years later, in *Oxford* magazine. When Gladys asked to attend her mother's 80th birthday party in England, the Foreign Languages Press refused. Only after she appealed to Premier Chou En-lai was permission granted.

In 1965, the Yangs' political problems increased. They were deemed politically unworthy of translating *A Dream of Red Mansions*, considered the greatest Chinese novel ever written. They were ordered to stop in mid-manuscript. The Communist Youth League, which took practically everybody, didn't accept their son until his fourth application. Then both Beijing University and

Qinghua University, China's top two schools, rejected his application. The reason: a "bad class background," namely Xianyi's aristocratic family and Gladys' missionary parents.

Once, Gladys glued two stamps side by side, a portrait of Mao and a PLA soldier. Unfortunately, that made it look as though the soldier was thrusting his bayonet at the Great Helmsman. The post office returned the letter with a stern warning. A note went into Gladys' dossier.

During the Cultural Revolution, Xianyi was denounced as a "counter-revolutionary revisionist," the most serious crime in the Maoist lexicon. Red Guards paraded him through the streets in a dunce cap and forced him to stand for hours in the painful "jet plane position," head bowed, arms raised behind. Like other children of embattled intellectuals, their son was pressured to disown them.

The Foreign Languages Press ordered Xianyi to write "confessions" and clean latrines. Several of his friends, including the novelist Lao She, had already committed suicide. Xianyi began to hallucinate. He heard voices. He thought his colleagues were plotting to murder him. One night in 1968, Xianyi was arrested on spy charges. He was led away in handcuffs, still in his pajamas. As a Chinese, he was tossed in a cell with 21 ordinary criminals. A day later, Gladys was strip-searched. As a foreigner, she was put in solitary confinement in Qincheng, the same prison as Sid Rittenberg and Israel Epstein.

In May, 1972, the Chinese released Xianyi after four years in jail. They declared him innocent of any wrongdoing. "As Chairman Mao always said: nobody is perfect," an official told him. But he wasn't talking about *their* blunder. He was talking about Xianyi's imperfections. "You have done good work for the Party, but you have also done bad things. There are always two aspects in a man. We hope in future you will keep doing good things and avoid doing bad things. You are free to go now."

That was it. There was no apology. Xianyi gathered up his pajamas and went home. Gladys was released five days later.

In all the time they'd been in jail, their children had not been allowed to see them or even write. Their two daughters had been banished to the countryside, their son to a factory in rural Hubei.

To make amends, China allowed the older daughter to study at Qinghua University. The younger daughter was accepted at Beijing University, where we became classmates. But the stress of being a mixed-race kid in the Cultural Revolution was too much for the Yang's only son. He suffered a mental breakdown and refused to speak Chinese, even at his factory in rural Hubei Province. After his parents brought him home, he still spoke only English. He fantasized that he was British and repeatedly tried to gate-crash the British Embassy, a dangerous act in the xenophobic years of the Cultural Revolution.

His parents took him to a Beijing mental hospital. It refused to admit him because Gladys was a foreigner. In desperation, the Yangs sent him to Britain for help. But those who befriended him in England did so because he was a Chinese and *because* they supported what was going on in China.

His name, Ye, meant Firelight. One Christmas, at his aunt's house, he bought some gasoline and burned himself to death.

As Beijing embraced capitalism, no one honored the Lifers any more simply for being red and white. The only color that mattered now was the color of money. China's economic reforms had eroded their privileged lifestyle. By the late 1980s, their special status was gone.

Many Lifers felt disillusioned and trapped. One of those who left, and returned in defeat, was a Brooklynite named Julian Schuman. Like Rittenberg, Julian had taken Chinese in the U.S. Army. In 1947, Julian took a Norwegian freighter to Shanghai, where he found a job at *The China Press*, one of the city's four English language dailies. In 1949, Julian was the only American reporter to stay on for the Communist victory. He filed stories for UPI, ABC, *Newsday* and the *St. Louis Post Dispatch*.

In 1953 when he returned to the United States, FBI agents met his ship. McCarthyism was in full swing. Suddenly, no newspaper would touch Julian's stuff. In 1959, he went on trial for sedition. As evidence, the Government cited articles he had written about China and the Korean War. Two years later, Washington dropped the case.

But Julian had had enough. He returned to China in 1963 with his wife, Donna Walker. The government assigned him a polishing job at *Peking Review*, at the Foreign Languages Press. Every break, he'd come up to our studio apartment for a cup of tea. Ever restless, he returned to the States in 1977. He and Donna began operating tours to China, using their Lifer connections to cut deals.

But as the new money economy flourished, friendship no longer mattered. By the time I returned as a foreign correspondent in 1988, Julian's company had failed and he was divorced. In his late 60s, he was back in China, polishing propaganda. Deeply disillusioned, he chose to work at the sports department of *China Daily*, the section least tainted by ideology. There, he became besotted with a Chinese typist half his age. Chinese cadres warned him that Yan Yan was no good. He ignored them. They forbade him to see her. He married her anyway. *China Daily* fired her.

I hired her. During the 1989 Tiananmen Massacre, Yan Yan helped me so enthusiastically that both Julian and I worried about her safety. With his support, she left for the United States to study English. He used the plane tickets given to him for home leave to visit her each summer in San Francisco.

Now that Julian was alone, Norman and I often invited him over for steaks and shots of Johnny Walker. He'd light up a cigarillo and carp about how everyone was bowing to the new god of materialism. He complained that Beijing didn't accord him the same perks as Lifers who arrived in the 1940s. He was annoyed that he wasn't invited to the same receptions and banquets to meet China's leaders. And he was bitter that, unlike them, he wasn't given a full pension. Hadn't he arrived in 1947? Why should he be penalized for having gone back between 1953 and 1963 to take McCarthyism on the chin? The final indignity was being unable to afford to eat in his favorite Shanghai-style restaurant. Currency devaluations and inflation had melted his "foreign expert" salary to nothing.

In April, 1991, Norman and I went to the first Passover Seder hosted by Israel's de facto representative in China. Most of Beijing's 80-strong Jewish community attended, including all the Jewish Lifers.

Their contact with Israel was a sign of the times. They had always been proud of their Jewish heritage, but for years most of them had echoed China's pro-Palestinian line. Now that China itself was making overtures to Israel, they had accepted the invitation to the Seder with a mixture of curiosity and nostalgia.

"The last Seder I was at, I conducted in Chongqing during World War II," said Sol Adler, then 81. He noshed on chicken soup and matzo balls, happy he didn't have to screen them for ginger or scallions.

Julian Schuman, then 70, was delighted with the gefilte fish and the apple-walnut paste, known as charoset. "It's the first Seder I've gone to since I was about ten," said Julian.

The Israeli host, Yoseph Shalhevet, said it was no accident that the leftists who went to China were disproportionately Jewish. "If Jews feel it's a movement for social justice, they join it."

He and his wife, Sheila, had arrived in Beijing a year earlier to open a liaison office. "Marx. I always mention Marx," said Shalhevet, 59. He liked to remind the Chinese that the father of Communism was Jewish. He also liked to remind them that their countries' birthdates, both ancient and modern, were roughly the same: China's early dynasties were contemporaneous with Abraham and Isaac, and modern Israel was founded in 1948, one year before the People's Republic.

There were some limits, though, to his enthusiasm. Most Chinese were unaware of Israel's unrestricted promise of a homeland to any Jew. Shalhevet, envisioning a billion applicants, preferred to leave it that way.

China itself had almost no indigenous Jews. During World War II, about 30,000 European Jews fled to China. Two-thirds — Germans, White Russians and Poles — settled in Shanghai, one of the few places that didn't require a visa at the time. The Japanese occupiers later herded the Jews into a ghetto, but did not exterminate them. Most Jews left after the Communist victory. In 1982, the *Los Angeles Times* reported that Max Leibowitch, the last Jew in Shanghai, had died of bronchitis at the age of 75.

But a thousand years earlier, Persian-Jewish traders had settled in Kaifeng, in central China. At its height, Kaifeng's Jewish population was estimated at 5,000. The Chinese Jews prayed in Hebrew, observed Jewish dietary laws, circumcised their sons and built at least one synagogue. By the late 19th century, they had basically been assimilated. Kaifeng's last Chinese rabbi reportedly died in the mid-19th century and the synagogue collapsed in disrepair soon after. Its Torah scrolls are now in Toronto's Royal Ontario Museum.

One of Shalhevet's first trips in China had been to Kaifeng. The city of 500,000 had optimistically established a "Special Economic Zone for Overseas Jews." There were few takers. He visited the site of the former synagogue and found about 70 Jewish families still there. "But," he said sadly, "there are no communal activities."

His wife, Sheila, had spent the week making 300 pieces of gefilte fish. That evening, volunteers read in Hebrew and English from the Haggadah, which celebrates the liberation of the Jews from their enslavement in Egypt. Among the guests were several dozen Chinese, including one man who was originally from Kaifeng and claimed to be Jewish.

"We preserve most of the Jewish traditions at home," Zhao Xiangru, 60, told me. He was now a professor in ethnic studies at the Chinese Academy of Social Sciences in Beijing. I sat at the same table with him, his wife and their two grown children. Professor Zhao showed me his blue velvet yarmulke, which he kept tucked in his pocket. He said he remembered his family daubing sheep's blood on their front door, a ritual that recalled the Israelites marking their homes so the Angel of Death would pass over them and instead smite the first-born in every Egyptian household.

Professor Zhao told everyone at our table that he wanted to visit Israel one day. "He doesn't have any money, but we might help him go some day," Shalhevet said. As Professor Zhao ladled out the steaming chicken soup and matzo balls at our table, a Jewish woman from New York looked him up and down.

"He looks," she said with a satisfied nod, "a little Jewish."

The Seder was the last time many of the Lifers were together. Sol Adler died a few years later. In 1992, Julian Schuman suffered a mild stroke. His doctors recommended a sanatorium, but *China Daily* balked at the cost. Then Julian had another, massive, stroke.

He couldn't walk or talk. In the hospital, he hit a nurse. After that, they tied him to his bed for the rest of his life.

I phoned Yan Yan right away. She never came back from San Francisco. It turned out that she had already asked for a divorce, but Julian had been too humiliated to tell us. With his prickly personality, he didn't have many friends besides Norman and me. We visited him as often as we could. As I had done with Sol, I told Julian all the latest news, even keeping him up to date on his beloved Yankees. He couldn't answer, but I was pretty sure he could understand. Every time I related a really juicy bit of gossip, the machine monitoring his blood pressure jumped. After a while, his doctor told me to take it easy.

We left China in 1994. Julian died, alone, eight months later. He was 74.

On my trip back in 1999, I phoned Joan Hinton and Sid Engst. Without preamble, Joan lit into me. She told me she and Sid were furious at me for *Red China Blues*. They had both tossed it away in disgust at page 15 after reading my summary of the years following Mao's disastrous 1958 Great Leap Forward. Why had I called it "one of the worst man-made famines in Chinese history"? (Because it was, but I was too stunned to do anything but listen.)

Joan accused me of telling lies to "sell the book" and to "please your bosses." She was particularly incensed that I had written that "40 million" Chinese had starved to death, when no one died from hunger. (Actually, I didn't specify any number in *Red China Blues*. But now that she mentioned it, Chinese friends who lived through the catastrophic famine of 1959 to 1962 – and respected historians – estimate that 20 million or more starved to death. Many others died shortly after, including many children, weakened by years of malnutrition.)

Call me a masochist, but I still loved Joan and Sid and I still wanted to see them. After lobbing a few more choice insults, Joan grudgingly agreed to let me visit them for old times' sake. I hung up the phone and burst into tears. Then I realized that I had landed right back in a Maoist-era criticism session. That didn't make me feel any better, but at least I understood.

Joan and Sid berated me some more when I arrived. They refused to accept a bottle of maple syrup and a still-usable old Chinese soldering iron I'd brought them until I said they were gifts from Fat Paycheck. When they calmed down enough to talk about China, they were pessimistic.

"So many people have no medical care. In Changzhi (a city in central China), half the elementary schools are shut down. Officially 30 million workers have been laid off. What's the real figure? Only God knows," said Sid, then 80. Joan, 78, said that Tiananmen was the turning point. "The army shot the people. It won't happen again."

After half a century of working for the Revolution, they were now the most senior Lifers in Beijing. They held the rank of Deputy Ministers, but still lived on a state dairy farm north of Beijing. Joan, who always wore a cap to keep her silvery hair out of her eyes while she drew blueprints, really had beaten swords into plowshares. Instead of making atom bombs, she was transplanting cow embryos and designing equipment for the Chinese dairy industry.

They remained True Believers. But over a lunch of dumplings and beer, I wondered if their political hearts were broken. All they had left, it seemed, was their love for one another. I asked if they had any regrets about coming to China. "No, because the first 30 years were so good," said Sid, with a grin, alluding to the years under Mao.

After lunch, we strolled over to the barn to look at their beloved Holsteins. With China's doors flung open to qualify for entry into the World Trade Organization, they were being undercut by cheap New Zealand dairy products. The farm produced 3.5 tons of milk a day, but they only had a guaranteed buyer for 2 tons. Recently, they'd been selling the surplus to McDonald's. Half a century of revolution had led to ... McFlurries and Big Macs?

"Ironic, isn't it?" said Sid.

9

The Dalai Lama's Revenge

Top: Tibetan children using sharpened sticks to write in the one-room school-house in the village of Cha.

Photo: Jan Wong

Bottom: Boy monks in Sera Monastery in Lhasa.   Photo: Jan Wong

Tibet was the most inaccessible place in China for a foreign reporter. It required a special travel permit routinely given to tourists, but rarely to journalists. For six years, I had telexed applications to the Foreign Affairs office in Lhasa. Mostly, they didn't bother answering, except for the memorable "not-enough-oxygen" response.

In 1994, as I was winding up my posting in China, I decided to make one last attempt – with or without official permission. My friend, Lena Sun of the *Washington Post*, wanted to try, too. Through a Hong Kong travel agency, we obtained Tibetan travel permits. That was the easy part.

The hard part was picking up the permits. The reason foreign correspondents couldn't get into Tibet unofficially was because our passports, stamped with journalist visas, automatically branded us as pariah reporters. In Chengdu, the gateway to Tibet, we knew we'd have to show our passports to the Chinese travel agent *before* he would release the permits. And we'd also have to show our passports to various authorities on arrival in Tibet.

So, we needed untainted passports. By chance, my Canadian passport was about to expire. It occurred to me that if I applied for a new one in Beijing it would be clean. Lena could do the same with a U.S. passport.

But what would we say when anyone asked why our passports were blank? How did we get into China in the first place? We "solved" that problem by photocopying the tourist visas of two Americans visiting Beijing. Then we concocted the following story: our old passports had expired in the middle of our trip through China, but here are our new passports and, uh, here are our new visas. It was so wild it just might work.

As someone frog-marched through the ethics course at Columbia University's Graduate School of Journalism, I had *some* scruples. But J-school had prepared me for working in a democracy. It didn't offer Ethics 101 for Dictatorships. My professors, for instance, had always taught me to identify myself honestly when interviewing someone. In a police state, that could endanger the interviewee. If I unburdened myself in the name of Western journalistic morality, authorities could later accuse anyone I talked to of *willfully* leaking state secrets.

Anyway, ordinary Chinese weren't stupid. Ask more than two questions, and they'd say, "You're a reporter, right?" The really smart ones knew better than to ask. On my 1999 trip, I hired the same taxi driver in Beijing for several days. Not only did he lend me his cellphone to book interviews, but he helpfully slowed down whenever Alister wanted to film sensitive shots from the car. The taxi driver saw our cameras, microphones and light. He even helped us carry the tripod. But he never, ever asked what we were doing. That way, he could truthfully say he thought we were tourists.

In July, 1994, Lena and I left Beijing in great secrecy. In Chengdu, the tour agent didn't bat an eye at our blank passports. The next morning, on the pre-dawn flight to Lhasa, I used a felt pen to alter the numbers on our Xeroxed visas so the deed couldn't be traced back to our tourist friends. I couldn't do anything about the watermarks. The high-quality photocopier had picked up the watermarks of shadowy American eagles. Belatedly, I realized I should have "borrowed" a visa from a Canadian. I just hoped nobody would notice that the eagles on my fake Chinese visa didn't match the maple-leaf watermarks on my Canadian passport.

Norman had come with us. Usually he stayed home with Ben and Sam whenever I traveled. But this time I feared that looking Chinese in Tibet would be a barrier to chatting up dissident monks. With his beard, he even looked like an aging pro-Dalai Lama backpacker. As a non-journalist, he had no trouble obtaining a Tibetan travel permit. But because his Chinese visa branded him as a journalist's *spouse* (Chinese bureaucrats left nothing to chance), we had to pretend to be old friends who had bumped into one another on the flight into Lhasa. Of course, that meant we'd have to sleep in separate hotel rooms. I told Fat Paycheck a good reporter had to make sacrifices.

On the flight, we popped some anti-edema pills and began guzzling water to prevent altitude sickness as our *Lonely Planet* guidebook instructed. Looking out the plane window, I saw moss-green massifs, some with a dusting of snow, poking through the clouds. But I didn't see any sign of human habitation until our descent onto the banks of the sparkling Brahmaputra River. At nearly 12,000 feet above sea level, Tibet's skies were deep azure, the same as Beijing's had been in the 1970s, before the veil of sulfur and coal dust closed in. With a bump, we landed on the single airstrip.

No one questioned our blank passports at Ganggor Airport. Pemba, our Tibet Tourism guide, bought our story about meeting Norman on the plane and added him to our package tour. After martial law, authorities tried to discourage backpackers by forcing "groups of one or more" to buy expensive packages.

At the Holiday Inn Lhasa, the reception clerk flipped through our blank passports. "Visas?" he said, with a puzzled look.

I whipped out our photocopied visas. He unfolded them. Without a second glance, he filled in the paperwork that would be forwarded to the local police station. We had made it!

Only one-fifth of the Holiday Inn's 500 rooms were occupied. Built in 1985, Tibet's only three-star hotel looked reassuringly normal. But its outdoor pool was polar-bear cold and its Himalaya Restaurant offered yak tartar. It also offered a gizmo in each room that piped oxygen directly into the bedside table so you could ostensibly lie in bed and gas up. But like the elevators, the oxygen system wasn't working. A call to housekeeping brought a Tibetan woman bearing a bag of room-service oxygen. Norman, who soon succumbed to altitude sickness, began stumbling around the lobby with an inflated khaki bag under one arm and a rubber tube stuck up his nose.

After a lunch of (cooked) yakburgers and fries at the hotel's Hard Yak Cafe, we rushed to the Barkhor, an open-air marketplace that wrapped around the Jokhang, Tibet's holiest temple. It was also the site of the 1989 riots. On March 8 that year, Beijing had imposed martial law on Lhasa after three straight days of rioting in the Barkhor. Like other journalists, I had been forced to follow the 1989 events by phoning hostels in the Tibetan capital. I had chafed at being unable to report first-hand. I had so many questions. Had Beijing destroyed Tibetan culture? Did Tibetans want independence? Did they hate the Chinese authorities – any more than the *Chinese* hated Chinese authorities?

Now we were finally here, and Norman was starting to feel queasy from the altitude. Suddenly, he upchucked his yakburger on the smooth paving stones where worshippers always prostrate themselves before entering Jokhang Temple. Now I knew why I never took Fat Paycheck on reporting trips. Barfing in the Barkhor was as bad as vomiting in the Vatican. A small knot of Tibetans surrounded us, but they weren't angry. They sympathetically patted their stomachs. "There's a good hospital over there," one young Tibetan said kindly, in perfect English.

Tibet felt like a movie set. Sealed off by the Himalayas to the south and the Qinghai desert to the north, it was a starkly beautiful land of glaciers and grasslands. Lhasa's white-washed buildings had tapering, deep-set windows, splashed with boxes of bright flowers. On the city outskirts, yaks grazed on purple wildflowers beside rushing, snow-fed rivers. Tibetan women, in kimono-like *chubas* and striped aprons of hot pink, cherry and lime green, strolled the streets, piously twirling prayer wheels. The paper money reeked of yak butter.

But a palpable tension underlay this Shangri-La. Fourteen months of martial law had ended the previous year. Sprawling military compounds were a stone's throw from Buddhist temples. Unsmiling Chinese soldiers manned checkpoints all around the city. In a single week, our Land Rover was stopped a dozen times by security forces searching for weapons and escaped prisoners.

The reality of Tibet was brutal. But the brutality didn't begin with Communist rule. Tibet had been a medieval theocracy in which even the monasteries owned serfs. Tibetan Buddhism forbade the taking of a life, but "iron-rod lamas" routinely flogged runaway serfs. And while there was no capital punishment, the landed gentry would gouge out the eyes of offending serfs, or inflict so many lashes the victim sometimes died.

Feudalism persisted until the 1950s. Local customs included one man marrying several sisters or several brothers sharing a single wife. One in every four boys were sent to monasteries. Most girls weren't educated at all. Traditional healers made pills from the Dalai Lama's excrement. And the average life expectancy was 30 years.

"The West believes Tibet was a Shangri-La, but it wasn't a fairyland," said Future Gu, my Beijing University classmate, who taught high school in Tibet for eight years in the 1970s. He remembered seeing a convicted thief who had had both arms lopped off. "His teeth were very strong. He could pick up anything with his teeth."

When the Communists ended theocratic rule in the 1950s, the biggest losers were the serf owners and the monasteries. The aristocracy lost everything when Beijing confiscated their vast estates and freed the serfs. The monks and nuns, the backbone of today's independence movement, endured the harshest repression. They must now swear allegiance to Beijing and undergo background checks for "subversion." Many have been jailed and hundreds more forced from the monasteries on suspicion of political activism. Beijing also imposes strict quotas for novices, just 15 or 20 a year per nunnery or monastery. Ani Tsang Kung, a small nunnery in the heart of Lhasa, had only 103 nuns, but a five-year waiting list.

Perspective helps. By 1999, Tibet had 46,000 monks and nuns. In a population of 2 million, that was 1 for every 43 Tibetans.

Pemba, our 28-year-old Tibetan guide, filled our itinerary with tours of famous monasteries. Outside, beggars clamored for alms. Inside, monks vied for pens and Dalai Lama pictures that Lena and I carried as ice-breakers. While we kept Guide Pemba busy, Norman chatted to the monks in Chinese. In a windowless prayer room at Sera, a large monastery on the outskirts of Lhasa, a 23-year-old monk whispered, "We want the Dalai Lama to come back." Norman asked why. The monk, his face illuminated by hundreds of flickering yak-butter lamps, whispered, "We don't like the Chinese. Tibet should be given back to the Tibetans. We want independence."

Drepung Monastery was a jumble of monumental white and maroon-colored hillside buildings that once housed 10,000 monks. By the 1990s, it had shrunk to 600 monks. We watched them, garbed in maroon, debating theology under gnarled walnut trees. At Drepung, a young monk told Norman, "To the monks and nuns, the Chinese are like this." He put one clenched fist over the other in a stranglehold.

On July 6, we'd heard rumors there would be a day-long picnic to celebrate the Dalai Lama's birthday. Tibetans were ordered to stay away. So were tourists. "If you go and are caught, the authorities will revoke your travel permit," Guide Pemba warned.

We had no idea where the picnic would be held. But the authorities posted notices, helpfully specifying exactly where we weren't supposed to go. Armed with the directions, Lena and I tied scarves over our heads in a hopeless attempt to look Tibetan. Then we hailed a pedicab and joined hundreds of revelers picnicking on barley beer and dried yak meat. The custom was to fling good-luck fistfuls of barley flour on everyone else. We returned for our afternoon tour, sheepishly brushing beige flour off our clothes, Guide Pemba and Lobsang, our burly Tibetan driver, grinned. But they said nothing. Just like Chinese interviewees, they wisely adopted a don't-ask policy, too.

To cross the Lhasa River, you climbed into a small round yak-skin boat and balanced yourself on one of its hardened wood ribs – trying to avoid punching your foot through the taut hide. As a joke once, Lena and I sang "Row, Row, Row Your Boat." The boatman picked up the refrain – in English. Then he sang a song of his own about rowing boats.

Tibetans, it turned out, had a whole repertoire of dirges that slowed the pace of every chore from hauling stones to harvesting barley. Norman figured the tradition originated in work-to-rule policies by brow-beaten serfs. Why exert yourself for someone else, especially at this altitude? At Drepung Monastery, I watched 15 Tibetans sing a hypnotic roof-repairing song while they leisurely tamped down a corner of the roof. The practice, endearing to tourists with video cameras, drove Tibetan contractors crazy.

"Tibetans prefer to hire Chinese construction workers because they work harder and better. Tibetans aren't as efficient," said Ma Drun, a Tibetan poet.

In the 1990s, the finely honed art of slacking off backfired. Tibetans began losing control over their economy to Chinese migrants. Sensing unbridled opportunity in the frontier, the Chinese poured into Tibet. They soon dominated every industry except yak-skin boat rowing. Chinese migrants operated restaurants, video stores, shoe-repair kiosks and the city's fledgling taxi service. They even sold prayer scarves outside the holiest temples.

"Tibetans are stupid," said one Tibetan, in frustration and despair. "Unlike the Chinese, we don't want to eat the bitterness that comes with making money." He told us the rags-to-riches story of a Chinese with a twisted spine who had arrived a decade earlier. Zhang Zehua had begged outside monasteries until he had saved enough to open a tiny food stall. Within a few years, he owned four restaurants and was rich.

We found him sitting outside his flagship Sichuan restaurant, called Hot, Spicy and Scalding. "Come in, try our hot pot," he urged Lena and me. When a beggar shuffled by, Zhang whipped out a large bill from his pocket and snapped his fingers. His assistant manager rushed over to make change. Then Zhang thrust some smaller bills into the beggar's hand.

Some critics have accused China of a genocidal "population-transfer policy." To me, the influx of migrants was an inevitable byproduct of capitalism. As a hundred million peasants left the countryside, every city was getting its share of of outside workers. But in Tibet, the wave of entrepreneurs from poor inland provinces strained already tense ethnic relations. "Lhasa is the Rome of Buddhism," a Western diplomat said. "How would the Italians feel if all the Germans started moving in?"

Tibet's original Chinese settlers had been Communist cadres, condescending, yes, but well-meaning types who at least had paid lip service to local culture. The new arrivals had no stake in political correctness. They gawked at Tibetans bathing in the river during the annual Washing Festival. And they snapped souvenir photos of Tibetans prostrating themselves at temples. Tibetan Buddhists ate meat. Several sects even permitted high-ranking lamas and abbots to marry. But the Chinese shocked the local populace by sometimes eating stray dogs, whom Tibetans believed might be humans reincarnated.

"Horses and snakes can't live together," was scrawled in Tibetan on a wall near a Chinese army base. Another graffiti, also in Tibetan, said, "Birds and wolves cannot co-exist."

The feeling was mutual. Chinese fruit vendors kept silent when Tibetan urchins snatched a piece of fruit. And a Chinese taxi driver, who drove one of only ten taxis in Lhasa, told me he never picked up Tibetans at night. "They're all drunk, and they all have knives. A drunken Tibetan is pitiless."

For Doje, the Tibetan cycle of life, death and rebirth had come full circle. A former monk and an ex-Red Guard, he was now growing highland barley in the shadow of the monastery he once served – and later destroyed. He was just seven when he took a vow of celibacy in 1956 and became a child monk in Ganden, one of Tibet's holiest monasteries. Three years later, when Beijing suppressed the short-lived theocratic rebellion and the Dalai Lama fled to India, Doje was forced back to his village.

At 17, he returned to Ganden, this time to destroy it. Fired up by Chairman Mao's Cultural Revolution, he and other Tibetan Red Guards stormed the monastery that glittered, like a diamond-and-garnet tiara, on a mountain peak high above his village. He helped tear apart its 15th-century stone walls and torch its Buddhist libraries. By the time he and his comrades left, Ganden looked liked the target of saturation bombing.

I'd always assumed Chinese Red Guards had destroyed Tibet's monasteries. But it turned out *Tibetans* had destroyed them. It made sense when you thought about it. *Chinese* Red Guards had been too busy trashing their own temples during the Cultural Revolution. Tibet's inaccessibility and debilitating altitude would have discouraged outsiders. And in the 1960s, why would Tibetan youth have been different from young people elsewhere in China?

We had spent the day sightseeing at Ganden, a dizzying 13,000 feet above sea level. Stung by international criticism and anxious for tourist dollars, China was rebuilding it stone by stone. Trucks wheezed up a dirt road with 17 hairpin turns. A crew fed whole trees into a whining electric saw. Amid the broken walls, square white and oxblood temples rose.

On the way down, we suddenly asked Driver Lobsang to stop at any village. A Chinese driver might have balked, but he bumped across the rock-strewn fields until we came to Cha, a hard-scrabble village with just 22 families, a half-hour walk from the nearest paved road.

We found Doje standing beside his adobe home. He had no radio, television, running water or electricity. Except for six shiny thermoses and a bicycle parked outside, we could have been in the tenth century. His cooking shed had a six-foot-tall pyramid of yak-dung fuel. Its thatched roof was black from smoke and grease. A yak-butter lamp glowed in offering to his father, who had died a few weeks earlier.

At 45, Doje was a slight, apologetic man in a battered fedora, soiled white shirt and torn canvas shoes, with a six-inch dagger on his right hip. He invited us into his home. As he stooped to pour us some salty yak-butter tea, he seemed full of regret. "At the time, I didn't care what I was doing," he said, his eyes filling with tears. "Now that I'm older, I feel bad." To make amends, he told us he had sent his eldest son to be a monk at Ganden. Outside in their dirt courtyard, Doje's wife, tall and silent in a dark kimono-like *chuba*, stirred a vat of maroon liquid, dyeing monks' robes for their son.

To me, Doje embodied Tibet's modern plight. He was impoverished and full of regrets, a victim of the vicissitudes of the Chinese revolution. But his confession elicited no sympathy from Driver Lobsang, who spoke fluent Mandarin and wasn't shy about sharing his opinions. "We have a saying," he said. "The villages below

Ganden destroyed the monastery, so fate decrees that they will be forever poor."

We wandered over to Cha's one-room schoolhouse. Even in summer, the children's noses dripped from sitting on the bare concrete floor. The one and only teacher, Phuntso, explained that the school had desks and chairs, but to make them last, the students used them only in winter.

Dipping sharpened sticks in an "ink" of ash and water, the children practised the graceful calligraphy of the Tibetan alphabet on homemade slates. Lena and I had brought bags of pencils and exercise books and several soccer balls as gifts. While Driver Lobsang inflated the balls with our tire pump, we asked Phuntso, 40, what else he taught besides the alphabet. Apologetically, he explained he only had a third-grade education. Outside, on an adobe wall, I saw the faded remains, in Tibetan and Chinese, of a Mao quotation: "Study hard. Make progress every day."

Was Tibet making progress? Or was Beijing committing genocide? Were Tibetans the pandas of the politically correct world, whose habitat was being encroached upon by the evil Chinese? The answers, I was beginning to see, were mixed.

The Chinese were equal-opportunity despots. Tibetan history textbooks spouted standard Communist pap, just as Chinese history textbooks did. Beijing abused human rights in Tibet, just as it did in China. And ever since the Cultural Revolution, Tibet, two or three times zones away, had been forced to set its clocks to Beijing time. But then, the entire country set its clocks to Beijing time. Iron-handed rule – interspersed with periods of brutal repression – was Beijing's modus operandi. The bloody suppression of Tibetan monks and nuns in the spring of 1989 was just the warm-up for Beijing's far, far bloodier massacre of its own people in Tiananmen Square three months later.

As the same time, average life expectancy in Tibet had doubled to 65 years under Chinese rule. The literacy rate was just 56 percent, but it was higher than at any time in Tibet's history. Like Teacher Phuntso, most rural Tibetan children quit in third grade. But that was no different from other poor regions of China. A 1998 decree forcing child monks back to school could be seen two ways, religious oppression or child-welfare protection. I personally favored educating children.

Tibetan remained the primary language on the streets, in homes and in schools. If anything was having a corrosive effective on local culture, it was Hong Kong pop music, which was having an equally devastating effect on Chinese traditional music in the rest of the country. In Lhasa as in Beijing, young people were more interested in buying tapes of Cantonese pop stars than attending local opera festivals.

Religion, the heart of Tibetan culture, was also thriving. More than 90 percent of the people were devout Buddhists. Every day, hundreds of pilgrims made a holy circuit around Lhasa, prostrating themselves and spinning prayer wheels. And while Beijing's quotas for monks and nuns was undoubtedly repressive, it also had the indirect effect of increasing the Tibetan population – by restricting the numbers of adults who practised celibacy.

Just as Doje symbolized Tibet's modern plight, Li Honghu symbolized China's failed Tibet policy. After devoting his life to the region, the Chinese cadre had been pressed into emergency police duty during the 1989 protests. The unrest fell on the 30th anniversary of the Dalai Lama's flight into exile. In the ensuing days, he helped the police arrest hundreds of Tibetans.

At 40, Li was bitter and disillusioned. All he dreamed about was getting out. He feared for his own safety. "I'm glad there are so many soldiers here because I'm afraid the Tibetans might slaughter all the Chinese."

The 1989 suppression was a turning point for Li, who ran a major government department in Lhasa. By day, the mild-mannered bureaucrat pistol-whipped and cattle-prodded Tibetan prisoners. At night, he donned riot gear and kicked in the doors of some of Tibet's holiest monasteries. "The monks," he said contemptuously, "were lying there asleep just like dead pigs. We trussed them up."

After the adrenalin faded, Director Li despised himself. "Once, our truck was surrounded by Tibetans as we loaded on some prisoners we had just beaten. People stood around us crying. I couldn't stand it." Director Li requested a transfer back to his old administrative job.

It seemed a lifetime ago that he had received a hero's send-off. In 1976, he had volunteered to work in Tibet after graduation. Amid clashing cymbals and fluttering flags, university officials pinned a huge, red silk flower to his chest. Then Li, a fresh-faced youth and a loyal Communist Party member, boarded a train to oblivion. "I sacrificed my youth, the best years of my life, for Tibet," he said bitterly. "I've just been a pawn of Communist Party policy."

Li got used to the altitude, and he eventually got used to rancid butter tea. But his Chinese wife, unable to adapt, had moved back to Beijing with their ten-year-old son. The only adornment on the walls of his tiny whitewashed cottage was a calendar, as if he were counting the days of a life sentence. He kept trying for a transfer back to Beijing. But bloated state companies were refusing to accept anyone. By 1994, after 18 years in Tibet, Director Li had hit a glass ceiling. "Affirmative-action policies mean the promotions are going to Tibetans," he complained.

Indeed, an elite group of Communist-trained Tibetan cadres was assuming power in the 1990s. They, not the rock-tossing pro-Dalai Lama monks and nuns, posed the greatest danger to China's grip on Tibet. Of 60,000 local officials, 70 percent were Tibetans, mostly ex-Red Guards who understood the strengths and weaknesses of the Chinese Communist Party.

"The same people who destroyed the monasteries are walking around today with their prayer wheels, talking about independence," said Guide Pemba.

For decades, waves of Chinese volunteers like Director Li had arrived as teachers, soldiers, builders, even playwrights. Initially, many Tibetans greeted them warmly. But as relations cooled, some began to view the Chinese cadres as failures who could not cut it inland or carpetbaggers lured by frontier pay. Guide Pemba didn't mince words when asked what he thought of them.

"They're not here to help us," he scoffed. "They get more pay and better housing than back home. And when they leave, they take home truckloads of possessions with them." Pay scales were 40 percent higher because Tibet was classified, even for Tibetans, as a hardship post. Most Chinese cadres planned to stay just a few years, so they often left children and spouses behind. Few learned to speak Tibetan. After all, that kind of career move could condemn you to life in Tibet.

Tibetans naturally assumed I was Chinese. In a region supposedly seething with ethnic hatred, they treated me with a lot more warmth than I have felt in some Chinese cities. At one roadside stall, some herdsmen even offered me a cup of their homemade barley beer.

Only twice did I have trouble. At one monastery, a young monk, miffed that I had run out of Dalai Lama pictures, tossed a stone at my back. The only other problem occurred at Lhasa's sky burial site.

Sky burials were a gruesome, but environmentally friendly, way of dispatching the dead. Crews of *domden*, or body breakers, chopped up corpses, then summoned a flock of resident vultures to feast. The souls of the dead were believed to have ascended to heaven if the bones had been picked clean. When Director Li suggested we visit the site, I hesitated, having read in the *Lonely Planet* guide that the burial workers sometimes chased off intruders with bloody bones. "All the burials take place early in the morning," he assured me. "No one will be there in the afternoon."

His Tibetan driver took us to the northeast edge of Lhasa, as far as possible, until the road ended. Then we all hiked half an hour toward a barren mountain where the body breakers lived like hermits. They were shunned by the rest of society; Tibetans despised any professions linked with death, including butchers and yak-skin boatmen.

As we rounded a corner, an old crone ambushed me, using my backpack to bind me in a straitjacket. She had matted braids streaked with gray and wore a coarse-spun black *chuba* and a long soiled apron. When I felt the iron grip of her hands and remembered what she did for a living, I was afraid. She unzipped my pack and grabbed my camera. Our Tibetan driver tried to grab it back. She wouldn't let go. A few other body breakers drifted out to watch in silence. She and the driver argued for a while, then disappeared around the side of the mountain to negotiate in private.

"She wants money. She's just extorting you," the Tibetan driver said in disgust, half an hour later. He told me to give her 50 yuan, which made the old woman so happy, I not only got back my camera, she even urged me to take pictures. I never had any intention of taking photos of a blank hillside, but I made a mental note to inform the *Lonely Planet* editors of the current price of ethnic sensitivity in Tibet.

The site itself was a huge sloping slab of rock that looked like the reverse side of a giant cheese grater. A dozen depressions the size of salad bowls pitted the smooth surface. Three or four holes still contained a trace of yellow-brown liquid. Others were stained with dried blood and stuck with a few strands of human hair. Some barley flour smoldered in a small bonfire, an offering to the dead.

The sky-burial workers processed about seven corpses a day. They began by stripping off the flesh and chopping it into mince-meat. Using the salad-bowl depressions like a giant mortar and pestle, they pounded entrails and other organs with a rock the size of a soccer ball. Then they blew a whistle, summoning the vultures down from the peak above. Later, the workers pulverized the bones and mixed them with barley flour. After the vultures had dined again, the workers burned any remaining hair and bones. The family later sprinkled the ashes in a river.

Our tour included dinner at a traditional Tibetan restaurant. As we sat at low, gaudily painted orange tables, *chuba*-garbed waitresses brought out coarse mutton dumplings, greasy mutton soup, dried mutton meat, dried yak meat, pungent sheep's yogurt and beige cigarillo-shaped lumps of *tsampa*, the Tibetan dietary staple of roasted barley flour mixed with rancid yak butter. Norman liked it, but to me, it was a dead ringer for window putty.

Dressed in an olive-green *chuba*, Chong Dron, the 49-year-old owner, smiled graciously at the polite Japanese tourists who ate all their *tsampa*. But when she came to our table, she glared at Lena and me. Perhaps it was because we were pushing our *tsampa* around on our plates. Perhaps it was also because we looked Chinese.

I kicked Norman under the table, and he took over the questions. It turned out Chong Dron longed for the good old days when everyone had to stick out their tongues as a sign of respect whenever she and other aristocrats passed. Her father-in-law had been one of Tibet's richest nobles. After he joined the abortive week-long rebellion in 1959, the Chinese government stripped him of his land holdings and tossed him in prison. "He died there," she said bitterly.

With his usual tact, Fat Paycheck asked if anyone in her family had married a Chinese. "No," she said, her voice stiff with disapproval. "We're not compatible."

Norman had asked about intermarriage because we were taken aback to find it flourishing. We wanted to find out more. Beijing had initially discouraged intermarriage when the PLA first marched in. Even including Sichuan and Qinghai Provinces, Tibetans accounted for a mere 0.5 percent of China's population. Beijing feared that if Chinese were allowed to freely intermarry with Tibetans, they would rapidly overwhelm the gene pool, a situation that could ignite ethnic unrest. "The government wanted to avoid causing conflicts," said Simon Hui, a Chinese friend who had been a soldier stationed in Tibet during China's 1962 border war with India.

Punishment was swift for Chinese breaking the ban. Soldiers could be court-martialed and Communist Party members could be expelled or transferred home in disgrace. In the 1980s, the ban was quietly dropped. A 1990 census revealed 2,600 mixed marriages, but the current number might be much higher. Many Chinese migrants deliberately sought Tibetan wives because they wanted someone already adapted to the harsh environment.

Others, like restaurateur Chong Dron, still opposed intermarriage. The late Panchen Lama, Tibet's second-highest spiritual leader after the Dalai Lama, married a Chinese, but was forced by public opinion to abandon his wife in the late 1970s, even though they had a child. More recently, Ni Drun, the Tibetan poet, spent a year persuading her parents to let her marry a Chinese editor in Lhasa.

The mixed offspring of such unions were called the "Unity Minority." These Chinese-Tibetan kids were usually bilingual and bicultural. They also had the right to choose their official ethnic group for their government ID card. ("Unity" was not an actual option, merely a creation of the overheated government propaganda machine.)

If Tibetans were as oppressed as many accounts contend, you'd think that the mixed kids would leap at the chance *not* to be classified as Tibetan the way light-skinned blacks sometimes tried to pass for whites in the Deep South before the Civil Rights movement.

In fact, virtually every "Unity" kid chose to register as a Tibetan. Guide Pemba's wife, for instance, was half-Tibetan and half-Chinese. "We consider her Tibetan, of course."

The reasons were illuminating. *Tibetans were treated better than Chinese.* As a "national minority," they were exempt from China's one-child policy, had a lock on boarding-school scholarships in major Chinese cities and were accepted into university with lower marks. They also enjoyed affirmative-action quotas for jobs and promotions. And, unlike the Chinese, they had the right to buy land in Tibet.

One evening we visited the home, or homes, rather, of a mixed Chinese-Tibetan couple. When Dejiquzi, a Tibetan, complained that her new concrete Chinese-style home aggravated her arthritis, her Chinese husband added a Tibetan one, with gaily painted eaves and a pretty blue-and-white canvas awning. They moved easily between the two houses, linked by a courtyard garden of purple petunias, yellow roses and giant dahlias.

Her husband, Zhang Rihe, invited us into his Tibetan living room, which had a spotless linoleum floor and carved wooden chests. He was Chinese, from Liaoning Province in the Northeast. He had arrived in 1960 as a volunteer truck driver, hauling cargo across some of the toughest terrain in the world. A mutual friend had introduced him to a stunning 22-year-old Tibetan who had learned to speak fluent Chinese at a police academy in Beijing. They fell in love. Defying the marriage ban, they married on October 1, 1961, China's National Day.

They were in their 50s now, but the relationship hadn't been easy. After 21 years of living in Tibet, he became terribly homesick. But when he moved his family to Liaoning in 1981, his wife became homesick. She soon returned to Lhasa — with their three children — while he stayed in Liaoning. In 1988, when he retired, he rejoined them in Lhasa and built the two homes.

Their three children, two girls and a boy, were grown now. They were educated in Chinese, but grew up speaking Tibetan at home. Each had a Chinese name and a Tibetan name and said they felt equally Chinese and Tibetan. But all three had registered as Tibetans because they each planned to have two children. And all three had already attended university, an opportunity open to just 4 percent of Chinese youth.

The son, Dawatsri, 26, worked in the Foreign Affairs Department of Tibet. He dropped in long enough to pose for a family photo and to bring his father a bag of his favorite steamed wheat buns, a northern Chinese staple. The younger daughter, Dramatsri, 24, worked in the Department of Foreign Trade in Lhasa. Both were dating other members of the "Unity Minority."

Drama, 28, the older daughter, had married a "Unity" man. "We feel comfortable with either group," she said. She had majored in English at the University of Tibet, and was about to go to England for further studies. With her even white teeth and flowing black hair, she could have passed for either Chinese or Tibetan.

Although both parents were Communist Party members, the children noted that their mother was becoming increasingly devout in her old age. Each morning, she prostrated herself before Buddha a ritualistic 108 times. "She says it's for exercise, but we know what's in her heart," teased Drama.

Zhang Rihe, who now worked as a driver for a Western aid agency, admitted to escorting his wife to temples. But he gently ridiculed her born-again Buddhism. "She never believed any of this stuff when she was young. She's gotten superstitious in her old age," he joked.

And what of his own Communist beliefs? "Me?" he said, with a chuckle. "I only believe in money."

Whose fault was it that Tibet, a territory the size of Western Europe, remained one of China's poorest regions? Wedged between several Chinese provinces and India, Bhutan, Sikkim and Nepal, Tibet had no railway, two highways in chronically terrible condition and the single airstrip at Ganggor. Lhasa didn't build a major hospital until 1985. Several of its main roads weren't paved until 1987. The first students at Tibet University graduated only in 1988. And Tibet didn't get a library until 1994, the very last region in China to get one.

In 1999, 90 percent of Tibetans were farmers and herdsmen. A mere 15 percent of gross domestic product was industrial. Even traditional Tibetan jewelry was made in Nepal. The butter for offering lamps came from India. And a sun hat Norman bought in the Barkhor was made in Tianjin. "Tibet's annual revenue isn't even as much as that of a township in a coastal province," said Director Li.

Tibet's Chinese name, Xi Zang, means "Western Treasurehouse." The exile Tibetan community has accused Beijing of plundering its vaunted timber and mineral resources. But forbidding geography, a primitive infrastructure and severe weather have meant that no one has been able to exploit Tibet's riches. "The Chinese have poured a lot of money in," said a Western diplomat who studied the region. "Everything is subsidized, but you don't see it, and therefore people don't feel grateful."

All the feel-good rallies in the West have emboldened a new generation of separatist-minded Tibetans. In part because China goes to such great lengths to keep us out, the Western media has paid inordinate attention to Tibet. A peaceful demonstration by two dozen Tibetans protesting Premier Zhu Rongji's 1999 visit to New York merited 16 inches in the *New York Times.*

Such coverage has given Tibetans an exaggerated sense of the importance of their cause. Hollywood has helped, too, by bequeathing pop-icon status on the Dalai Lama. Martin Scorsese made a film about his childhood, Brad Pitt starred in *Seven Years in Tibet* and of course, there is the tireless Richard Gere. Tibetans think that because heads of state and movie stars seek audiences with the ever-smiling Dalai Lama, public opinion will force Beijing to let them have a country of their own.

But the dream of independence is hopeless. Neighboring Chinese provinces have already absorbed two-thirds of Tibet's original territory, home to the bulk of six million Tibetans. Despite the Dalai Lama's 1989 Nobel Peace Prize, not a single country recognizes his government-in-exile. On the contrary, every nation, including the United States, Britain, Canada, Russia and India, supports

Beijing's claim. To other nations, Tibet is a remote backwater with a population the size of Cleveland's. "To be blunt, Tibet is of zero strategic importance," said a Western diplomat in China. "It is a crime to encourage these people."

China's claims to Tibet date back to 650 AD. But its hold on Tibet waxed and waned, reaching a nadir in 763 AD when Tibetan troops sacked the Tang Dynasty capital of Changan (now Xian). In 1911, Lhasa squandered a golden opportunity to make a clean break when the Qing Dynasty collapsed. Instead of swiftly establishing diplomatic relations with other countries, theocratic Tibet remained closed. After Mao Zedong took power in 1949, Tibet belatedly sent four officials on a desultory tour of India, China and the United States. By the time the delegation returned two years later, the Communists had conquered all China.

Tibet's xenophobia was part of its allure, and part of its problem. Many 19th-century travelers perished trying to reach it. Those that made it were peremptorily turned away. Heinrich Harrer, the Austrian Olympic skier and author of *Seven Years in Tibet*, was allowed to stay only because he offered to tutor the young Dalai Lama. In his 1953 memoirs, Harrer wrote that while stores in Lhasa sold Elizabeth Arden cosmetics and Bing Crosby's latest records, Tibetan scholars still believed the earth was flat. The only person in Lhasa able to communicate with the outside world was the local British representative. Tibet was not even a member of the World Postal Union.

"No one received permission to come to Tibet," Harrer wrote. "The unchangeable policy was to present Tibet as the Forbidden Land. The foreigners whom I met during the five years of my stay in Lhasa were not more than seven in number." They included the British representative, the resident Chinese minister and a few Nepalese.

Although 80 million Chinese live below the poverty line, Beijing's annual subsidy to Tibet was nearly $300 million a year. But to Tibetans, China was a tyrant. Beijing may have built 500 hydro power stations in Tibet, but it also stationed 40,000 troops there.

Again, perspective helps. Put another way, Beijing had stationed nearly one soldier in Tibet for every monk and nun.

Since the 13th century, every Chinese government has counted Tibet as Chinese territory. The region, which accounts for one-seventh of China's land mass, acts as a buffer with Burma, India, Nepal and Bhutan. Still, I believe there is a chance that China's policy could change. The new generation of pragmatic Western-educated Chinese technocrats is more sensitive to world opinion – and the bottom line. They will consider what Tibet gives them – an international black eye – and what they give Tibet – millions of dollars in aid each year.

Tibet will make it easy for them to walk away. The Dalai Lama has proposed limited self-rule, leaving foreign affairs and defense to Beijing. But the 15,000-member exiled Tibetan Youth Congress has formally rejected the Dalai Lama's position and called for an independent nation. It has also refused to rule out the use of violence.

Without constant infusions of Chinese aid, the Roof of the World could easily slip back into its medieval past. No one is clamoring to invest there. Do the people of Tibet want independence if it means a drastic drop in their standard of living? It is clear what the monks and nuns think. And it is clear what the exile community overseas thinks. But what about Tibet's silent majority? My sense was that while they were unhappy with Chinese rule, they weren't yet angry enough to cut the umbilical cord.

For their part, many Chinese were puzzled as to why Tibetans weren't grateful for being dragged into the Communist era. The truth is, Beijing's ham-fisted techniques have not won the hearts and minds of Tibetans, just as the same techniques have backfired in China. "When all is said and done, the Tibetans will know in their hearts whether our intentions were good or bad," said a Chinese official who was on the verge of retiring after 32 years in Tibet. "Did we oppress them? Exploit them? Suppress them? Or did we raise their standard of living and guarantee them food and clothing?"

The answer was that China did all of the above. It gave the Tibetans their very own version of Hong Kong pop music, with whips and chains.

The Chinese never caught Lena and me in Tibet. Lena was forced to leave China four days after we got back to Beijing, but not because of our trip. It was fallout from the earlier search of her office by State Security agents.

Months after my return to Canada, I began suffering stomach pains. In the shower one day, I encountered a small, flat worm in my nether regions. I screamed. Then it *moved*. I screamed again. Over the next few days, more of these tiny critters emerged without warning, creating my very own in-house horror show.

My doctor in Toronto, who had never seen anything like it, sent me to a tropical-disease specialist. He was so thrilled that he called in all his residents: I was a textbook case of the perils of sampling yak tartar. Two very expensive tiny white pills later, I was cured. I can't remember the name of the disease. I just called it the Dalai Lama's Revenge.

10

Farting at Ferragamo's

Chowing down on Kentucky Fried Chicken in Shanghai.

Photo: Wang Gangfeng

As the first Canadian to study in China since the Cultural Revolution, I felt an obligation to experience everything, even the boring stuff. So in 1972, I'd grab my khaki folding stool each evening at seven and join my dorm mates in front of a small black and white television set to watch robotic announcers in Mao suits describing the latest bumper harvest. This would be followed by a documentary, say, on cow vaccinations. Occasionally, there would even be a death rally, complete with a bullet to the back of the head.

"Television," the official New China News Agency opined, "must play an increasingly important role in the struggle to consolidate the dictatorship of the proletariat."

Television sets required ration coupons and cost several years' salary for the average worker. With just one for every 4,000 Chinese, my dorm mates and I weren't the only collective couch potatoes. Anyone lucky enough to own a set found themselves hosting their neighbors every night. Everyone watched the daily three-hour broadcast. There was nothing else to do.

No wonder everyone went ga-ga in 1979 with the airing of the first U.S. television show. *Man from Atlantis*, a dud back home, was a smash hit in China. It gave audiences their first Technicolor glimpse of six-lane freeways, bikinied blondes and on-screen kisses.

The crime rate dipped whenever it aired. And at least one classical piano concert I attended pushed back its starting time so no one would have to miss an episode.

Chinese audiences would watch anything. I know, because in 1980, I made my own television debut. Along with several friends, we put together an English-language special explaining a strange ritual called Christmas. It aired over Chinese New Year's to fabulous ratings – 400 million viewers.

In the 1980s, a color television set became *the* status symbol. By the 1990s, there were 500 state-run television stations. An average of 700 million viewers tuned in daily. Chinese Central Television (CCTV), the original monopoly station, still held the number one spot.

As a foreign correspondent, I still felt an obligation to experience everything, even the boring stuff. So one Friday night in 1993, I slumped on my couch, determined to tough out an entire evening of Chinese state television. At 7 p.m., just like in the old Maoist days, I tuned into CCTV's half-hour national newscast. It was still the top-rated show in China and, come to think of it, the world.

"Good evening, viewers," said the female announcer, dressed in a bright yellow blouse. That was a good sign. Whenever the political situation was tense, as it was after the Tiananmen Massacre, the announcers wore Mao suits and called us "comrades."

The lead item denounced Britain's plan to introduce democracy in Hong Kong. Just as in the old days, this was followed by a report on a bumper peanut crop in Hubei Province. The only violence was some footage of a chest operation, performed by some army doctors. There was still no sex.

"This just in," the announcer said. I sat up and grabbed my notebook. Real news? Oh, just Communist Party chief Jiang Zemin and Premier Li Peng in a photo op with 40 Hong Kongers. It lasted two minutes, an eternity on television.

International news occupied the final ten minutes. Talks were breaking down, again, between Bosnia and Serbia. Bill Clinton proclaimed his support, again, for Boris Yeltsin. And Los Angeles was bracing itself for yet another race riot.

Since its first transmission in 1958, Chinese television had been commercial-free for 21 years. Now, capitalism had arrived. After the news, I sat through nearly an hour of unbroken commercials for cough drops, air conditioners, industrial tires, skin cream, Chinese motorcycles, Honda motorcycles, hot dogs, a military-industrial complex ("investors welcome!"), cold capsules, diesel engines, longevity potions, cooking oil, toothpaste, farm tractors, water heaters, diet pills and Beck's beer. One for insomnia pills appeared to be a public-service message – anyone who was still awake could probably really use them. Plus the voice-over said they also cured nervous breakdowns.

After the sixth air-conditioning ad in 50 minutes, I switched to Beijing Television to catch a new soap that was starting at 8:18. (Except for the nightly news, Chinese programs always had chaotic starting times.)

A Path Goes Beyond the Horizon was about a female film producer who has an affair with, gasp, a married scriptwriter in Beijing. She's broken-hearted when he won't leave his wife. So she moves to tropical Hainan Island. He ends up divorcing his wife and resurfacing in Hainan. *Horizon* had lots of aviator sunglasses and Hawaiian shirts, but no bikini scenes. Although televised kissing was no longer banned, when the two lovers finally meet in his *hotel room*, they give each other a chaste hug.

"It's you," he says.

"How are you?" she replies.

"I'm fine," he says.

"How's your leg?" she says.

"It's all better," he says.

Another chaste hug. Then, like heads of state at a summit, they sit down in armchairs, separated by a tea table.

I switched channels again, trying to stay awake. The late-evening newscast began at 9:56. The lead story: delegates to the National People's Congress checking their bags at the airport. Pass me those insomnia/nervous breakdown pills.

At 10:06, a program called *Across China* featured a spot about a Pepsi bottling plant once visited by George Bush. More pills, please. Then there was a pop video, featuring a busty Chinese woman in a white tank top and jeans. This was followed by a short documentary on Chinese Muslims eating shish kebabs and another on the life cycle of a 12-legged insect.

At 10:29, another program, inexplicably called *Bell and Drum Tower*, featured an investigative report on counterfeit Kent cigarettes, pirated books and knock-off designer shoes. It ended with a public-service announcement on fire safety. Do not pack aerosol sprays, the host warned air travelers. To illustrate, he pressed the nozzle on a can, flicked on his cigarette lighter and *voila!* A do-it-yourself blowtorch.

That woke me up in time for *Let's Meet Tonight*, a series of one-minute matchmaking videos. The first of six eligible bachelors was a bespectacled computer nerd in a green windbreaker. The video showed him in his fluorescent-lit office as his vital statistics were flashed across the screen ("age 27, 1.72 meters tall, graduate degree"). The only female contestant was Yang Liu ("age 28, 1.64 meters tall, university graduate"). She was filmed shopping for clothes. Interested parties were instructed to write in.

At 11:05 p.m., I watched a dubbed German soap opera. Someone rich had died, and the potential heirs had gathered in a baroque hall to hear the will read out. As one of them stomped out and sped away in a red sports car, I decided it was time to bail out, too. I wanted to be up to catch the 6:55 a.m. disco-dancing show for seniors.

In the 19th century, Western capitalists dreamed of selling oil for all the lamps of China. Civil war, invasion and revolution intervened. At the end of the 20th century, the dream recurred, and it was still all about oil. Three Chinese McDonald's held worldwide records for opening-day sales. Kentucky Fried Chicken, Pizza Hut and Dunkin Donuts also opened for business, as did Baskin-Robbins, Dairy Queen and Häagen-Dazs.

In 1999, millions paid $8 apiece, a huge amount in China, to see *Titanic*. They bought Ikea kitchens, Jeep Cherokees, Nike shoes and Tampax. Starbucks, which opened its first outlet in Beijing, figured that if every Chinese drank just one cup of coffee a year, it could unload 40 million pounds of beans in China.

The hour-long barrages of television commercials helped spark an insatiable appetite for Western goods. Many people moonlighted at second jobs. In Guangdong Province, factories hummed through the night. Traffic was so clogged that enterprising peddlers hawked food to captive motorists.

Nike Inc. liked Guangdong because the people worked hard and the central government was safely distant. "'The heavens are high and the emperor is far away.' That could well be the motto on the Canton city crest," said Charles Brown, quoting a Chinese proverb to explain why Nike had set up a joint venture in Guangdong.

I asked Brown, the general manager, if there was any Marxist study at Nike. He turned to his Chinese assistant, who was typing furiously at her word processor.

"Monica, do you have to go to political meetings?"

She looked blank. "What?"

"Political meetings," he repeated.

"Oh." She laughed. "No."

"Does anybody?" Brown persisted. Monica laughed again and shook her head.

Then I asked if Nike had any Communist Party members on staff. "No," he said promptly. "I know that for sure. The last one emigrated to the States."

In 1990, the world's biggest cosmetic company also moved into Guangdong. China's richest province, with 70 million people, was virgin territory for Avon Products Inc., the first company authorized to sell directly to the Chinese public. This was, after all, a populace scarred by decades of dealing with surly salesclerks who gave new meaning to the term, "hard sell." In state stores, even toothpaste was kept out of reach. If you wanted, say, a flashlight, clerks would slam two or three of them on the counter, then drum their fingers impatiently while you tried to figure out which one was least defective.

"Any direct selling should do well in China," said Ben Mok, a McGill classmate who headed China operations for Electrolux. In 1989, he conducted a three-week experiment selling expensive vacuum cleaners door to door in Shanghai. One of every two calls resulted in a sale, Electrolux's highest success rate ever. Consumers bought on the spot, even though many didn't own carpets.

"One factor is guilt," said Ben. "The salesman demonstrates for an hour, and Chinese people feel sorry for him. They're so surprised someone bothered to come to their homes."

Chinese consumers were putty in the hands of smooth-talking Avon ladies. State enterprises invited them to tout "cell renewal formula" in the same halls where Party cadres once lectured on the evils of capitalism. Business was so brisk that two Avon ladies teamed up to handle the crush.

The company initially predicted annual sales of $1.5 million. But first-year sales broke company records worldwide. By the second year, Avon had posted $50 million in sales. By the third year, it wouldn't discuss figures anymore. No one wanted Mary Kay and other rivals coming around.

When Avon called, Li Xiuxian answered. She and 18,000 others became China's first Avon ladies. By day, Li Xiuxian (Fairy Li) dozed at her state job at a meat wholesaler. At night, lured by 30 percent commissions, she sold lipstick and eyeliner. In just ten months, she had also signed up 40 of her own Avon "sub-ladies," whom she supplied with cosmetics and catalogues. They reported to her, and when they did well, she rewarded them with trinkets she bought herself. In return, she got a 5- to 10-percent cut of their sales. Not bad for a 19-year-old.

Chinese Avon reps averaged 1,000 yuan a month in sales, twice their counterparts in Malaysia, a country with a much higher per-capita income. Top Chinese reps sold 30,000 yuan of cosmetics a month and earned 10,000 yuan or more in commissions, a staggering sum considering the average state worker then earned just 200 yuan a month. "They've tasted blood. Now the motivation is money," said Samantha Kong, acting sales manager for Avon in China.

Fairy Li was coy about her take, but it had to be at least five times her state salary. The previous spring, her sales were so good that Avon awarded her a bicycle. She even managed to sell novel products like deodorant and after-shave to male colleagues at her day job. The only person she couldn't convince was her own mother, who was appalled at the thought of spending a day's pay on a lipstick.

In Canton one sticky summer night, I followed Fairy Li on some sales calls. She looked businesslike, all 90 pounds of her, in her slim black skirt, white blouse and patent leather pumps. Her first stop was to a regular customer who lived in a third-floor walk-up. Tan Junyi wasn't back from her job at a power station, but her teenaged sister let us in. As we waited, sipping oolong tea, Fairy Li cast a practised eye over the girl.

"How old are you?" she asked.

"Sixteen," the teenager mumbled.

"Hmm, you can wear makeup at 16," said Fairy Li, who permed her hair to make herself look older.

The Tans cramped apartment was one small room partitioned in two. Three adults, two teenagers and a two-year-old slept on one double bed and several mattresses arranged on a plywood loft. The housing was typical – and state-subsidized. That was why Tan Junyi had disposable income to splurge on cosmetics.

"People here are quite affluent," said Samantha Kong, the Avon manager. "They pay six yuan (75 cents) a month for an apartment. How much can they spend on food if they don't eat in restaurants?"

While some Western companies were apprehensive about doing business in China, Avon found the creaky state system suited it fine. About 95 percent of its sales force had subsidizing housing, plus free medical care, state pensions and a place to take afternoon naps. Fairy Li, for instance, installed a cot at the meat wholesaler and rested during the day to fortify herself for knocking on doors at night. Like many Chinese, she didn't yet have a home phone, so she used her office phone to set up evening appointments.

Tan Junyi finally arrived home, sweaty and tired. Fairy Li tugged a catalogue from her red Avon bag and launched into her sales pitch. "This new cream is good for oily skin, especially in the summer," she said, scrutinizing Tan's perspiring brow. She flipped the page. "This lotion cleans your pores and prevents pimples." Tan Junyi, who had mild acne, bought a small bottle of lotion.

Next, Fairy Li hit a night school. Brandishing her Avon bag, she accosted a student in the courtyard. "You have skin that's both oily and dry," she declared, brushing the surprised young woman's bangs aside for a better look. Then she whipped out a brochure and pointed to photos of blue-eyed blondes. The student listened shyly, but didn't buy anything. Undaunted, Fairy Li took down her name and phone number, confident of making an eventual sale.

"To be an Avon lady, you must be thick-skinned," she said later, over dinner in a nearby restaurant. "Not everyone is so polite." She broke off the conversation to size up the waitress. "Your haircut is lovely," she said. The waitress blushed, and took our order. After she left, Fairy Li thought about recruiting her. "She'd make a great Avon lady. She meets so many people every day." She made a mental note to return.

Others followed in Avon's footsteps. In no time, several thousand companies unleashed more than one million salespeople to knock on China's doors. Some were less than honest. Consumers began complaining about pyramid scams and other con jobs. In 1998, China banned all direct selling. The prohibition directly affected Avon. At last report, it had negotiated a deal to set up exclusive counters in Chinese department stores.

Chinese yuppies, called *ya pi shi* (literally, elegant-skinned beings), disdained cheap stuff like Avon. They wanted designer goods. Louis Vuitton SA opened its first luggage shop in 1992 at Beijing's *luxe* Palace Hotel. Next door at La Perla, film stars paid $1,000 for an Italian swimsuit. When Salvatore Ferragamo set up a boutique in the Palace, too, film actress Gong Li stuffed her ample bosom into a lovely gray suit to preside over the opening.

The glitzy Palace arcade soon became the Great Mall of China. Ermenegildo Zegna offered cashmere polo shirts for $700 and suits for $2,000. "At first we expected to sell to expatriates and foreign tourists," said Frank Zhang, the manager. "But after a year, locals account for more than half our sales."

Who were these Chinese dropping two grand for a suit? Many were *bao fa hu*, or "exploding-wealth households." Using Party or government connections, they had acquired scarce items, such as concrete and steel, at state-controlled prices and resold them at huge profits. When money washed in that effortlessly, you didn't pinch pennies.

Joanne Lee-Young got a close-up look at "exploding-wealth households." As retail coordinator in Beijing for Yves Saint-Laurent, Prada and other luxury boutiques, the energetic young Canadian met clientele who had gone, quite literally, from rags to riches. At least one of her customers arrived from the provinces toting an Adidas sports bag stuffed with cash.

The stores were elegant. The clients sometimes weren't. One of her boutiques displayed only 20 pairs of shoes, like jewels, on padded beige suede under pale green lights. "One time, a man from northeast China – we could tell by the accent – was standing at the back," said Joanne, "and he let out a large, large fart." Another time, a woman demanded a refund, annoyed that the heel of her new shoe snapped on the second wearing. "She took out a bag, and the heel was stuck in a bike pedal," said Joanne. "I laugh now, but at the time, it wasn't fun to be caught between two worlds. Head office in Hong Kong wasn't amused."

Joanne was actually living in three worlds. In addition to her luxury-goods job, she polished propaganda at *China Pictorial* monthly and worked as news assistant for my successor, Rod Mickleburgh. Her *China Pictorial* monthly salary of 3,000 yuan (or $375) was enough to buy one pair of Prada loafers. But "exploding wealth households" didn't balk at the prices. A Ferragamo scarf cost $300, a silk tie $140 and twinsets – cardigans with matching short-sleeved sweaters – $1,200.

Sometimes her sartorially-challenged clients sought out her advice. Once, a young businessman brought in a suit he'd just purchased in Hong Kong. He'd heard of Hugo Boss, Versace and Yves Saint-Laurent, he said, but who was Armani? His wife, who was about to move to Beverly Hills, had advised him not to wear it until he showed it to Joanne. "I assured him it was 'okay – no problem'," she said, "and he put it on right away."

Joanne once okayed a 10 percent discount for a man buying a black Prada women's jacket. "When I saw him next, I said to his wife, 'Oh, how's the jacket?' The salesgirls in the store started glaring at me." Joanne belatedly realized the man had bought it for his teenaged girlfriend.

The salesclerks privately classified the mistresses into three groups: *gaozi*, or high-class ones with their own credit cards; *zhongzi*, or mid-level ones, who had to shop with their man and *putong*, or ordinary ones, who shopped first, then begged their boyfriends to come to the store for a look.

The fancy boutiques became a place for "exploding-wealth households" to pick up "elegant-skinned beings." Joanne once refused to discount a beribboned Ferragamo hairband for a young woman because, at $100, the item was relatively cheap. "Oh, c'mon, give her a discount," a male customer urged. When Joanne wouldn't budge, the man ended up buying the headband for the young woman. "Then they went downstairs for a drink," Joanne recalled.

Unlike most Chinese, who could be breathtakingly frank about bad haircuts and fresh zits, Joanne's clerks quickly learned that flattery did wonders for sales. Once, a customer tried on a white suit with black trim. Patting her dark bouffant flip, she turned to the salesclerks and said, "I *do* look like the young wife of President Kennedy in this, don't I?" They immediately chorused, "Yes, yes, you do."

The young salesclerks themselves wore Esprit clothes and breakfasted at Dunkin Donuts. They changed their names as often as their hairstyles. One month they'd be "Marie," the next month "Pearl." Joanne didn't mind. But to spare head office confusion, she decreed that when dealing with Hong Kong, "you had to be what you were when you applied for the job."

11

Pandora's E-mail

At Stock Market Corner, an impromptu meeting place for small investors in Shanghai, in 1999.

Photo: Robin Benger

Back in the 1970s, entire phone conversations went like this.

"Hello?"

"Hello!"

"Hello?"

"Hello!"

"Hello?"

And finally,

Caller: "Who are you?"

"Who are *you*!"

Caller: "Who are you?"

That's when I'd snap, "If you don't know who you're calling, don't call." That wasn't very understanding of me. The hello-hello duel was a test of static soup to see whether real conversation was possible.

Telephone etiquette was in its infancy back then because almost no one had home phones. In an emergency, you called from one pay phone to another. These weren't coin-operated pay phones. A human being sat beside each one. If you received a call at your local pay phone, for instance, the person in charge would send a runner out to your home. You'd hurry over, pay your four fen (half a penny) and take the call – while everyone in the room listened in.

That's why people preferred writing letters. Mail arrived twice daily, six days a week and once on Sundays. With same-day delivery within cities, you could invite a friend for lunch later in the week, and get a reply by return mail that evening. It was better than Fed Ex. This being a dictatorship over the proletariat, no one ever dared go on strike.

The post office was one of China's few efficient organizations. That, and the secret police. Or maybe the two were in cahoots. During the Cultural Revolution, a letter from abroad could sometimes get you a stint in the gulag. Chinese assumed overseas mail was inspected and read. The post office even sent me formal notices whenever it confiscated my Hong Kong magazines as "reactionary material." But I digress.

Or not. It was no coincidence that a single ministry was in charge of the post office, telephones and telegraphs. For efficiency of eavesdropping, the ministry issued telephone exchanges by category, not geography. All foreigners, for instance, were given numbers beginning 532 and later, 6532. The People's Liberation Army had its own distinctive exchange, too. After the 1989 Tiananmen Massacre, China rewired its phone system so that no foreigner could dial through to any military-related number, and vice versa.

But it was too late. The Information Age was already knocking at China's door. Eager to expand its economy and become globally competitive, Beijing signed deals with Canadian, Swedish, Finnish and U.S. phone companies. The growth was exponential. In 1990, only a handful of my friends and contacts in Beijing had home phones. Today, I can't think of a single one who *doesn't*. By 1995, Beijing had three million phones, forcing it to expand the numbers from seven digits to eight. By 2000, it is expected to have seven million phones.

Communist control freaks freaked out. A billion Chinese talking to one another was an unprecedented national-security risk. "Communications are the nation's nerve system and involve the nation's secrets," fretted the *Economic Daily*. "If China's information system is spread about and not grasped firmly in hand, how can people feel safe?"

One way was by keeping phone numbers a secret. At Montreal West High, Mr. Cooper, my band teacher, enjoyed telling this really bad joke.

Question: Why don't they have any phone books in China?

Answer: Because they always wing the wong number.

I had no idea he was right. China had no Western-style phone books. Adding to the confusion, people's phone numbers and exchanges seemed to change every six months. I learned to keep a bottle of White-Out beside my Rolodex.

Despite the phenomenal growth, phone etiquette remained primitive. Few people knew how to take a message. Government phones rang unanswered. And in this country of massive over-employment, nobody understood answering machines. Callers kept trying to elicit a response – until the tape ran out.

There was also no decent phone word for "goodbye." Some callers did it their way, holding the receiver farther and farther away in a Sinatra-style fade-out. Others simply warned: "Hanging up now!" Modern types said, illogically, *zai jian*, which meant, "See you again."

In the late 1990s, there was no more need for static-soup checks – except when peasants digging manure pits accidentally cut under-ground telephone lines. Some digging was deliberate, to harvest the valuable copper wire. When the phone company levied fines, the peasants quickly patted down the earth, forcing technicians to test the entire line to pinpoint the problem. So the phone company began rewarding anyone who reported a cut wire. Then the peasants cut the lines and made a report to collect the reward.

Nobody felt sorry for the phone company. Initially, Chinese paid the equivalent of two years' wages to install a phone. Even so, in the early 1990s, the waiting list was nearly one million long. Many people skipped a whole generation of hard-wired phones and went straight to cellphones. Others waited and waited.

Take Du Weiwei, who paid his installation fee in December, 1990. As a member of Nanking's municipal People's Congress, he was clearly a man of some importance. But not important enough, apparently, to get a phone. Two and a half years later, on his deathbed, he asked friends to intervene with the phone bureau. In vain. Du died, phone-less, that May.

Huang Lixin was alive and well in Nanking when the big day arrived. Alas, he hadn't thought to have a ladder ready. The installers left in a huff and Huang never got his phone.

If you were lucky enough to be a customer, there were other headaches. The phone company didn't take checks. So each month I'd count out a two-inch stack of cash, which Driver Liu then schlepped to the main phone bureau on Dongdan Street, along with 184,000 other residential customers. A policeman, armed with a club, would survey the crush.

Billing problems? Queries? In Beijing, the phone company didn't accept questions over the phone. You had to go in person – but only on Saturday mornings. And one last thing: the phone company dictated where you put the phone in your house. Move it, and face a stiff fine.

By 1999, the push to join the global economy had changed everything. That February, Beijing dropped phone-installation prices 75 percent, to 1,000 yuan from 3,800 yuan. In March, it announced it began charging a mere 100 yuan, about $12, to install a second line for computers and Internet access. Also that March, Shanghai slashed cellphone prices 93 percent to 1,500 yuan from 20,000 yuan. There were even, praise Mao, real phone books. Shanghai's Yellow Pages were seven volumes thick. Or you could call directory assistance.

Hotlines specialized in everything from unemployed workers to consumer complaints. By 1999, 11 percent of Chinese had home phones nationwide. Some 30 million people had cellphones. In a sign of the times, the new Shanghai Museum didn't care if you photographed its bronze collection, but it banned cellphones.

Every night, my cousin Qiu Hai, a factory manager in Hangzhou, called his teenaged daughter in Tianjin, 700 miles to the north, to check up on her homework. Taxi drivers had cellphones, too. During my 1999 trip, I sometimes paid the cab driver a little extra to borrow his phone. It seemed an especially safe way to call my contacts. How could authorities track journalists anymore?

Phones directly impacted human rights. The current Party Secretary of Waterdown had a home phone, a cellphone and two office phones. But his villagers were getting wired, too. If they got fed up with corruption, help was now just a phone call away – in the guise of a crusading Chinese journalist.

With state subsidies dwindling, the media suddenly had to worry about profits. Like us, they've learned that muckraking draws readers, and readers draw ads. *Southern Weekend*, a Canton newspaper, doubled its circulation to 1.3 million by running page-one exposés. "Focal Point," a daily prime-time investigative television show, won top ratings for stories on corruption.

The most important new electronic battleground was the Internet. "The State is in charge of overall planning, national standardization, graded control and the development of all areas related to the Internet," declared a Big-Brother law, signed in 1996 by Premier Li Peng.

But his successor, Premier Zhu Rongji, felt that China couldn't pause at the brink. President Jiang Zemin, whose son is an info-tech czar in Shanghai, also feared global competitors would zip past China. In 1999, authorities dropped Internet-access fees 75 percent to a user-friendly 4 yuan (50 cents) an hour.

In February, 1999, reporters and editors at the *People's Daily* also got Internet access. They even hooked up Wang Ruoshui, a former deputy editor who had been purged in 1983. Wang had retained his salary, his access to free cars and his apartment, even though he was now a board member of New York-based China Human Rights. In essence, the official Communist Party mouthpiece was wiring dissidents, too.

Late one Saturday night in 1999, I dropped into an Internet café in Shanghai. Decorated with posters of *Titanic* star, Leonardo DiCaprio, it was called 3 C+T (for "Coffee, Computers and Communications plus Training.") It had become famous after President Clinton visited it in 1998. I sat down at a computer under a framed photo of a grinning Clinton from said visit. Unsolicited, the latest news on Monica Lewinsky popped up when I signed on. Beside me, a handful of customers were slurping noodles and surfing the Net.

I typed in "democracy in China." Long pause. Then this response: *Internet Explorer cannot open the Internet site. A connection with the server could not be established.*" Using a search engine, I typed

"June 4, 1989." Same response. I typed "human rights in China." Same response, again.

That didn't mean the cyber cops were winning. The government had erected a Great Firewall of China to filter e-mail and block politically incorrect Web sites. But anyone willing to pay long-distance rates could bypass the electronic "firewall" through international direct dialing.

Beijing also blocked Internet access to most of the Western media, too, but Chinese had ways. When Wan Yanhai, an AIDS activist, helped some peasants sue the government after their son was infected by a blood transfusion, friends in San Francisco e-mailed him a *New York Times* profile of the boy. And when angry Beijing consumers protested shoddy construction in their apartments, Wan heard about it by e-mail the next day.

"The Internet will break the government's control of society," he said. "When the government wants to prevent people from knowing something, the Internet works against them. When they say we can't publish something, we just publish it on the Internet."

Indeed, anyone with $100 could break the state's monopoly on publishing. It cost even less to access electronic newsletters, webzines and on-line chat groups. Gays, who have long remained underground, now have a Web site listing gay bars. One gay man in Beijing downloads interesting articles on homosexuality from the Internet, translates them into Chinese and distributes them to friends. And they can now talk to one another through such e-mail addresses as chinagay@hotmail.com.

Despite China's attempt to police cyberspace, dissidents overseas have been quick to set up Web sites. To mark the tenth anniversary of the Tiananmen democracy movement, Wang Dan and Wuer Kaixi, another exiled student leader, launched two Internet sites: www.6-4.org and www.june4.org.

As quickly as firewall techies block Web sites and e-mail addresses, the dissidents set up new ones. Chinese pro-democracy activists in the United States send their e-mail newsletter to 250,000 computer users inside China. When authorities blocked e-mail from the dissident group's address, they dodged the barrier by e-mailing the newsletter from a different American address every day.

Flummoxed, authorities finally cracked down the old-fashioned way. The first casualty of the Internet wars was Lin Hai, a 30-year-old Shanghai computer executive with a shock of wavy hair. In early 1999, he was sentenced to two years for giving 30,000 Chinese e-mail addresses to "hostile foreign publications," namely the dissident electronic newsletter. Significantly, Lin Hai wasn't a dissident himself. His wife said he exchanged e-mail addresses to build a database for his business: setting up Web sites.

Authorities are fighting a losing battle. When Lin Hai was first arrested in March, 1998, China had 670,000 Internet users. By his trial that November, eight months later, the number had doubled to 1.2 million. And a mere two more months later, when he was sentenced in January, 1999, the figure had nearly doubled again, to 2.1 million users. IDC, a Boston-based worldwide information-technology information provider, forecasts that by 2001 – when Lin Hai completes his two-year jail term – China will have 27 million Internet users.

In March, 1999, while Lin Hai was languishing in prison, the chairman of Microsoft Corp. journeyed to China for the seventh time. Bill Gates signed an Internet deal to allow Chinese to download movies, music, e-mail and other services in their homes. "By delivering this technology in a low-cost and easy-to-use format, we hope to increase access to educational software and, ultimately, the Internet, for China's consumers," said Gates, who also signed an anti-piracy pact. His partner in the deal was the state telephone monopoly, China Telecom Group, which operates Chinanet, the nation's biggest Internet network.

In Beijing's "Silicon Alley," the streets were jammed with peasants on pedicabs loaded with computer monitors. Sprawling stores sold laptops, hard drives, keyboards, circuit boards and modems. China's high-tech industry sprang up here, in the university district, to feed off Beijing and Qinghua universities. In 1999, after looking around a computer store, I slipped onto the campus of my alma mater to check out The Triangle, the nickname for a bulletin board where Beijing University students once put up protest posters in 1989. A decade later, it had nary a political statement. Instead, it was plastered with Internet ads. One, for www.loginchina.com, blared, "Get your own Internet address for 30 yuan ($3.75). Terminal time: 2 yuan (25 cents) an hour. Set up your own Web page for 200 yuan ($25)."

As I left Beijing University, a scruffy-looking guy approached me. "CDs, CD-ROMs?" he whispered. China had to heed copyright law if it wanted admittance to the World Trade Organization. Yet, clearly, the pirating business was booming. With Alister Bell filming me from a distance and my radio mike turned on, I followed the young hustler down a dirt alley and around a corner to a rundown shack. Inside, two women and a man displayed suitcases full of pirated Celine Dion and Rolling Stones CDs, video games, DVD movies such as *Prince of Egypt* and Microsoft Windows '98 software. (Memo to Bill Gates: this was ten days after you signed that anti-piracy agreement.)

When Alister and Robin walked in, camera rolling, the place erupted. "What are you doing!" one woman shouted. To buy time, I acted dumb and translated as slowly as possible. I also kept buying, which mollified them somewhat. I held up a CD-ROM of *The Encyclopedia Britannica*, so Alister could get a good shot. It sold for 45 yuan, or $5.60.

The vendors shut their suitcases and pushed us out. As Alister filmed the outside of the shack, three lookouts appeared from nowhere and covered up his camera lens. We beat a hasty retreat. For once I was glad Tweedledum and Tweedledumber were two huge guys.

In 1992, China passed the point of no return. For the first time, the number of people working for private companies surpassed the number of Communist Party members. Private-sector output also exceeded state-sector output. The government had lost a key means of control over a majority of citizens: paychecks.

"No one wants to talk about this subject in public. It's too sensitive," said Cheng Yuanzhong, a social scientist. He summarized his findings in a book, *Heroes of the Wilds*, which was published only after censors slashed all positive comments about capitalism.

On the brink of the new millennium, the world's fastest-growing economy had 30 million private entrepreneurs and 40 million pager customers. Want to interview a dissident? Just e-mail him. Or her. Chai Ling, the female student who launched the hunger strike with Wang Dan, earned an MBA and became an executive with an Internet company in the United States.

Therein lay the Chinese communist dilemma. It needed the Internet and related technology to rush down the capitalist road. But technology was a Pandora's Box. Plug in a phone, switch on a computer, and suddenly, you can't turn off the flow of information. I remember when the first photocopiers arrived in China in the late 1970s. Authorities carefully padlocked them to stanch the leaking of state secrets. It was hopeless. Every little stationery shop soon had a photocopier.

Phones, faxes, beepers and the Internet were shredding Beijing's efforts to censor news and limit debate. Whether China's leaders liked it or not, that basic pillar of democracy had arrived. China had freedom of information, including, for $5.60, the entire collected wisdom of the Western world. And freedom of information is precisely the one freedom that will bring down the Chinese Communist Party.

On a gray Sunday afternoon in 1999, I waded into Shanghai's Stock-Market Corner, a weekly outdoor gathering of Chinese investors. "What's it like in Canada?" a woman asked me. Before I knew it, I had my own little chat group. I told them about a gold-mining swindle called Bre-X. They nodded understandingly. "We lose money, too," said one man. Then I tried explaining insider trading, and more people nodded. "We have that, too," said one old lady. "Here, they get a token fine. It's nothing."

Everyone was having a good time. Several swore that as soon as the lackluster market recovered a bit, they'd cash out and never gamble their savings again. But you could tell they were hooked. We were standing outside a brokerage house. Someone pointed out that it was once a Workers Union Hall.

"There's no more workers now. We're all bosses," joked one elderly lady.

"You're all capitalists," I teased. The crowd laughed uproariously.

China was becoming a country of capitalists. In Fujian Province, the pitched roof of a Tudor country house rose from the paddy fields like a surreal joke. It wasn't. Lin Mei, a factory owner, had asked a British friend if his father could design her a home. To humor her, the father, a prominent London architect, sent over some old blueprints for a 4,000-square-foot mansion.

Lin Mei (Plum Blossom Lin) immediately had it built, down to the last fireplace and wooden beam. She installed a Poggenpohl kitchen and a swimming pool. That latter mystified local peasants, who couldn't figure out how the water stayed fresh day after day.

But running her many businesses from a paddy field proved a logistical headache. You had to hand-crank the phones. You couldn't get taxis. And curious neighbors dropped in at will. A year later, Plum Blossom sold the house to a Taiwanese businessman for $378,000 — a 200-percent profit. That whetted her appetite for real estate. She quit her factories and began buying condos in Xiamen, a booming port. By the time I met her, two years later, she was 35 and her net worth exceeded 10 million yuan ($2.2 million.)

Xiamen (pronounced hsia-mun) was a go-go port where smugglers shipped humans out and Marlboros in. It was the perfect place for a budding entrepreneur like Plum Blossom. She was part of China's new generation of risk takers who believed in little but themselves. Abstract concepts of freedom and democracy bored her. But she was just the kind of citizen most likely to change the system — by making the Communist Party irrelevant.

Plum Blossom was short, wiry and supremely self-assured. Her formal education had ended in second grade when the Cultural Revolution shut down her primary school. Self-taught and street-smart, she had the system figured out. In the countryside, she avoided hard labor by convincing the peasants she could teach their children English. She neglected to say she only knew the alphabet. In 1979, when the rural enterprises were just taking off, she jumped to a metals factory. Eight years later, she became one of the first to "plunge into the sea," slang for going into private business.

In a country where 99 percent of females married by 25, Plum Blossom flouted convention. She was a single mother. She adopted a baby girl, whom she named Pearl. Plum Blossom lavished everything on her daughter, which gave her another idea. With China limiting boomers to a single child, Plum Blossom figured they'd be suckers for upscale children's clothing. She sketched some designs and recruited peasant seamstresses.

A year later, she'd saved enough to open a rural factory and build her Tudor mansion. When she switched to real estate, her first property was modest: a single parking spot in an office tower. Then she invested in a dozen condos – and nearly went bankrupt when she couldn't meet the mortgage payments. "But I didn't really lose because the deal made me famous," she said. "After that, anybody who wanted to buy a building here would come to me."

Plum Blossom showed me around the site where she was building a $400,000 home for herself. It had four bedrooms, five bathrooms and a palm-fringed lake view. As we walked around the half-finished house, she pointed out where the marble floors would be laid, where she'd put her grand piano, where she'd hang the chandelier.

At the moment, she was running her real-estate business out of a bedroom in her mother's cramped apartment. During the day, and every night while her five-year-old slept, Plum Blossom worked at a small desk, piled high with business journals and home-decorating magazines, She slept four hours a night, sipping cups of black Lipton tea to stay awake.

She had the new system figured out, too. Foreign investors enjoyed tax advantages, so her brother would smuggle out cash to Hong Kong for her and register her company as a "foreign firm." To exploit more loopholes, she also hired an accountant and a secretary in Hong Kong. Finally, to burnish her *guanxi*, or contacts, in Xiamen, she retained a well-connected lawyer who was not only a Communist Party member, but dean of the local law school. She also bribed officials to have their photos taken with her, which she then used to cajole the local bank into giving her loans.

Like her company, Plum Blossom wanted the tax advantages and the status of a foreign investor. She planned to apply for New Zealand citizenship, through its foreign-investor program. Her favorite book, she told me, was *Gone with the Wind*, which she'd read in translation. She identified with Scarlett, who knelt in the ashes of her plantation, and vowed to rebuild it from scratch. "Maybe I have a lot in common with her," Plum Blossom mused. "Scarlett valued land above all else. To protect her property, she was willing to do anything."

His father starved to death under Communist rule. He himself was sentenced to death during the Cultural Revolution and languished in prison for nine years, including four in solitary confinement. In 1983, the government accused him of "economic speculation" and tossed him in jail for another year. All of which made Mou Qizhong (Middleman Mou) an unlikely cheerleader for the Chinese Communist Party.

Oddly, he couldn't do enough for his former oppressors. During the Tiananmen protests, he threatened to fire any employee who supported the students. He later endorsed the massacre. "I'm afraid of social disorder," he told me. "Only socialism can maintain the stability of society."

Naturally, authorities were grateful. State banks lent him money. His company was the first to be allowed to sell stock. Land Economic Group soon grew into China's third-largest private company.

Middleman Mou first gained attention with a 1992 socks-for-Soviet planes deal. It netted him $18 million, even after paying bribes to officials on both sides of the border. Spotting a scarcity of planes and a surplus of consumer goods in China, he bartered 800 railway cars of canned goods, thermoses, surplus pork and 600,000 pairs of socks for four Russian Tupelov-154M passenger jets.

"We're taking advantage of the dissolution of the Soviet Union. There's a chance to make obscene profits there," said Mou. Other grandiose plans included buying four Russian-made satellites, building a 100-storey office tower in Beijing and humidifying China's deserts by blasting a pass through the Himalayas to suck moist air from the Indian Ocean.

By the mid-1990s, both the *People's Daily* and *Forbes* listed Middleman Mou as one of China's ten richest men. The youngest son of a salt-mine financier, he was nine at the time of the Communist victory. For 30 years, he suffered because of his capitalist background. Then, in 1979, the first year Chinese were allowed to start a business, he parlayed $75 into a barter company. A decade later, he became the first private entrepreneur from China to attend the World Economic Forum in Davos, Switzerland, beating Premier Li Peng by three years.

Everyone said Middleman Mou must have had extremely good *guanxi*, or contacts. He denied this. "I stay far away from leaders. I don't have a powerful backer in the government." In the next breath, though, he mentioned he played bridge with Wan Li, then-president of China's rubber-stamp parliament.

Nor did he mind anyone knowing that Zhao Ziyang, then Party chief of Sichuan, had stayed his Cultural Revolution death sentence. (After Zhao was purged during Tiananmen, Middleman Mou quickly distanced himself. "If I got too close to him, when he fell, I'd be finished, too. People in business should maintain their independence," he said sagely.)

I went to see China's leading deal maker one Sunday morning in Beijing. In 1992 Middleman Mou was 52 and worked seven days a week. That morning, nine staff came in to help receive me. One switched on a tape recorder. Five others sat at an oval table, taking down their boss's every word. A sixth poured tea. A seventh snapped photographs. Downstairs a waitress and a cook, the latter imported from Mou's native Sichuan, prepared a gourmet lunch.

His personality cult would have shamed the most egotistical Western executive – or the late Chairman Mao. Chairman Mou was a Mao wannabe, although only a psychiatrist could have sorted out how anyone who spent years in a Maoist prison could end up combing his longish hair straight back like Mao's. When I asked if the coif was a coincidence, several assistants vied to answer. "Everyone says how much he looks like Chairman Mao!" exclaimed one. Another gushed: "Not just his face, but even his physique!" The Great Helmsman once swam the Yangtze River to demonstrate his vigor during the Cultural Revolution. Likewise, Middleman Mou made it known that he sidestroked in icy water. And just as Chairman Mao's outsized quotations once dominated building entrances, Chairman Mou adorned his lobby with his own turgid quotations, in gold characters on red velvet. Sample: "Revitalize state-owned enterprises for the promotion of the socialist economic system."

His staff pronounced his name with a Sichuan accent, a gesture as obsequious as American employees dropping their "g's" to suck up to a boss from Alabama. Even the company's Chinese name, Nan De, became "Land" in English, not because it was involved in real estate, but because in Sichuanese *nan* is pronounced *lan*. For such devotion, employees earned outsized salaries, plus a 2.5 percent commission on any business they brought in.

"The desire to get rich is the only way to motivate the whole society," said Middleman Mou, adding that he planned to give each employee a Russian-made car as a bonus. Staff also got free housing and a daily lunch of spicy Sichuan cuisine.

Authorities, who wanted to divert young people's attention from democracy to dollars, often asked Middleman Mou to speak to students. "I can be a role model," he said modestly, as we moved into his private dining room for a lunch of tea-leaf-smoked duck. He wasn't a member of the Communist Party, but he frequently declared his allegiance, unbidden.

"I'm a Marxist," he said. When I nearly choked on my rice, he added, "You just don't understand our concept of socialism."

Or maybe others just didn't understand *his.* In 1998, dozens of disgruntled investors, included several major Chinese cities and banks, sued him, alleging soured business ventures. Police raided his headquarters, impounding cars and other assets. Middleman Mou was ordered to repay nearly $100 million in overdue loans. He told everyone he was the victim of a conspiracy. Then he disappeared. Chinese newspapers reported that police arrested him on January 6, 1999.

12

Great Leap into the Driver's Seat

Xiao Yang, governor of Sichuan, China's most populous province.

Photo: Jan Wong

Li Xiaohua first dreamed of owning a car during the Cultural Revolution. For years, the labor camp convict harvested wheat behind a belching East Is Red tractor. In 1981, he realized his driving ambition when he bought a used Toyota from a Libyan diplomat. But he never dreamed he would one day roar down the Avenue of Eternal Peace in a red Ferrari.

China was taking a great leap into the driver's seat. Not long ago, people lusted after clunky Flying Pigeon bicycles which came in black, black or black. But by the late 1990s, cars had become the ultimate status symbol in the world's fastest growing economy. "Private cars are a measure of the standard of living of a country," said Li Xiaohua, whose acquisition of a $175,000 Ferrari Testarossa put him on the cover of a new Chinese magazine called *Car Fan.* Li, 42, who had made millions in real estate, owned seven cars, including two Mercedes-Benz 600 sedans.

With so many "exploding-wealth households," Ferrari, Rolls-Royce, Mercedes-Benz and BMW all opened showrooms. Rolls-Royce adapted the engines of its China-bound cars to low-octane fuel, the only kind available at the time. Most Chinese buyers chose the Silver Spur, which cost $250,000 and was four inches longer than the Silver Shadow.

Legitimate imports couldn't meet demand. So thieves stole luxury cars in Hong Kong and smuggled them in speedboats to the mainland. Theft was so rampant Hong Kong insurers refused to cover certain popular models. Sometimes the smugglers worked with the People's Liberation Army. The *South China Morning Post*, Hong Kong's leading English daily, photographed a boat-to-boat smuggler's showdown between the PLA and Hong Kong police. (The PLA, which was armed, won.)

Cars weren't always a driving desire. Mao eschewed one in Yanan when the Communists were battling for power. Deng Xiaoping, who died in 1997, had no such compunction. Late in life, he swapped his Chinese-made Red Flag limousine for a bullet-proof Cadillac.

In the 1980s, car ownership was beyond the reach of 99.99 percent of the population. In 1981, when Ferrari Li bought his used Toyota, he became one of only 20 Beijingers to own a car. The others were worthy celebrities, like math genius Shi Fengshou. As late as 1988, a friend of mine parked his Polish-made Fiat several blocks from work to hide it from jealous co-workers.

Even state-owned cars were so rare that most Beijing intersections lacked traffic lights. Stop signs were non-existent. At night, cars were *required* to douse headlights to avoid blinding cyclists. With only a handful of vehicles on the road, no one worried about one car smashing into another in the dark.

In the 1990s, China gave car ownership a green light. It halved import tariffs to 110 percent. Domestic production doubled, from 220,000 cars in 1993 to nearly 500,000 in 1998. Canton began allowing car purchases on the instalment plan. And in a sign of the times, Beijing's first drive-in movie theater opened for business in 1999. That same year, state lotteries began selling tickets for $15,000 Citroens at 24 cents a piece.

Beijing signed joint ventures with Chrysler, Volkswagen and General Motors. Some stalled. Peugeot, for instance, quit its plant in Canton. Chrysler cut production of its Jeep Cherokee by two-thirds. But GM remained optimistic. If only 1 percent of the Chinese people could afford to buy a car, those 12 million cars would be "roughly the size of our market share in Europe," a GM official enthused, as the first made-in-China Buick rolled off an assembly line in Shanghai in 1998.

GM's new Buick had adjusted airbags "suitable for the Chinese physique." The Chinese version of the Volkswagen Santana was designed with extra legroom in back because everyone assumed the new rich would hire chauffeurs. But it turned out that China's 30 million entrepreneurs were self-driven. Chen Yi, the twin businessman, mastered the art of chatting on his cellphone while swerving around bicycles and, at 26, had already traded in his old Soviet-made Lada for a new $14,000 red Daihatsu Charade.

By the late 1990s, Beijing had one car for every five bikes. That meant 1.3 million cars competing for road space with 6.5 million bikes. Here's the scariest statistic: *one million first-time Chinese drivers.* To cater to demand, dozens of driving schools opened for business in Beijing.

Zhang Yamei, 37, wrinkled her brow as she backed the rusting Toyota between two bamboo poles. Her instructor, standing outside, slapped the roof. "Once more!" he barked. She obeyed meekly. If she annoyed him, it was possible he would order her to shift into neutral – and get out and push. For this, she had forked over ten months pay.

Chinese driving school was no crash course. Programs lasted four to six months, compared with 12 hours in, say, Quebec. They were boot camps in which you rose at dawn, attended classes six days a week and obeyed orders, including to push cars, as opposed to push-ups. The results spoke for themselves. In 1990 alone, 50,000 people died and 155,072 were injured in 250,297 "serious" traffic accidents, according to the official New China News Agency. Since then, the volume of cars has quadrupled.

Driving in China was a never-ending game of chicken. Slow cars hogged the passing lane. Fast ones passed on the right. And if too many bikes clogged one side of the road, well, by all means go down the wrong way. Yellow caution lights lasted one second, compared with four in Canada. When a light flashed green, left-turners zipped first across the intersection, trying to beat oncoming traffic.

There were traffic lights now, but most drivers ignored them at night. The higher your status or the nicer your car, the more you or your driver felt entitled to go first. In Anhui Province, 80 percent of government officials put police plates on their cars to ensure they got the right of way.

With driving school the only way to get a license in China, Zhang Yamei had signed up for lessons at the Beijing-Toyota Driving School. So named because Toyota had donated dozens of rusting 1973 Coronas, it offered an "accelerated" two-month course, which skipped the mechanics portion. Still, this was life in the slow lane. Every morning, Zhang Yamei began by hand-washing a car. Then she made tea for her instructor. Only then could she practise maneuvers – with three other classmates in a single car. While one student drove, the teacher sat in front and the three other students became backseat drivers.

Surrounded by corn and wheat fields north of Beijing, the school was a Disneyland version of the capital. It had well-marked streets, a fake underpass and not a single crazy cyclist, stunned jaywalker or missing manhole cover. Even so, the teachers always dismissed classes whenever it rained. In Zhang Yamei's group, the instructor often sent the other three students home early because he was besotted with the fourth and wanted to joy ride with her to the local hot-springs bath. After Zhang Yamei complained, the trysts ended and her own lessons resumed. But her deeply annoyed teacher froze her out.

Zhang Shaowei, a young Chinese newspaper reporter I knew, spent the entire first month at another school memorizing motorcycle and bus regulations. The second and third months he studied the engine. The fourth month, he learned to park. Only then did he actually hit the road. For reasons that escaped him, he had been assigned a two-ton truck. "I found it exhausting. The truck was very heavy when I turned the wheels."

The day of his driving test, it rained. The whole class panicked. Their teacher had also sent them home when it drizzled. Everyone failed but Zhang. "I just thank heaven I passed the exam," he said. The other seven in his group went back for two weeks of remedial lessons. Five passed the second time. The last two passed the third time around. Luckily. Fail three times and you were doomed to take the six-month course over again.

By 1999, some driving schools had cut the course time to 80 hours. So many people now owned cars that parking had become a headache. When my old roommate Scarlet and her husband took me out for Mongolian Hot Pot in Beijing, they invited along their friend with the Toyota minivan chiefly to avoid taking their own Opel out of their apartment parking lot. "I wouldn't be able to find a parking space later," her husband explained. Even at my classmate Future Gu's apartment complex, where his neighbors faced job cutbacks at the History Institute, the yard was jammed with private cars.

On my 1999 trip, I was late for every appointment in Beijing until I learned to factor in the worsened traffic. It now required 90 minutes to get from Beijing University to Tiananmen Square, a drive that took half an hour in the 1970s. As I sat fuming in a taxi, 40 minutes late for a meeting, it occurred to me that in the good old Maoist days I could have biked it in less than an hour.

In Shunyi County, on the way to the Great Wall in 1999, I got stuck in massive rural gridlock. Hundreds of tractors, trucks, cars, jeeps and buses piled up at the intersection. There wasn't any accident. It was simply that there was no traffic light, and no one would give way. Even the unpaved shoulders were clogged as everyone crept up as far as they could. "The problem is," said my taxi driver glumly, "this intersection has no policeman."

That traffic jam symbolized China today – chaotic, in a hurry and in terrible need of authority. Perhaps that was why the Chinese continued to tolerate the Chinese Communist Party. At least it was good at giving orders.

Car ownership spawned other boomlets. State-employed drivers had always washed their own cars, but the new rich patronized car washes, or rather, car washers. Budding entrepreneurs waved damp rags at passing vehicles. They were better than squeegee kids. For one yuan, they hand-washed your entire car.

But for $10, I could get a car wash *and* a few state secrets.

When an American friend tried to organize a tour of the local fire station for our kids, they turned her down. "They told us there were state secrets inside, believe it or not."

Later, I noticed the fire station had put out a big sign: "Car Wash." I strapped Ben, then two, in his car seat and drove over. A sentry tried to stop us. I gave the secret password: "Car wash." He waved us through. Inside, I asked a fireman in military green the price. "Are you expensing this?" he countered. "Depends," I hedged. He suggested $10 for a car wash, including the motor and chassis. Done.

While they washed our Jeep, Ben and I wandered at will. We counted seven fire trucks. Was that a state secret? They were all tankers. Was that a secret, too? Perhaps. I only realized Beijing had virtually no hydrants after Ben kept pointing at them in Canada and asking what they were.

Four of the trucks were ancient Chinese models with the improbable brand name of Chicken Globe. The others were good-will gifts from Japan and Austria. I couldn't remember the last time I had seen a fire truck racing through the streets of Beijing. "Basically, we have nothing to do," one fireman admitted.

Dialing 119, the emergency number, sometimes elicited an argument rather than action. Norman and I were having dinner atop one of Beijing's new skyscrapers when he spotted a fire below at the Beijing Number One Machine Tool Factory, a place where I'd once toiled during the Cultural Revolution. He called 119. After much prodding, the skeptical dispatcher still wouldn't send a fire truck. But she finally agreed to call the factory itself. She apparently never did. The fire was still burning as we finished dessert.

The car wash took an hour, and then some. Ben and I watched a fireman blasting away with a high-powered hose. That shorted out the ignition. Out came a red hairdryer. For another 40 minutes, the fireman blow-dried our engine. The lunch whistle blew. The other firemen drifted away, returning with chopsticks and bowls full of food. One of them told me that they'd made $1,000 in their first two months of operation. And what did they do with the money? He paused between mouthfuls. "We eat better," he said.

In 1998, China spent more than $20 billion on a new national highway system. By 2010, it expected to create an American-style interstate system. But while the new roads boosted local economies, they also spread crime, venereal disease and pollution.

In the 1970s, I remembered sunny days when you could see clear across Beijing. But as more and more vehicles clogged the road, I sometimes had trouble seeing past the next block. By the mid-1990s, pollution in Beijing had become nine times worse than in Toronto, which itself sometimes issued smog alerts.

On February 11, 1994, I awoke to a rare Beijing snowfall. Ben was so excited I took him outside to make a snowman. As we scraped up the thin layer of snow, I noticed yellow patches underneath. I assumed the pet dogs in our compound had left it. I moved to another patch of snow. It was also yellow underneath. Disgusted, I tried another patch, and another, before giving up. There must be more dogs in our compound than I thought, I mused as Ben and I headed back inside in disappointment. Then I noticed the snow mantling the railing on our building was also stained deep yellow. "It's pollution," said a guard.

China was stewing in its own wastes. It could claim five of the world's ten-worst polluted cities. In 1991 alone, China dumped 25 billion tons of industrial sewage into its waterways, creating more toxic pollution than in the entire Western world. The Yangtze River, crystal blue at the dawn of the 20th century, was now coffee-colored and flecked with clumps of chemical foam. In Jiangsu province, water was shut off for days while a vast black tide of industrial effluent passed downriver from factories upstream.

At the Earth Summit in 1992, Beijing pointed an accusing finger at developed nations. China had become an offender only recently, it said. Meanwhile, the West had ruined the global environment during more than a century of industrialization. China was the developing world's largest emitter of greenhouse gases, but it argued that, on a per capita basis, it produced just one-ninth that of the United States. Its per capita carbon-dioxide emissions were one-third that of North Americans.

Environmental degradation didn't begin with China's recent economic reforms. Beginning in the Ming Dynasty, a desperate search for fuel denuded mountain ranges and levelled ancient forests. By the 20th century, no country was more dependent on coal than

China. With only limited oil and natural gas, it consumed 900 million tons of soft coal a year, burned in primitive household stoves and technologically obsolete factories. The result was a major contribution to global warming. Each year, 15 million tons of sulfur dioxide floated up chimneys, returning to earth as acid rain; 20 million tons of coal dust darkened the skies.

Pollutant levels were two to five times World Health Organization guidelines for safe exposure. Respiratory disease, five times the U.S. rate, became a leading cause of death in China. Lung cancer was common, even among non-smokers. The World Bank estimated air pollution caused 178,000 premature deaths each year.

When I was pregnant with Sam, I developed a bad cough. The doctor at the Australian Embassy blamed the air and said his wife had the same problem. What could he prescribe? "Get out of Beijing," he said. "That's what I tell my wife." My hacking worsened whenever I lay down. So for six months, until I went to Hong Kong to give birth, I slept sitting up. Fat Paycheck took refuge in the guest room.

In Beijing, one of the five worst cities in the world, I always kept our windows closed, but could never keep out the grit. Papers on my desk would be coated by day's end. Sam's baby snot was black. And Ben suffered constant ear infections, which stopped only after we moved back to Toronto.

Until recently, Chinese cars only used leaded gasoline and produced 10 to 15 times the exhaust of their American counterparts. In 1998, Beijing finally banned leaded gasoline and decreed that all new cars had to have catalytic converters by 1999. China also claimed to have installed dust filters in 74 percent of industrial furnaces. But a technician who worked in an environmental lab in Beijing told me she had been ordered to give out doctored statistics. The real numbers were a state secret. That reminded me of the Maoist days. Factory workers were supposed to get the day off when temperatures spiked past 104°F. The day off never materialized. When temperatures soared, the government would routinely shave a few degrees off the official weather report. And that was that.

In 1998, 39 Chinese cities, including Beijing, began issuing regular air-quality reports. The uncharacteristic candor suddenly dovetailed the government's economic agenda. By scaring everyone with pollution statistics, Beijing hoped to win support for shutting inefficient state-owned enterprises, a move that inevitably would idle millions.

China pledged to spend 1.2 percent of GNP on pollution control. At the same time, it was trying to wean itself from its dependency on coal. But the economic revolution was unlikely to slow down because of environmental concerns. The Chinese Communist Party was racing against time to improve living standards. If it failed, it could be swept from power. If it succeeded, the whole world could pay an environmental price.

Xiao Yang grimaced as an aide accidentally spilled scalding jasmine tea on his lap. "What is this?" he deadpanned. "The Cultural Revolution?" The Communist Party Secretary of China's biggest, spiciest city was a Chinese Bob Hope and a master of the one-liner. With all of the problems in Chongqing (population: 30 million), you needed a sense of humor. As the aide, who wasn't laughing, frantically mopped up his boss, Xiao Yang (pronounced See-ow Yang) grew nostalgic.

"Everything happened to me during the Cultural Revolution – jail, forced labor, criticism," he said. "I was the target of the dictatorship of the proletariat."

Now, as party chief of Chongqing, he *was* the dictator. He could and did block plans for the Three Gorges Dam, a $29 billion megaproject. The world's largest dam would force the relocation of 1.3 million Sichuanese, trap silt, cause landslides and worsen upriver flooding. But Xiao Yang's concerns weren't environmental. He actually wanted the central planners to make it bigger so oceangoing ships could call at his city. So they did. Now, the 400-mile-long dam, scheduled for completion in 2009, will flood the Yangtze River upstream all the way to Chongqing.

Xiao Yang also negotiated a bigger share of electricity for Sichuan Province and hefty relocation sums for the 32,000 people displaced from Chongqing. "Of course, we asked for a lot," he said with a grin. "It's a once-in-a-lifetime chance."

Most Chinese officials shun foreign reporters, but Xiao Yang talked to me at length several times in Beijing and Chongqing, once over a memorable Sichuan banquet of spicy noodles and sweet date pancakes. He once even offered to provide a helicopter so I could tour Jiu Zhai Gou, a scenic Sichuan mountain range. (I declined.)

Although Xiao Yang never deviated from the official line, he did give me a rare look at the workings of power at the regional level. At 62, he was barely five feet tall, with naturally wavy hair, glasses and the confidence born of a lifetime in power. The year after our first meeting, he was promoted to governor of Sichuan, China's largest province, with a population of 120 million. Through his father-in-law, Wan Li, then chairman of the rubber-stamp National People's Congress, Xiao Yang hobnobbed with China's ruling elite. His former bridge partner was Chinese Communist Party chief Hu Yaobang, whose death in 1989 sparked the Tiananmen demonstrations.

"I sneaked to his house to play," Xiao Yang recalled. "We were both in the doghouse back then. We moaned a lot about our problems."

"Back then" was the Cultural Revolution. In 1966, Xiao Yang was attacked as a "capitalist roader" and stripped of his post as director of the Beijing General Glass Works, a plant with 23,000 workers. After a year in a makeshift jail, he was released on parole. To survive, he became a roofer, mason, electrician, carpenter and street sweeper, experiences that helped him retain a common touch. "Need a carpenter?" he joked. "Just call me."

The son of a Sichuan warlord, Xiao Yang grew up in comfort, surrounded by nightmarish poverty. He remembered peasants selling their babies for food. He knew others hanged themselves in despair from the rafters of their homes. When he was ten, his father died fighting the Japanese invaders. At 17, Xiao Yang joined the Communist Party, then enrolled in electrical engineering at Beijing's prestigious Qinghua University. After the Communists took power, he quit school to head the Beijing General Glass Works.

While many officials isolated themselves in walled compounds, Xiao Yang believed in talking to people. As mayor of Chongqing, he set up a complaints hotline. Soon people were phoning about power failures and backed-up drains. "On average, I got criticized 41 times a day," he recalled. "It's the same as being village head. Everybody's always bugging you."

Built on a rocky promontory at the confluence of the Yangtze and Jialing Rivers, Chongqing was a Chinese city without bicycles. People took buses or hiked up streets so steep some were actually flights of stone steps. Known in the West as Chungking, its unrelenting shroud of fog had helped foil enemy bombers during World War II. In the 1990s, the air had an added spice. Sulfur dioxide gas weighed in at a poisonous 338 micrograms per cubic meter, compared to 94 in unbreathable Beijing and 8 in smoggy Los Angeles.

The culprits were the city's crumbling state enterprises, including southwest China's biggest steel factory. These smokestacks pumped out enough acid rain to kill thousands of hectares of crops in the surrounding countryside. But Xiao Yang couldn't just shut down polluters; he also had to worry about state jobs. Each year, 100,000 new high-school graduates streamed into the market. In a good year, he could find 70,000 jobs. That still left 30,000 without. When he weighed the risk of unrest, he kept Chongqing's factories smoking.

Another big headache was population control. Half Sichuan's rural labor force was surplus, and the number was growing. "The peasants think: 'One more child is one more pair of hands,'" he said. "People have a feudal tradition here. To be without descendants is to offend the ancestors. And girls don't count as descendants." His subordinates sometimes forced women to have abortions. That didn't bother him. He disagreed only when they bulldozed homes. "Why tear their house down?" he said. "The third child is still there."

As the father of three himself, Governor Xiao agreed he wasn't the ideal family-planning spokesperson. "I tell them, 'Please forgive me. It was a different era.'" Bored and on parole during the Cultural Revolution, Xiao Yang decided that he and his wife should have a third child. "I was not permitted to speak freely or move about. But I checked the regulations. Nowhere did it say I couldn't have a child," he recalled with an impish grin. Their daughter was born in 1970. With his wife sent away to toil on a farm, Xiao Yang cared for his infant daughter. "I kept her baby bottle in my pocket," he said proudly. "Her first word wasn't mama, but papa."

Although he enjoyed a generous expense account, two servants and a chauffeured burgundy BMW, his official salary was hardly higher than the average state worker's. His two sons, however, earned good money. So Xiao Yang would drop hints. "I say, 'Your mother worked so hard for you. Why don't you buy her a fur coat?' Then they give me 6,000 yuan split between them. I don't buy the coat. So we're rich. No orders. No meetings. No discussions."

13

In the Chinese Closet

Top: With Guo Bin, a lesbian in Beijing, in her secret "clubhouse."
Photo: Private collection

Bottom: Cui Zi'en, a novelist in Beijing who writes about gay topics and doesn't mind being mistaken for a woman. Courtesy Cui Zi'en

In the 1950s, a Chinese lesbian couple lived openly in Beijing. But no one dreamed they were anything but two spinsters. Red Guards persecuted them during the Cultural Revolution, not because they were lesbians, but because they had money. The older woman had been a nurse to Sun Yat-sen, the first republican president of China, said Simon Hui, my matchmaker's husband, who knew them.

There was no concept of being "out" in China. At the same time, the culture provided excellent cover for gay men and women. China was a feudal country where people were still shy about touching the opposite sex, but where same-sex slow dancing, hand-holding and nuzzling were socially acceptable.

For those in the know, a gay subculture always existed. At the turn of the century, a fancy restaurant called Feng Ze Yuan was famous for its waiters in drag. Opera singers, always male by tradition, were coveted as homosexual lovers, especially the ones singing female roles. Many top chefs were also gay, for some reason. In a famous ditty, apprentices, again always male, were advised: "If you want to really learn, then sleep with the cook."

In Shanghai in the 1930s, Christopher Isherwood, the British playwright and travel writer, told of cruising the city's bathhouses with W. H. Auden. "Towards the end of their visit, Wystan and

Christopher began taking afternoon holidays from their social conscience in a bathhouse where you were erotically soaped and massaged by young men. You could pick your attendants, and many of them were beautiful. Those who were temporarily disengaged would watch the action, with giggles, through peepholes in the walls of the bathrooms. What made the experience pleasingly exotic was that tea was served to the customer throughout; even in the midst of an embrace, the attendant would disengage one hand, pour a cupful and raise it, tenderly but firmly, to the customer's lips…. It was like a sex fantasy in which a naked nurse makes love to the patient but still insists on giving him his medicine punctually, at the required intervals."

In the 1990s, ignorance among the general population didn't mean tolerance. It meant that homosexuality was beyond the pale. Gays had to lead lives of utter secrecy. Most married, had children, and otherwise appeared heterosexual. They kept their sexual orientation a secret from parents, siblings, friends, colleagues, even their wives.

"Foreign homosexuals get very angry if a lover gets married. Chinese gays see it as normal. Their filial duty is to produce descendants to carry on the family name. And they need to cover up their homosexuality," said Beijing University sociologist, Li Yanhe, who co-wrote *Their World*, a groundbreaking book on Chinese gays.

A pervasive ignorance of homosexuality plus a severe housing shortage meant no one blinked when house guests shared a bed with their host — as long as they were the same sex. In the 1990s, one married taxi driver in Canton carried on a homosexual affair under the nose of his unsuspecting wife. Whenever his lover stayed the night, the wife would move into their child's bed, leaving the two men to sleep together.

"The attitude is permissive because nobody realizes it actually exists," said Dr. Li's husband and co-author, Wang Xiaobo. Dr. Li herself added, "When Chinese leaders are asked about it by foreign guests, they always say, 'You have it. We don't.'" In conducting her research, she added, she had never met anyone who was openly gay.

Some historians contend that China had a rich homosexual past. Many emperors were at least bisexual, as far back as the

Spring–Autumn Period (770–475 BC) and as recently as the Qing Dynasty (1644–1911). Nobody minded as long as their dalliances didn't interfere with the procreation of an heir. The only succession crisis occurred during the Han Dynasty (206 BC–220 AD), when a dying emperor tried to pass the imperial seal, the symbol of state power, to his boyfriend.

Indeed, the literary euphemism for homosexuality, "cut sleeve," originated with an emperor in the second century BC. One afternoon, a Han Dynasty emperor awoke from a nap to find his sleeve trapped under his still-slumbering boyfriend. Rather than disturb his beloved, he cut the sleeve on his imperial robe. Another euphemism for homosexuals also has imperial roots. "Sharing the peach" was coined after an imperial lover bit into a peach and found it so delicious, he saved it for the emperor. (Later, when the boyfriend fell out of favor, the emperor was said to have complained about getting leftovers.)

Under the judgmental Communists, who weren't shy about denouncing imperialists, capitalists and reactionaries, there were no insulting terms for gays. The popular slang was *tu zi* (rabbit), which many Chinese gays insist is not pejorative. And when "comrade" fell out of favor as Maoism itself declined, gays embraced the word as their own. "Comrade" (*tong zhi* or "same will") echoed the Chinese for "homosexual" (*tong xing lian* or "same-sex love"). Many, however, just used the English word, "gay."

Mainstream culture regarded homosexuality as decadent, but considered it more an act, and less an identity. Perhaps for that reason, Chinese heterosexuals have felt far less threatened. Homosexuals in China, for instance, were never burned at the stake as they were in medieval Europe, to test whether a bonfire was hot enough to incinerate a witch. (The pejorative "fag" or "faggot," comes from the bundles of firewood.)

China has no tradition of gay-bashing. In the classic Qing Dynasty novel, *Dream of the Red Chamber*, one passage does depict a gay being beaten by a straight man who rejects his advances. But four other homosexual incidents are positive.

In the 1990s, gays said that if they were arrested, say for having sex in a public toilet, they weren't beaten or mistreated or cattle-prodded – any more than the average citizen. Indeed, China has no law against homosexuality. That didn't stop police, of course, from arresting gays on vague charges of "hooliganism." One male doctor was sentenced to eight years in prison for having sex with 19 men, including patients. A gay graduate student at Beijing Foreign Studies University was denied his degree after his arrest. In Hunan Province, a gay schoolteacher, who also happened to be a Deputy Communist Party Secretary, killed himself after a student informed on him.

The police also sent gays to mental hospitals. In Harbin and Tianjin, some doctors showed homosexual erotica to gays, then administered electric shocks to discourage pleasant thoughts. At the Mental Health Center in Shanghai, a psychiatrist told me he treated about ten gays a year, all sent by the police. "We use behavior-modification therapy," said Dr. Yan Heqin. He'd instruct transvestites, for instance, to don women's clothing, then inject them with apomorphine to induce vomiting. Dr. Yan would repeat the process half a dozen times, though he admitted the "patient" was rarely "cured."

Gays were so deeply in the Chinese closet that for years, I never knowingly met one. Eventually, I called a gay friend in the West who had grown up in Beijing. He advised me to check out the public toilets at a certain downtown park.

That's when I told Fat Paycheck we were going for a walk in Dongdan Park. One warm autumn day, we made a beeline for the latrines. Half a dozen young men were lounging on nearby benches. Were they, or weren't they? It wasn't the kind of question you could just walk up and ask. So I told Fat Paycheck to find out. As Norman self-consciously sauntered by, a young man with blow-dried hair, eye makeup and a pastel T-shirt patted the empty spot beside him on the bench.

To my dismay, Fat Paycheck didn't stop. Instead, he chose an empty bench just past him. Immediately, several young men joined Norman. After a little chitchat, one of them touched his hand, then his knee. When Norman jumped up, the young Chinese burst into laughter. "Not interested, eh?"

I approached them a few moments later. But I still couldn't figure out a subtle opener. "You're gays, right?" I said.

"What makes you say that?" one of them boldly challenged.

I explained I was a Canadian reporter and suggested that anyone willing to talk should meet me in ten minutes at the cafe across from the park. I would buy the coffee. And I promised to use pseudonyms.

Half a dozen showed up. A conservatively dressed young man in navy pants and a green sweater spoke up first. "I didn't come to the park to find a man, but to find people who understand me," he said. "I can't tell my closest friends about this, but here I can talk."

A 22-year-old, flamboyant in a peach polka-dot shirt, a single earring and a lock of permed flame-red hair, offered me a cigarette. When I declined, he teased, "What's wrong? You think I have a disease?" He told me that, despite his fashion sense, no one suspected his sexual orientation. Secrecy was paramount to him and the others. "They'll tell your work unit and you won't be allowed to work anymore," he said. "They'll tell your family and you can't live at home anymore. You're finished."

Through my gay friend in the West, I also met a slender 31-year-old named Tang Libin. He told me friends gathered in his apartment several times a month to talk about being gay in China. "We don't think of having sex, but they may bring a newcomer who is beautiful," said Tang. "We have an unspoken agreement to introduce new friends to each other so we don't have to cruise."

His gay-consciousness-raising group was tolerated by his gay-unconscious neighbors, including the nosy retirees of his local Street Committee. "China is a paradise for gays because people are so naive," said Tang, who spoke fluent English and liked to use the word "gay" even in the middle of Chinese sentences. "They're worried about dissidents. They haven't thought about gays yet."

Tang grew up not realizing he was gay. He dated women initially, but always "felt nothing." Even after he had sex with a man for the first time, at age 26, he wasn't sure what had happened. "What we just did – is this homosexuality?" he asked his more experienced partner. That was five years earlier. It took him two more years to pluck up the courage to go to a gay pickup spot.

He liked to cruise in the shrubs outside Diaoyutai, the vast state guest house famous for putting up the likes of Richard Nixon and Prince Philip. One night in 1991 Tang had just loosened his trousers and was embracing a stranger when two militiamen appeared from nowhere and shone flashlights in their faces. Stunned, Tang hugged his coat around him to prevent his pants from falling down.

"You must be hiding something!" barked one militiaman, knocking away Tang's arms. His coat fell open and his pants dropped to his ankles, exposing his underwear.

"You guys are rabbiting!" the militiaman shouted, turning the slang for gays into a verb.

The two militiamen, local factory workers on neighborhood security duty, began punching Tang. When he kicked them back, they handcuffed him and threw him on the ground, still with his pants around his ankles. They interrogated the other man, but didn't beat him, Tang believes, because he was older.

The militiamen checked Tang's papers. He remembered feeling relief that he had just quit his job at the Customs Bureau to go into private business. Without a state "work unit," he was beyond control. He didn't have to worry about his Party Secretary dressing him down. The militiamen also understood this. They removed his handcuffs, gave him a hard kick in the pants and sent him on his way.

Tang had come out to his family, one of the few Chinese gays to do so. They accepted him now, but breaking the news had been traumatic. "My mother burst into tears and hugged me and said, 'I want my son back.' My father said, 'When you're an old man, you're going to sodomize little boys.' "

Homosexuality was so rarely mentioned in the official media few Chinese were even conscious of it. One translator for a Western television bureau told me he thought homosexuality only affected foreigners. He'd always felt different himself. But he didn't figure it out until he and the foreign correspondent interviewed some Chinese gays. "I realized *that's it. I'm gay.*"

Surveys put China's gay population at 1 to 4 percent, compared with Western population estimates of 4 to 10 percent. If true, that meant China had 13 million to 52 million gays. A landmark study of 254 gays in six cities found that gays – surprise, surprise – existed in all age groups and all walks of life, according to Liu Dalin, China's foremost sexologist and president of the Shanghai Sex Sociology Research Center. He told me another of his studies found that at least 2.3 percent of China's married rural population had taken part in homosexual kissing, fondling and intercourse.

Just as there were "corners" for English fans and stock-markets buffs where like-minded strangers could gather, in the 1990s, nearly every major Chinese city had developed a "gay corner." Every big city had gay cruising areas, too. In bathhouses, the soaking pools were shared by a dozen people, providing ample opportunity for contact. "The water is murky," said my Western gay friend who grew up in Beijing. "It's all terribly furtive."

I heard about a gay cruising area in Shanghai. It was, ironically, a sidewalk bulletin board where the masses could read state-controlled newspapers for free. Late one night, I stood there, pretending to read the *Liberation Daily*. Beside me, a man in a gold shirt sidled up to another man in a white shirt. Gold Shirt pressed his body against White Shirt, who responded by leaning backward almost imperceptibly. I watched them leave separately and meet up, moments later, around the corner in a dark alley.

In Beijing, through my fledgling gay contacts, I met a 38-year-old I'll call Yang Tao. His odyssey of confusion, despair and, finally, self-awareness is the story of Chinese gays in microcosm. He first faced up to his homosexuality in 1989, the night of the bloody crackdown at Tiananmen Square. He'd gone there to demonstrate. When the army suddenly started shooting, he leaped over a fence and ran to safety. "It was a narrow escape. I could have been killed," said Yang, a researcher at a Beijing institute. "That made me think: Why should I live with a mask? This is the way I am."

For Yang, Tiananmen Square was a rebirth. He had spent half his life trying to be heterosexual. By 35, he was still a virgin. But four months after the crackdown, he had his first sexual experience, with a male college student he met at a public toilet.

Yang was the youngest of four children born to a senior Communist Party official. If the father was red, the son was pink. "I realized when I was 16 that I was different. I had no interest in girls," said Yang, a tall, soft-spoken man in blue jeans, a gray windbreaker and glasses. Because of his father's status, he was able to study English at an elite language school. In foreign books, he encountered the words "gay" and "homosexual." Burning with curiosity, he looked up the entry for "homosexuality" in the *Encyclopedia Britannica*.

"During those years, I had a very, very hard struggle with myself," he said. "I lived in darkness. There was nowhere to look for help. Very often I asked myself: 'To be gay, or not to be gay,' just like in *Hamlet*. To live in this world was just too hard for me." His adolescence was filled with loneliness and self-doubt. "We get very depressed because we think we're the only people who feel like this. When I go cruising now, the first thing we talk about is: How did you know? Were you taught or was it self-awakening?'"

Over the years, he dated what he described as "battalions" of women. He was a good catch – tall, handsome and well-educated, with an impeccable political pedigree. Each time, he dutifully dated the woman once a week. The correct Chinese pattern consisted of several months of chaste courtship followed by a marriage proposal. But Yang could never bring himself to propose. Sometimes the woman hinted that she wouldn't mind being kissed or hugged. Again, he did nothing. Most thought he was shy, and fell harder. "They wanted intimacy, but I couldn't respond. In the end, I couldn't stand the relationship, and just said goodbye."

In 1986, he spent a year in the United States as a visiting scholar. Elated, he bought gay magazines, watched gay videos and frequented gay bars. But he never went home with anyone. Back in China and well past the conventional marrying age, he tried once again to start a heterosexual relationship. In 1987, he dated yet another nice young woman, but broke it off again. By 1988, he was 34 and desperate. Friends introduced him to one more woman.

"I told myself: This is the last one. I must marry her," he recalled. The relationship lasted until Tiananmen Square. A few days after the killings, he wrote his girlfriend a farewell letter, telling her the political situation was hopeless in China and that he would try to go abroad. She said that she supported him.

He fled south to Canton where he bided his time, wondering if he could slip across the border to Hong Kong. One day, in a department store restroom, he noticed other men staring at him. One of them followed him out and tailed him for several blocks. Already paranoid in the aftermath of Tiananmen Square, Yang confronted him. The man explained he was gay. They went to a park to talk.

"He told me about being gay. He used the English word. It was the first time I heard a Chinese say the word for 'homosexual,'" said Yang. "He also told me that many cities had gay cruising grounds." Although the man, a taxi driver, propositioned him, Yang demurred, saying politely, "I'm very sorry, I'm not gay." But when he returned to Beijing that July, he began frequenting the gay hangouts the man had described. In September, he became lovers with a young man he met in a public toilet.

Because he hadn't married, Yang said, he had been passed over for several promotions. But what he found most irritating was being forced to live in a collective dormitory at his age. His state-run institute wouldn't allot him an apartment unless he married. "They told me, 'Come on, Yang, get married.'" Under the rules, he had to wait until age 40 to apply for an apartment if he wasn't married, "What will I say when I get older and people ask me why am I not married? What will I say when I'm 40?"

Yang was keeping his homosexuality a secret from his brother and sisters and his mother, who were all Party members. His father had been persecuted during the Cultural Revolution and had died in 1968. His mother, he said, had suffered enough. "If I told her, she could not bear it."

One Saturday night in March, 1999, I stopped by Bar 101, on New Happiness Road in Shanghai. I was the only female. About 20 attractive young men sat on zebra-patterned banquettes or sipped drinks at the black granite bar. Some couples sat close together, but it was all very sedate. One loner flipped through a copy of *Esquire*. Overhead, two television monitors played silent videos of very soft porn. I checked out the bathrooms or, rather, the bathroom. There was no women's room. The men's was a spotless, perfumed urinal, complete with a fresh flower and a flickering votive candle.

Kennly, the soft-spoken owner told me he had recently moved to Shanghai from Hong Kong. In a gold and brown velvet Gucci shirt with exaggerated cuffs, he chatted with customers and served Perrier and scotch. "My clientele are quite rich, quite upper crust," he said, setting down a zebra-patterned coaster and my drink. The police left his place alone, he said, although Asia Blue, another Shanghai gay bar, had been recently shut down.

In the four years I'd been gone from China, the gay community had undergone a revolution. The first gay bars had opened for business and authorities, more or less, turned a blind eye. Several gays I'd previously interviewed were now halfway out of the closet, known to close friends, but still not to their families. They had begun networking – through gay newsletters, gay hotlines and gay Web sites.

China even had gay novelists. A week later in Beijing, I had dinner with Cui Zi'en. It was a sign of how much things had changed that he didn't mind my using his real name. He was 40, and if you didn't look closely, you could mistake him for a woman, which he also didn't mind. He was baby-faced, with soft, tiny hands, a swept-back pompadour and a single dangling earring in his left ear lobe. He wore, unusual for a man, a brown silk brocade vest.

Cui had lost his job teaching at the Beijing Film Academy after a student complained he'd tried to seduce him. Now he made a living writing screenplays and gay novels, including one called *Peach-Colored Lips*. I asked Cui if he went cruising. He shook his head and said he preferred straight men. "They're not gay," he said in a soft, breathy voice. "They're all married. I usually just say I like them. But more and more, they approach me."

Unlike the Judeo-Christian tradition, Chinese philosophy had no corresponding concept of fire and brimstone. It rejected moral absolutes. Chinese Buddhists ate meat, Chinese Moslems drank and everyone was tolerant. Maybe that was why a homosexual encounter was not such a cataclysmic experience for a straight Chinese male. I asked Cui how straight men felt after their first homosexual encounter. "Some worry they won't be able to father a baby in future, or they worry about the AIDS virus," he said. "But half don't even think about anything."

As gays began to live more openly, they did become targets. But it wasn't gay-bashing, so much as mugging. One gay man told me he'd been lured by a man pretending to be gay who then stole his wallet and jewelry. Another gay man told me a friend had been similarly robbed. This time, the other man blackmailed the gay – threatening to scream and say he'd been attacked – unless the gay man forked over a stack of cash.

In 1999, Chinese lesbians were half way out of the closet, too. There was even a lesbian support group in Beijing. Through contacts, I became the first foreign journalist to attend one of their gatherings. After dinner with Cui Zi'en, I rushed off to meet them. I got lost a few times in the dark, but kept calling on a cellphone for instructions. Finally, I located their "clubhouse," an ordinary apartment in an ordinary neighborhood on the west side of the city.

Although they had agreed to let me visit them, the women were deeply suspicious of my motives. Instead of letting me interview them, they interviewed me. Or rather, they interrogated me. "What's your position on lesbianism?" one woman demanded, as soon as I sat down. "Do you think lesbianism is good?" said another. "What percent of the population do you think is lesbian?"

There were nine women present, including a banker, an engineer, a businesswoman, an importer and several students. I sat meekly on the couch in their meeting room while the three most aggressive hammered me with questions. They wouldn't answer any of mine until I revealed my "attitude." That in itself told me reams about what it was like to be a lesbian in China. Certainly, I'd never encountered this with the gay men I'd interviewed.

It felt like a 1960s consciousness-raising group, or maybe the Cultural Revolution. Poor Robin and Alister had tagged along, hoping to film them. But, as two hairy heteros, they were doomed. The women snookered them into donating 100 yuan to their communal fund – then kicked them out into the night.

They called themselves the Beijing Female Comrades Working Group, but I should really translate it as the Beijing Lesbian Working

Group. They used the slang, *nu tongzhi*, or "female comrade," for lesbian. As someone who learned Chinese during the Cultural Revolution, it took several minutes for me to click. Come to think of it, I still don't know the proper way to say "lesbian" in Chinese.

They were mostly in their 20s. All but one had short hair and wore jeans, vests and hiking boots. The prickliest one, a medical student, had long hair and wore sleek black pants and a purple blouse. After I had answered all their questions, they finally let me ask a few myself.

They said they had found one another through a hotline and the Internet. Lesbians, they declared, always approached one another with the question, "*Ni shi?*" which means, "Are you?" They claimed they could easily tell who was a lesbian and who wasn't. Hillary Clinton was one, for sure, they said, and so was Florence Nightingale. When I asked what the secret was to telling a lesbian from a straight female, they said it was too obvious for words.

Their "clubhouse" resembled a million other nondescript apartments in Beijing. It had concrete floors, whitewashed walls and a fluorescent light. It was furnished with a double bed, an L-shaped sofa and a coffee table. The only things that set it apart were a bookcase with volumes on sado-masochistic sex and, in keeping with the combative tone of the evening, a lesbian manifesto in English on one wall and a movie poster of a sweaty Demi Moore, in *G.I. Jane* garb, on another. The women met here weekly, over a bottle of white wine and a platter of sliced oranges and apples. They each contributed 30 yuan ($3.75) a month toward the rent.

"Lesbians have nowhere to meet. We don't like to go to bars. We need a place to get together," said one.

With my questions being lobbed back to me as "meaningless," I eventually stopped asking and started observing. All but one of the women smoked cigarettes. When I jotted that down, several of them demanded in annoyance to know why that was significant. Fleetingly, I thought of saying, "You've come a long way, baby."

Only two defied the general opprobrium to talk to me. And only one agreed to let me take her picture. Guo Bin, 23, tried to encourage the others to have their photos taken, too. She had been severely burned as a child in a fire, and didn't want to give a distorted idea of what a Chinese lesbian looked like. But the others refused. So Guo Bin posed, her disfigured face turned away, in front of the *G.I. Jane* poster.

She was a vivacious woman in a white hooded sweater and black jeans. Around her scarred neck, she wore a necklace looped with rainbow-colored rings, the universal gay symbol. Guo Bin, a law student, said she was completely "out" at school and at home. But that didn't mean anyone accepted her. "My professor said I was just being trendy," she said, lighting a cigarette. "And my parents are always trying to match me with a boyfriend. They think I'm just immature, that my hormones haven't developed yet. But this is the way I am."

14

The New Opium Wars

At the Yunnan–Burmese border in 1992.   Photo: Jim McGregor

The crowd came early. Children munched peanuts and spun pirou-
ettes. Chinese pop music blared over the loudspeakers. Suddenly,
the wail of sirens filled the air and a convoy of 13 army trucks sped
onto the damp red earth of the Mangshi Youth Sports Stadium.
The death rally had begun.

It was mid-morning in Mangshi, a sleepy city of 50,000 in semi-
tropical Yunnan Province. A squad of bayonet-toting soldiers jogged
onto the roped-off basketball court. Several hundred others kept
the huge crowd at bay. One soldier positioned an ancient tripod-
mounted machine gun on the roof of a battered army truck. Everyone fell silent as soldiers in green riot helmets frog-marched 28
convicted drug dealers across the field. Right after the rally, they
would be taken to a secluded execution ground and given a bullet
to the back of the head.

This was China's new Opium War. And one of its battlegrounds
was Mangshi, on the old Burma Road, carved from the jungle in
World War II. The front line was Yunnan Province, which bordered
the opium-rich "Golden Triangle" of Burma, Laos and Thailand.
Faced with a growing number of addicts and an incipient AIDS
crisis, China was fighting back.

But experts predicted that brute force would only drive drugs
further underground. "Every drug dealer knows there is a death

penalty, but they sell it anyway. Every addict knows he'll be sent to labor re-education, but they don't stop," said Li Jianhua, a psychiatrist and director of the Drug-Abuse Research Center in Kunming, the provincial capital. "The penalties just frighten law-abiding people who wouldn't get involved in drugs anyway."

I'd come to Yunnan in 1992 with the *Wall Street Journal*'s Jim McGregor. Someone had tipped us off about the Mangshi death rally, one of a dozen staged that year to mark International Drug Day. Tickets had been distributed at offices, schools and factories. Four thousand spectators showed up, including the entire graduating class of the National Minorities Teachers High School. One woman in a flowered dress brought her three-year-old daughter.

The 28 doomed traffickers included four Burmese. There were also 29 addicts, sentenced to between 2 and 15 years in labor camp. White cardboard placards hung from their necks, their names and crimes – "drug dealer," "addict" – written in large, black brush strokes. Thick rope hobbled their feet, encircled their necks and trussed their arms high up behind their backs. If they lowered their arms, they would choke themselves.

After months of detention, some appeared dazed in the bright sunshine. Each knew death was near. They would have been informed 15 days earlier, the period criminals are allotted to appeal their death sentences. One man in a red-and-white sweatshirt looked defiant, his eyes hard, his crew-cut head held high. Others seemed terrified.

There was only one female, a statuesque woman wearing the white cloth cap of a Muslim. She descended from the troop trucks last. Calmly, she scanned the crowd. The three soldiers guarding her let her move next to a fellow Muslim, a short man in a shabby, black Mao suit. They chatted animatedly for a few moments, like neighbors who happened to meet at the vegetable market. The crowd gawked and pointed, for they were the only prisoners acting as if they weren't about to die. Finally, the soldiers jerked on their ropes and ordered them to be silent. I heard later they were partners in trafficking – and love.

Few Chinese opposed the death penalty. Rape, murder and even embezzlement sometimes, were capital crimes. Given China's

Opium War history, drug dealing was an especially grave offense. Authorities once ordered a German restaurant in Beijing to stop serving poppyseed cake. "Something to do with opium," a waitress said, with a shrug.

In the 19th century, Britain remedied a growing trade deficit in tea and silk by selling China an addictive commodity. A weakened imperial court protested in vain. Two Opium Wars later, from 1839 to 1842, and from 1856 to 1858, victorious English gunboats forced a trade agreement with China that legalized the import of opium. By 1949, when the Communists took power, China had 20 million addicts.

Mao Zedong himself was a regular opium smoker. But after proclaiming the People's Republic, he banned all opiates. Authorities sealed China's borders, destroyed vast poppy fields, arrested 80,000 traffickers and encouraged ordinary citizens to snitch on anyone still taking drugs. Three years later, in 1952, Beijing boasted that it had eliminated the problem.

Now, China was once more awash in drugs. The bulk of the opium and its powerful derivative, heroin, came from Burma. It was the unhappy confluence of a porous border between two friendly dictatorships and flourishing jungle refineries, which were operated by remnants of the Communist Party of Burma.

"The Chinese are a bit naive. They seem to think: 'We've solved the problem before and we can do it again,'" a U.S. drug enforcement official told me. "I don't think they are prepared for the proliferation of drug use and crime that is beginning to happen."

Selling a couple of grams got you 2 to 15 years in the gulag. Fifty grams or more was an automatic death penalty. "This fear approach cannot work. There is no country in the world where it has worked," said Christian Kroll, a UN expert who ran a drug-abuse program in Ruili, the Chinese border-town and major entry point for Burmese heroin.

Fueled by high profits in a country where state workers made a pittance, trafficking was on the rise. Between Ruili and Kunming, a $12 bus ride away, the price of heroin jumped tenfold. Peasants carrying a kilo or two easily blended into the ceaseless flow of humanity along the back roads of China. From Yunnan, the drugs flowed across south China to Hong Kong, and on to Canada, the United States and Europe.

Fear only made it harder to treat addicts. "Anybody who has a problem with addiction is going into hiding," said Kroll, the UN expert. "You don't have a chance to do any prevention because everybody is lying like hell." Jim McGregor and I got a taste of that when we visited Da Deng He, a village of 136 families. According to a UN report, it had 25 addicts. But when a local policeman insisted on escorting us there, the village head nervously claimed that Da Deng He had no addicts.

The United Nations gave China $6 million to fight drugs. It mostly went to buy fancy Mitsubishi police jeeps. One recipient was Bao Zhihong, who headed Ruili's police task force on drugs. Scratching his legs and burping his way through a morning interview with Jim and me, Bao insisted he had the drug problem under control. He arrested addicts, he said, and forced them to stop cold, followed by 20 days of lectures on the evils of drugs and several months in the gulag. "The poison is still in them. Through labor, they can sweat it out," he said. "We make it so painful for them they're afraid to come back."

Liu Huiyin was mainlining heroin at a friend's house when the police burst in. They handcuffed him, beat him and zapped him with a cattle prod. Then they dumped him into a "forced detoxification center," levying a 100-yuan deposit against "damage." Forty agonizing days later, Addict Liu was set free, supposedly cleansed of his habit. The police returned his deposit.

"The first thing I did was spend it on heroin," said Addict Liu, an emaciated 19-year-old with a smart-aleck grin. I met him in Kunming's Drug-Abuse Research Center, where he had enrolled in an experimental program. Unlike the police-run addicts prison, the center took a kinder, gentler approach to detox. It was housed in a wing of the Yunnan Mental Hospital, amid paddy fields and bamboo groves. There were no beatings. And although the police disapproved, addicts could purchase two weeks of methadone treatment.

Even so, the center felt like a prison, with barred windows, high brick walls topped with barbed wire and a locked metal door to the outside world. No family visits were allowed. The addicts slept two or three to a room on scarred metal beds with hemp mattresses. Every two hours during the day, they had to sign a roll-call sheet. They wore faded, pink-striped pajamas to distinguish them from the mental patients, who wore blue stripes and were allowed to wander freely.

The doctors provided counseling during withdrawal. They administered acupuncture and herbal medicine to alleviate the pain. And they worked on antisocial behavior, such as lying. When Addict Liu told Jim and me that he mainly "chased the dragon" – heated heroin on foil and inhaled the vapors – his doctor grabbed his arm and pulled up his sleeve, revealing an arm scarred with needle marks.

"Tell the truth," Dr. Zhang Ruimin ordered.

Later, when Addict Liu talked about how much his habit cost him, Dr. Zhang prompted him. "Did you steal a television set?" Addict Liu insisted he hadn't.

Nine out of ten patients returned to drugs within a year. As a reminder to those who couldn't kick the habit, a forced-detox center, run by the police, was next door. The failure rate there was worse, nearly 100 percent, despite three-year sentences in the gulag for repeat offenders. "Drugs are everywhere," said Addict Liu. "As long as you know someone, you can get it, 24 hours a day, in someone's home, on the street, in barbershops, at dance halls."

Dr. Zhang agreed. The crackdown, he said, had little impact on users. "Executions only affect those who haven't taken drugs. It has no effect on addicts." A few places in Yunnan were beginning to understand the psychological chains of addiction. Several villages had formed soccer teams for ex-addicts to keep them busy and enable them to monitor one another for relapses.

In the city, drug addicts didn't play soccer. On Great Prospect Street in Kunming one evening, a young man sat on a stoop, rhythmically banging his head against a brick wall. In the bad old days before the Communist takeover, this street of elaborately carved Qing Dynasty buildings had been a magnet for opium addicts. Now, the drug of choice was heroin. Down the street, a shaggy-haired teenaged boy squatted on the sidewalk, his eyelids half closed, his hands limp from the wrist. Minutes later, he bought a small white packet from an even younger boy, and tucked it into the pocket of his Mao jacket.

The street price of first-grade heroin in Kunming was about the cheapest in the world. In a futile attempt to counteract the bargain-basement prices for drugs, the local media broadcast virulent anti-drug commentaries. Authorities pasted comic-strip tales of hell and redemption on walls. And on International Drug Day, Yunnan authorities ordered addicts to turn themselves in within 30 days, or face forced detoxification at police-run centers. "Every unit and every citizen has the duty to report drug users," a poster declared.

"Propaganda doesn't help," said Li Jianhua, director of the Drug-Abuse Research Center. "We did a survey of addicts and found they don't read newspapers, watch television or listen to the radio."

At his center, I met a pretty 19-year-old named Wang Jingfang who had checked in after her shocked parents discovered her shooting up at home. Her parents initially hired a folk doctor who prescribed a daily intravenous drip. "He would never let me see what it was," she said, playing nervously with her waist-length hair. After each drip, she would go into withdrawal. In desperation, her parents let her take heroin again. Then they sent her to the center.

After 40 days in detox, Wang Jingfang had joined a special rehabilitation program. It involved Western-style group therapy, unusual because baring one's soul to strangers was antithetical to Chinese culture. Only four addicts had signed up. "People don't understand the need for psychological rehabilitation," said Dr. Zhang, the same physician who treated Addict Liu. "Everybody thinks you just go to detoxification and that's enough. But it doesn't solve the root problem of why the person turned to drugs in the first place."

In the center, patients adhered to rigid schedules, cooked their own meals and learned to care for themselves. Like residents in an old-age home, they tended vegetable beds and made handicrafts. Peng Ruibo, a skinny, sad 26-year-old, had collapsed, blackened veins on his arms and seemed barely aware he had a two-year-old son. His wife had recently asked for a divorce. Peng said he had no plans to return to his business, wholesaling herbal medicines. "Who would trust me, a former drug addict?" he said, looking down at his lap.

Ma Yan, 22, another addict, was a former Communist Youth League member. She had undergone detoxification the previous year, but still wanted to mainline. Her father, a Communist Party member, locked her in their home. Her brother, a bank security guard, took time off from work to watch her. Three months after entering rehab, she stopped craving heroin. But when Jim and I met her after she'd spent nine months in the program, she said she still didn't feel ready to cope with the real world. "I get up. I eat. I sleep," she said, with a tired shrug. "I try to lead a normal life."

Heroin abuse quickly spread from Yunnan to other areas of China. By the mid-1990s, China acknowledged having 250,000 drug addicts. The press began reporting busts, such as the two traffickers who shipped 325 kilos of cocaine by train as chicken feed.

In Ruili County, a finger of land jutting into the Golden Triangle, Zhuang Xiangsai (pronounced juong Siang-sy) lay on the bamboo floor of his platform home, chewing pellets of raw opium. Outside, his wife and 16-year-old daughter were bent at the waist, sarongs tied high, laboriously transplanting rice seedlings. Every able-bodied person was needed during the planting season, but Addict Zhuang was adrift in his own world. When Jim McGregor and I stopped by, he could barely rouse himself. At 42, his eyes were dull, his pupils dilated, his frame so wasted that his bones seem to poke through his threadbare cotton pants.

"Sometimes I cough up blood. If I didn't take opium I'd feel worse," he said, trying to suppress an explosive cough.

Neither Addict Zhuang nor his family knew it, but he also had AIDS, probably contracted while mainlining heroin. He would probably die within a year. China, as a matter of policy, did not inform AIDS victims or their families.

About two-thirds of China's confirmed AIDS patients lived in this strip of Yunnan, smack against the opium-growing hill country of Burma, Laos and Thailand. The actual number may have been much higher. Ruili County was one of the few places in

China to test addicts, even while ignoring other high-risk groups, such as prostitutes and addicts' families.

China had blanketed its AIDS crisis in secrecy. Officials wouldn't even admit Ruili was building the country's first AIDS hospital. Stumbling upon the site, Jim and I learned from construction workers that it would have 100 beds. We also heard of one village where every single adult male, including the village chief, was an addict. But the Foreign Affairs Office in Ruili refused our request to go.

"They're very sensitive about this problem. They don't want foreigners to know," said a concerned Chinese doctor. At great political risk, he took us to see Addict Zhuang because he wanted the story of China's AIDS problem to get out.

In 1992, the official line was China had no AIDS problem. The head of Ruili's Health Bureau qualified that statement. "No one *alive* (my emphasis) at the moment has AIDS here," he said. Indeed, 11 addicts had already died in Addict Zhuang's village of Handeng, probably of AIDS-related illnesses, according to Christian Kroll, the UN expert. Their average age was 29.

About 3 to 4 percent of Ruili County's 83,000 people were addicts. From 1983 to 1990, 234 had died of overdoses. Most people in Ruili were hill tribesman and ethnic Dai (Thai) minorities who were at additional risk because they practised a local custom of whole-body tattoos. Addict Zhuang's own arms were blue from tattoos.

His village of Handeng was a hamlet of 305 people. With its water buffalo and lush banana trees, it couldn't have been a bigger contrast to a drug-infested urban ghetto. But because it was a 15-minute stroll from the Burmese border, it faced the same problems as Vancouver, New York and Amsterdam. One out of every ten villagers in Handeng was a drug addict, including Addict Zhuang's father, brother and brother-in-law.

To see what the Burmese border was like, Jim and I followed the villagers' directions and strolled along a muddy water-buffalo path. Only a small wooden sign and a granite marker in the dirt told us we had reached the border. There were no officials, no checkpoint, no customs inspectors. Two hours away by foot was the source of 80 percent of the world's opium. In the toxic poppy fields of Burma, refineries processed raw opium into the world's purest, most potent heroin, "China White." No wonder you could buy it for 50 cents a fix in Handeng.

The United Nations had targeted the village for an experimental drug-rehabilitation program. A Narcotics Anonymous group met weekly in the village temple, surrounded by Buddhist icons and vases of plastic flowers. Just like an inner-city ghetto in the West, Handeng had built a basketball court so ex-addicts could occupy themselves with something wholesome.

Addict Zhuang was too far gone for basketball. He had chewed opium pellets for years. When heroin became available, he began shooting up, but switched back to cheaper opium when he ran out of money. When Jim and I visited him, he offered us burlap sacks to sit on. He had already sold the family's hand-woven cotton mats. To feed his habit, Addict Zhuang had also sold his tractor, the family's only bicycle, all their furniture, even the seed for the following year's rice crop. Indeed, he had just sold the current year's crop, still green in the fields, though it brought half the price of a mature harvest. His younger daughter, Han Pin, had stopped going to school because he wouldn't pay the $6 annual fee. His older daughter, Han Rong, a beautiful 19-year-old with almond eyes and glossy dark hair, left home when he tried to sell her for $300. We found her through the UN workers.

"My father will do anything for money," said Han Rong sadly. Both sisters were co-operating with the UN project, but neither knew their father had AIDS. All they knew was that he had ruined their lives. Han Pin, 16, toiled in the fields and helped translate for the UN health workers. Han Rong washed dishes in town at the county hospital. Each month, she sent money home. "I give it to my mother," she said. "I don't tell my father."

AIDS was a ticking time bomb in Ruili. Spiraling heroin abuse, unscreened blood transfusions, dirty needles and prostitution were rapidly spreading the disease throughout Yunnan Province to the rest of China. In Ruili County, authorities wouldn't allow health workers to demonstrate how to sterilize needles. Condoms weren't available, either, except through prim family-planning officials. At the same time, a thriving economy attracted long-distance truck drivers, needle-sharing addicts and Shanghai salesmen. Ruili's prostitutes catered to all – at \$4 a trick – and acted as a national crossroads for AIDS.

In 1993, China set up hotlines in five cities. It opened its first AIDS agency. By 1999, everyone disagreed on the statistics. The New China News Agency reported 200,000 Chinese were HIV positive. The Chinese Ministry of Health put the number at 300,000. The United Nations estimated it at 400,000, and Chinese AIDS activists claimed it was 2 million. Probably no one knew for sure. Testing was erratic, and drug addicts understandably avoided authorities.

Whatever the true number, Ruili – where it mattered most – had no AIDS-awareness campaign. According to a survey of more than 1,000 villagers, half the people there thought AIDS could be transmitted through handshakes, mosquito bites and the air. Decades of government propaganda had taken its toll. "Peasants think AIDS is a government plot to scare them into stopping taking drugs," said Dr. Li of the Kunming Drug-Abuse Research Center.

Not only did a squeamish government fail to educate the public, it consciously avoided notifying the AIDS victims themselves and their families. Big Brother could know, but not the little people. What authorities feared the most was someone who had nothing to fear. "What if the patient went to a restaurant, didn't pay the bill and took out a knife? He says: 'I'm going to die anyway. Come and get me,'" Dr. Li explained.

Terminal cancer patients in China weren't told the bad news either. Yet the smoking-related death rate among Chinese men was 12 percent and rising, according to a massive study published in 1998. It was the largest epidemiological project ever to examine the link between smoking and dying. The researchers, from China, the United States and Britain, traced the death certificates of one million people who died in China between 1986 and 1988. The epidemic was "still in the early stages," they concluded.

China represented one-third of the world tobacco market. In 1978, the year Deng Xiaoping launched his economic reforms, Chinese smoked 500 billion cigarettes. By 1998, China had more than tripled consumption, to 1.75 trillion cigarettes. That compared with 700 billion for all Eastern Europe *and* the former Soviet Union, and 555 billion for North America. As China has grown more affluent, cigarettes have become the Chinese way of death.

Smoking-related diseases take decades to develop, so China's sharp rise in cigarette consumption won't show up in mortality tables until well into the 21st century. Experts warn that, over the next few decades, smoking could result in the deaths of one of every three Chinese men. Put another way, 50 million Chinese children alive today will die of smoking-related diseases. The toll will dwarf all deaths from tuberculosis, malaria and AIDS.

Then again, these predictions may not hold up. The Chinese are already telescoping the Industrial Revolution in time. In the West, in one generation we have gone from an era where hostesses offered cigarettes to an era where hostesses won't allow smoking in their homes. I only hope that the Chinese, too, will go through their smoking phase – and then hit the non-smoking phase – at the same telescoped rate.

Currently, about 70 percent of Chinese males smoke. Among females, the rate fluctuates, sometimes hitting 10 percent. In the *Globe and Mail* office, the cook, the driver, the housekeeper and my news assistant all smoked. Only Nanny Ma didn't, but both her husband and son did.

Confronted with aggressive anti-smoking campaigns and multi-billion-dollar lawsuits in the West, tobacco companies have turned to other markets, particularly Asia. And within Asia, China was the most coveted market because of its sheer size, soaring personal income and pathetic naiveté. Surveys showed 50 percent of Chinese didn't think smoking harmful. Over 60 percent were unaware it could cause lung cancer.

In 1987, Chinese health authorities launched an anti-smoking campaign. It was miserably financed and generally ignored. Years of government propaganda had created 1.3 billion cynics who assumed the smoking-hazard campaign was one more lie.

China later banned smoking on all flights, domestic and foreign. It also banned cigarette advertising, although tobacco companies were still allowed to promote brand awareness on television and radio. They also sponsored fashion shows, car rallies and tennis and soccer championships. Philip Morris Co. plastered the Marlboro man on Shanghai phone booths and sponsored a daily American music radio show. Marlboro became the number one imported brand in China.

It is easy to draw parallels between the Opium Wars and the modern-day sale of foreign cigarettes in China. But it wasn't that simple. Foreign tobacco companies were actually having a hard time breaking into the China market. Even by 1998, stiff import duties kept their market share down to a mere 2 percent.

The world's largest cigarette producer was in fact the Chinese government. China grew more tobacco than any other country on earth. By 1998, its tobacco monopoly, called Chinese National Tobacco Corp., had become the most profitable corporation in the world, single-handedly producing 12 percent of the Chinese government's revenues.

Yunnan, where opium once flourished, became the heart of China's tobacco industry. With its high elevation, strong sunshine and abundant rainfall, it was ideal tobacco country. At the province's biggest cigarette factory, the equipment rolled cigarettes so fast I got dizzy. The general manager told me the factory might print health warnings on each pack.

Some packs already have health *recommendations*. Jin Jian filter cigarettes, produced at the Beijing Cigarette Factory, were labeled in Chinese and fractured English: "It contains Chinese medicinal herbs, being new type and, therefore, safe to use." The Laifeng Cigarette Factory in Wuhan even claimed to have invented an anti-cancer cigarette.

Li Musheng, a grizzled worker in a Mao jacket, struck a classic revolutionary pose. Fist clenched, back erect, eyes focused dreamily ahead, he said, in a conspiratorial whisper, "I'm an underground Communist Party member. That's why I've been put here."

I nodded politely. "Here" was the Psychiatric Research Institute in Wuhan, a gritty industrial city on the banks of the Yangtze River. His doctors said that Li suffered from mania and needed chronic care. Unfortunately, he had been in and out of hospitals for years.

Like other Chinese cities, Wuhan was critically short of psychiatric beds and staff.

Mental illness was on the rise in China, sparked by the economic boom turning the world's most populous country inside out. Decades of political campaigns had taken their toll. In the 1990s, the new stress point was choice. For the first time, millions had to make their own decisions. Plant peanuts, or sweet potatoes? Stay in the countryside, or make it in the big city? Cling to the state sector, or go into private business? Get a divorce, or stay married? Change apartments, or countries? The choices might not seem that traumatic to a Westerner, but in just a few years, the Chinese had gone from zero choice to every choice.

With choice came risk, and the possibility of personal failure. In 1993, when a six-year-old child would not stop throwing glass shards at a wall, Ge Yunbao, a 36-year-old martial-arts expert, flew into a rage and beat the child to death. He dismembered the corpse and left the severed head on a bus. His colleagues told the *China Sports Daily* that he had been a model employee at his state-owned company, but had been passed over for a promotion.

"In the old days there was no competition, and the incidence of mental illness was much less than 1 percent," said Dr. Bai Xueguang, a psychiatrist at Wuhan's Psychiatric Research Institute. "Today, it's much higher than in the Cultural Revolution."

China was a country under stress. This manifested itself in what I called Chinese Jiggle Disorder. Men, especially, flapped their knees, like geese taking flight. Or they'd cross their legs and furiously wiggle an ankle, like a podiatric eggbeater. In meetings, you sometimes felt like the whole room was vibrating.

If I talked to myself in Toronto, most people would give me a wide berth. But in China, when I had to memorize a couple of monologues for Robin Benger's documentary, I chanted them aloud while walking down a busy street. Nobody gave me a second glance. I assume they assumed I was just one more mentally disturbed Chinese.

In 1991, the official suicide rate was similar to the West's, about 12 per 100,000. But by 1999, the rate had soared to 30.3 per 100,000 people. Among Chinese women, the rate was five times that of other countries. And the overall suicide rate was triple the world average, according to a combined study by the World Bank, Harvard University and the World Health Organization.

Statistics on mental illness were more problematic. China sometimes classified homosexuals as mentally ill. At the same time, severely depressed people weren't always classified as having psychiatric problems. But in 1993, the *China Daily* reported that the number of mental patients had doubled over the previous decade to 13 million, or 1.1 percent of the population. It also noted that surveys showed nearly 30 percent of Beijingers believed they had some kind of mental problems, compared to a common estimate of 6 percent in the West.

Decades of suspicion about Western-style psychiatry and psychology had decimated the ranks of mental-health workers. "We have a terrible shortage of doctors – about 1 psychiatrist for every 100,000 people," said Dr. Zang Dexin, vice-director of Wuhan's Psychiatric Research Institute. "The whole area of psychiatry is rather backward."

In the 1990s, 40 medical schools began offering courses in psychiatry. In the meantime, telephone hotlines and radio call-in shows stepped into the breach. Most calls to the Women's Hotline in Beijing were from women who had lost their jobs.

"Demand for psychological counseling way outstrips supply," said Lu Xiaoya, who ran a youth hotline in Beijing. "It's like throwing a cup of water on a truckload of burning kindling. The social changes are happening so fast. Those who can adjust are okay. Those who can't are under great psychological pressure." Half the calls to her hotline were about sex and love. "There's sexual stimulation on television, in magazines and in books," said Lu Xiaoya. "In my day, girls were supposed to be as pure as jade. My mother said I wasn't allowed to have a boyfriend before I was 25."

For years, China adopted the Soviet model, including shock treatments and lobotomies. (Unlike the Soviet Union, however, Beijing rarely put political dissidents in mental asylums.) In recent years, Chinese doctors began relying on modern medications, such as clozapine for schizophrenia. Occasionally, they still performed lobotomies.

Popular attitudes remained stuck in the dark ages. The colloquial term for a mental patient was *feng zi*, or "madman." On the eve of important Party meetings, police would sweep through neighborhoods rounding up the mentally ill, who were considered a social blight and a security risk. At Beijing's Ankang Hospital, doctors told me that more than half the mental patients had exhibited behavior such as "making faces," "causing accidents," or "disturbing the public order."

Prejudice ran deep. Many offices and factories refused to take anyone with a history of mental illness. To avoid losing face, some people kept mentally ill family members locked up at home and didn't seek treatment until quite late. "The patient who comes here isn't in the early stage," said one Shanghai psychiatrist.

Perhaps because of the stigma, mental hospitals were often set in remote areas. Beijing's was at Zhoukoudian, a three-hour bus journey away. Getting to Taizhou's psychiatric hospital required a 42-mile trip over twisting mountain roads. In Shaoxing, the nearest mental hospital was in a mountain gully, 20 miles away. Outpatients arriving for treatment had to walk seven miles from the closest bus stop.

Kunming's was 50 miles away, deep in the Yunnan countryside. After interviewing drug addicts there, Jim McGregor and I had rashly promised the doctors a lift back to the capital in our taxi. But we couldn't all fit in at once. So Jim, the biggest person, stayed behind. By the time I returned, he was entertaining the mental patients in the garden with his own rendition of *Jingle Bells.* That was the moment, he said, when he made up his mind to quit journalism and become a corporate executive. Soon after, he became Dow Jones' representative in China and president of the Beijing American Chamber of Commerce.

If ordinary citizens lacked human rights, Chinese mental patients had no rights at all. Unlike in the West, they couldn't refuse treatment or hospitalization. Most were committed by family members. At the Mental Health Research Institute in Beijing, Feng Huibin, 63, was committed by her children after she tried to give away her husband to a widow. I watched nurses urging her to take her "vitamins," actually anti-psychosis tranquilizers.

As with its AIDS crisis, China didn't like foreigners seeing this so-called dark side of society. The Shanghai Mental Health Center was one of the few institutes open to foreign visitors. With 880 beds, its cavernous wards reminded me of *One Flew Over the Cuckoo's Nest*. Patients slept on iron cots, several dozen to a room. Most were schizophrenic and had been committed by family members. Only patients with specially marked pyjamas could leave the locked ward.

"The facilities are pre-World War II, but the place is very progressive and well-run," said Dr. David Marsh, a psychiatrist at Brooklyn's Maimonides Hospital, who was visiting at the same time. "But there's a very high reliance on equipment. For instance, they do no psychotherapy with schizophrenics."

Some treatments looked scary. Patients diagnosed with neuroses donned Velcro headbands to receive electric pulses. The patients told me the treatment was painless and said they took it twice daily. Day patients on reduced medication actually worked six hours a day making safety pins, a task subcontracted from a Shanghai factory. Doctors said the work was rehabilitative and also supplemented the meager allowances patients received from their workplaces.

The Wuhan Psychiatric Research Institute was off-limits to reporters. But I managed to get in with *guanxi*, or connections, through a friend whose aunt was a psychiatrist there. Inside a crumbling three-storey building with barred windows and locked wards, I found Luo Xiaonian, a 29-year-old peasant, tied spread-eagled to a bed frame. She moaned continuously: "No more money. No more money." In the next room, a grieving relative watched over a 35-year-old woman who had destroyed her lips and esophagus by drinking acid in a suicide attempt.

At mid-morning several dozen patients with less serious disorders were allowed to roam the yard. That's where I saw Li, the "underground Party member," declaiming his undying loyalty to Communism. A few patients played basketball. One young man pirouetted to music only he could hear. In a recreation room decorated with tinsel and Mickey-Mouse cutouts, a few patients played table tennis. Three just held their heads. Chen Fang, a 21-year-old patient, told me her parents were dead. A doctor later said she was schizophrenic, that her parents weren't dead and that she ate her own feces to punish herself.

15

Holding Up Half of Hell

With new assistant Stella Wu (left) at farewell party for former assistant Yan Yan (right), in 1990.   Photo: Catherine Sampson

Quickly now, what's the definition of a Chinese sex film? Answer: One without sex. China's first film touted as "adults-only" opened in Beijing to sellout crowds. That sunny afternoon in 1989, scalpers were out in force selling tickets to *Widow's Village* at triple the regular price. "I was curious," said Zhang Jun, a 24-year-old factory technician who took his girlfriend. Like him and everyone else, I went expecting sex scenes. After all, a lurid poster showed a man burying his face in a woman's breast.

It was packed inside Cinema No. 3501, a thousand-seat theater run by a military-uniform factory. In the first row of the balcony, three men even squeezed into two seats. Everyone hooted when the documentary short began. *Sterilization* showed actors dressed as peasants earnestly discussing birth control. Choice scenes include vasectomies, tubal ligations and a close-up of a testicle.

When *Widow's Village* finally started, the crowd fell silent. Ten minutes later, everyone booed as the lights suddenly went on. Technical difficulties, apparently. "My eyes are bulging," hooted a youth, breaking the tension as everyone awaited their first bit of Communist-era nudity.

Widow's Village depicted the customs of an ethnic tribe in Fujian Province that limited newlyweds to three conjugal nights per year – and forbade them from consummating the marriage in the first three years. But *Widow's Village* left the audience cold. There was just one chaste kiss and zero nudity.

"It's just an ordinary film," Zhang Jun, the factory technician, grumbled as he left the theater. "There's no need to make it for adults only. I feel like I've been fooled." An airline worker, who bought expensive tickets from a scalper, agreed. "It was a lousy film," he said disgustedly. "I'd have been better off staying home for a nap."

In a telephone interview from Canton, Wang Jin, the 47-year-old director, denied that the "adults-only" hype had been a publicity stunt. "A film doesn't have to have nudity in it to be for adults only. In this case, I don't think children can understand the film."

Beijing's first nude art show, also in 1989, definitely had nudity in it. When it closed after 18 record-breaking days, it left in its wake some very rich artists and some very angry models. The 120 Western-style oils ranged from abstracts to photograph-like details of nipples and, sometimes, pubic hair. Tickets at the state-run Beijing Art Gallery sold for ten times the normal price. Ten thousand art lovers a day poured in, twice the previous record set by an exhibit of 18th-century French landscapes.

Jammed cheek by jowl, art lovers at the front were pushed to within an inch of the paintings. Those at the back glimpsed only the tops of frames. "I couldn't study any of the paintings. I kept getting shoved past them," complained Li Shili, 26, an art student, who went twice before she got a decent look.

One male nude was modestly clothed in a wispy pair of pants, but the erotic poses still elicited clucks of disapproval. So did the outsized breasts. "They look like Chinese heads stuck on foreigners' bodies," muttered one young woman.

The models disapproved, too. Some of them stormed the show, weeping and demanding that at least five paintings be removed. They never dreamed, they said, that the paintings would actually be displayed. One model, who had kept her career a secret, said her husband found out when he saw her nude portrait on the television news. Several said their husbands were seeking divorce. The models, all regulars at the Central Academy of Fine Arts, went on strike. At least two hired lawyers and were suing for a share of the profits. Their privacy had been violated, they said, because they had never agreed to an exhibition.

On the last day, fans mobbed the artists for autographs. Ge Pengren, who organized the show, was running a fever from over-excitement. Half of the 28 other artists, all young teachers at the Central Academy of Fine Arts, booked off sick from exhaustion.

A decade later, I visited the new Shanghai Museum. In 1999, it was abuzz with visitors to its magnificent collections of porcelain and ancient bronzes. On a whim, I stopped by a special exhibit of female nudes by the Belgian painter Constant Permeke. To my surprise, the gallery was deserted except for a couple of middle-aged Chinese cadres shuffling past an olive-green oil painting of a nude. "I just don't understand this," one cadre muttered to the other, pointing to the painting. "I just don't understand this."

Female nudes were okay, but beauty contests remained taboo. A few attempts to revive them in the late 1980s petered out under a storm of criticism. Then pageants sneaked back under a different guise. One cold spring morning in 1989, I watched 36 high-heeled finalists vie for the title of "Miss P.R." That didn't stand for "Miss People's Republic." A soft drink company was hunting for a "Miss Public Relations."

In an unheated classroom of a Beijing high school, Yang Haiying adjusted her overcoat, batted her eyelashes and boldly stared the judges in the eye. "Some people call this a beauty contest, but it doesn't matter," she said, tossing her mane of glossy hair. "It spreads the name of Changlee soda."

The judges beamed.

Each contestant performed a one-woman skit of her own creation promoting Changlee products. Then each had to remove her coat and dance before the judges – without music. "I'm trembling," whispered Fang Fang, a 22-year-old accountant with a sleek chignon, in the gloomy hallway where the contestants were awaiting their turns. A 21-year-old in skin-tight pants flounced into the hallway and pouted, "I wasn't finished my dance and they kicked me out."

The contestants, aged 17 to 26, were all unmarried. Five judges, including a marketing professor and a retired English teacher, graded them on beauty, poise, etiquette, "public relations eloquence" and conversational English. Eight finalists would be notified by mail. The grand prize was a two-year contract, cash and a chance to go abroad on promotional tours. About 300 women in Beijing had handed over a day's pay to register. Organizers said many more would have, but were stymied by a minimum height requirement of 5 feet 6 inches. (Chinese women average slightly under 5 foot 2).

"*I'm* not even 5 foot 3," chortled Chen Ming, Changlee's chain-smoking sales manager. He watched approvingly as Zou Wei, a mini-skirted contestant, performed the role of a patriotic salesperson trying to wean an imaginary customer away from Coca-Cola. "Changlee is made in *China*," she said, smiling brilliantly into space. "Why drink a *foreign* soft drink?"

Other contestants extolled the virtues of Changlee soda, which came in cola, orange, lemon and lichee flavors. One blithely announced the soft drink cured cancer and "paralysis." Others promised Changlee would bring true love or prowess in sports. Some contestants were unintentionally funny. One woman played a vendor on a train. "Comrades, I have soft drinks to sell," she announced. When the imaginary passengers asked what was for sale, she said, "Just one brand."

Another contestant launched into a tortured debate over Changlee's steep price, playing both the saleswoman and the irate customer. "Are you trying to rob people?" the customer demanded. "With inflation, 2.50 yuan isn't so bad," she countered. The customer grudgingly consented to try Changlee, then spat it out in disgust. The saleswoman, the picture of contrition, proclaimed that Changlee products are made with the "latest scientific methods." She promised to have the sample tested in the lab. As the customer stumbled off, she called after him, "You forgot to pay for the drink."

The judges looked pained. "Public relations is a new thing in China," explained Chen.

After their skits, each woman removed her coat to perform her dance. Some launched into self-conscious disco steps. One contestant tangoed, holding her purse aloft as a partner. Still another, humming under her breath, performed a foot-stomping flamenco, then groaned as she leaned too far backward.

"At least we don't have to wear bathing suits," muttered Fang Fang, the 22-year-old accountant.

Some contestants flatly refused to go through with the silent dance segment. "I've always played basketball," said one mortified young woman. "I don't know how to disco." One of the judges gently suggested she do calisthenics instead. So she did.

Here comes the bride. And another. And another. And another. In all, seven brides for seven comrades. Purple House, Beijing's first and only wedding center, sold everything from the ring to the double bed. At this, its first group wedding, the blushing couples bowed to one another in unison. Then a master of ceremonies exhorted them to obey family planning laws.

"Just have a single darling," he said, as the room dissolved into giggles. Purple House managers laughed, too, all the way to the bank. Each couple paid several months wages for the ceremony, which included renting their finery, the artificial bouquets and the red-carpeted hall. Even the bridesmaids were strangers hired for the occasion.

"We're fully booked for the month," Yang Yi, a deputy manager, whispered happily. She was wearing high heels, a cream blouse, pearls and, of course, a wedding band. In an earlier career, she had been a Communist Party official in charge of ideology at the Beijing Textile Bureau. "Then, we were revolutionaries," she said, with an embarrassed laugh. Her own wedding, in 1969, was in the midst of the Cultural Revolution. Like all newlyweds, she had bowed not to her spouse, but to a portrait of Mao. As for wedding presents, "everybody got busts of Chairman Mao or his *Collected Works,*" she said. "We had a drink of water and a piece of candy."

I sympathized. When Norman and I married in Beijing in 1976, we treated guests to jasmine tea and peanuts. We certainly had no honeymoon, unless you count an outing to a coal mine. Yang Yi's honeymoon consisted of borrowing a vacant room at her factory. A month later, she and her husband returned to their separate dormitories. It wasn't until their 20th anniversary that her husband finally got around to buying her a wedding band.

Now puritanism was out and Purple House was in. The Beijing Textile Bureau had opened it on the theory that fancy weddings involved lots of cloth. From there, it branched into banquets and ceremonies. That day's couples all worked for the Mining Ministry, where the Communist Party Secretary thought it would be neat to have a group wedding and offered to subsidize expenses. Seven couples signed up. Their friends and family sat at little tables, sipping tea and munching candies.

Inside the dressing room, the seven brides, two in frilly pink and five in white, were having last-minute jitters. Everybody kept stepping on everyone else's veil. Someone applied the identical shade of lipstick on everybody, including the grooms.

"Brides on this side," ordered a Purple House staffer, handing out bouquets of fake flowers. "Who's first? Make sure you pair up with the right groom." The flower girls, neighborhood children hired for the occasion, did double duty, escorting one couple to the front, then racing back to fetch another pair. The seven couples took turns reading their vows. One groom held up a prompt card with large print on it for his nearsighted bride.

Purple House was founded in 1934 by a businessman named Yu Zhichang. A lavish wedding there soon became a status symbol among Beijing's elite. After 1949, it was converted into a state-owned photography studio. "We felt it only served the bourgeoisie," said Deputy Manager Yang, sounding very much like her old Communist Party self.

Purple House had just hired back the original owner, now 85, as a consultant, to avoid muffing some of the more arcane details. It wasn't just the rent-a-bridesmaid service or the lipstick for bridegrooms. When it came time to exchange rings, one bride instead gave her new husband a tie clip. Another bride gave her spouse an electric razor. "We're going on a honeymoon," she confided later. "I thought it would be more useful."

My husband has been impotent for years. I can't have the warmth and happiness a woman should have…. I want a divorce and my husband agrees. But the officials object, citing Marxist Leninist principles.
Signed: *"Hoping for Springtime."*

Dear Springtime: I've tried my best to search through the works of Marx and Lenin, but nowhere do I find any discussion of whether divorce is permissible if a husband and wife can't have a normal sex life. If you and your husband want a divorce, that's entirely your own business.
Signed: *Qiu Ming.*

Qiu Ming was China's Ann Landers. With her tongue sometimes firmly planted in her cheek, she breezily dispensed advice to the lovelorn in the *Chinese Women's Journal* (circulation: 500,000), the same newspaper that printed my Yellow Banana interview.

"I have had a love affair, a marriage, a baby and a divorce," she told readers in her debut column in 1988. "I have tasted all the bitterness … a divorcee can experience."

What she didn't tell them was that she had also attempted suicide five years earlier. A woman wrongfully accused her of sleeping with her husband, and smashed her across the face with a wooden stick, breaking her nose. Qiu (pronounced chew) protested, but everyone assumed she must have been guilty. After all, she was a divorcee. The woman later attacked her again, at a bus stop at rush hour. "She screamed, 'Look at this whore.'"

Humiliated, Qiu Ming threw herself in front of a passing car. The driver stopped in time, but it was a turning point in Qiu Ming's life. She regained her courage and tried to sue the woman. When she failed, she quit her job as an engineering technician and began studying law. Later, she became a legal-affairs reporter and a lawyer for women's groups. By the time I met her, she was 41 and a full-time editor and writer. Her weekly column, called "Qiu Ming's Mailbox," covered such previously taboo subjects as wife-beating, unrequited love, frigidity and extramarital affairs.

Everyone wrote to her: brides whose husbands didn't believe they had been virgins, peasant women forced into marriage, adolescents in the throes of their first heartbreak, disgruntled husbands, even prisoners. One convict complained that his wife wanted a divorce. "You should have thought about your wife at the time you embezzled," Qiu Ming snapped.

The daughter of China's Vice-Minister of Metallurgy, she grew up amid servants and privilege. During the Cultural Revolution, her college classmates were peasants and workers. She fell in love with one of them, a peasant, and married him. They had a daughter, but because of China's then-strict system of residence permits, he was unable to live with her in Beijing. Using her father's *guanxi*, or influence, Qiu Ming eventually got her husband transferred to the capital. A month later, he asked for a divorce.

"I found out then that he had always loved a woman in his village. But she wouldn't marry him until he got his urban residence permit," said Qiu Ming, who had soft hair and a girlish, heart-shaped face.

As a divorcee in the early 1980s, people treated her like a fallen woman. Some prim male colleagues avoided her. Others insisted on keeping the door ajar at meetings. Her Party Secretary was afraid to be alone with her, even though Qiu Ming herself was a Communist Party member. "I'm not going to throw myself in your arms," she once told him in exasperation.

Others assumed she was available. "Some men pawed me at the office or tried to stroke my face," she said. When she complained about one colleague groping her, the man's wife accused Qiu Ming of tempting him. The experience that finally transformed her from victim to advocate was the beating at the bus stop.

She got custody of their daughter, but received no child support. Qiu Ming wanted a man in her life. How she would have the time wasn't clear. Advice to the lovelorn was just one of her jobs. She also edited two magazines, was writing a non-fiction book about Chinese women and had written several novels, so far unpublished. In her spare time, she studied English, Japanese and German. She accomplished all this by rising at 2 a.m. most days, after just four hours sleep. She also skipped lunch, sipping only a soft drink or a bit of juice. The regimen was taking its toll – her hair was threaded with white. To sustain her energy, she practised *qi gong*, a yoga-like system of breathing exercises.

"Women have to be tough," she said. "I always say in my letters, let others know you have needs, too. Young women are always trying to make their boyfriends happy. They're not thinking enough about what makes themselves happy."

By 1999, Beijing had sex shops and sex-advice call-in shows.

Viagra was the most talked-about drug, though it had not yet been approved for sale. Called *Weige*, or "Mighty Brother," it would have been just the thing for "Hoping for Springtime." That is, if she hadn't already gotten a divorce.

In Chairman Mao's time, China's divorce rate was zero. For decades, even when both sides wanted out, the busybodies of the Street Committees would mediate endlessly between squabbling spouses. Then, in 1980, divorce became automatic if one side, such as Qiu Ming's husband, was "completely alienated." Years of economic reform reshaped traditional attitudes. Increased mobility and cellphones made it easier to cheat on mates. And rising expectations meant it was all right to dump a spouse who was too old or earned too little. Marital disputes soon topped the list of civil cases handled by the courts. By 1996, China's divorce rate hit 24 percent.

One great advantage of looking Chinese was getting to see the real China, unedited. As traditional life unraveled, I paid a visit to the Hujialou Neighborhood Matchmaking Center. All morning, I sat in the waiting room, observing the comings and goings of Beijing's lonely hearts.

"People are too relaxed about sex," sighed Tang Ni, 36, a divorced sales clerk with even white teeth and a cascade of permed hair. Her marriage had disintegrated two years earlier after her husband had had an affair. She had dropped by the matchmaking center several times to look for a new husband. "I've never found someone I liked," she sighed.

Unlike in the West, where divorce has been a fact of life for decades, some Chinese were bewildered by their new-found freedom. Tang Ni's first marriage, for instance, had been arranged by her parents. The second time around, Chinese like herself were unsure of the protocol of finding a new mate. Still, only the truly desperate risked public scorn to come to Hujialou.

A mere 5 percent of its introductions ended in marriage. About 3,000 hopefuls, mostly middle-aged women, had signed up since the service began three years earlier. They paid the equivalent of $1 as a registration fee and 15 cents for each blind date. All couples first met, during office hours, in the whitewashed waiting room.

The ambiance was not especially conducive to romance, although the matchmakers had tried. They strung up tinsel garlands and set out vases of plastic flowers. But they could do little about the distinct odor emanating from a nearby latrine. Most couples quickly fled to a park across the street.

I watched a middle-aged man, dressed in a Western-style suit and clean shirt, sitting on the couch. He must have been awaiting a blind date. Each time someone came in the room, he looked up expectantly. But after an hour, he realized he had been stood up. With a sigh, he flipped through a well-thumbed folder labeled, "Women, age 40–50." "They're all too short or too old," he muttered, tossing the folder aside.

He told me he'd been divorced four years earlier. He'd looked for a new wife on his own, without success. A year ago, he had come to the center, bringing a small black and white photograph of himself. He filled out a one-page form that asked, among other things, his age (47), his height (5 feet 8 inches) and his job (bank accountant).

Chinese matchmaking was pragmatic. The form allotted no space for favorite pastimes, but it did want to know if you were a member of the Chinese Communist Party. (It wasn't clear if this was a plus or a minus.) It also asked your monthly salary, the square footage of your state-assigned apartment and who else lived there. Your aging mother, for instance? "I lived with his parents *and* brothers *and* sisters," recalled Tang Ni. "We were always fighting."

A 30-year-old unemployed housemaid named Li Shuang came in to fill out a form. Before the ink was dry, she grabbed a file marked, "Men, age 30–40." Her three-month marriage had ended four years earlier, and she flipped through it as if she were perusing a mail-order catalogue.

"How about this one?" she said to me, as I peered, in Chinese busybody fashion, over her shoulder. She pointed to a photo of a handsome young soldier.

"He's taken," said one of the matronly matchmakers. The housemaid looked crestfallen. "What about this one?" she said, pointing to a description of a divorced intellectual. His résumé seemed ideal.

"His child is handicapped," the matchmaker said.

"Oh," said Li Shuang, putting the file down. She was looking for Mr. Right, not any old Mr. Wong. She herself was short, plump, poor and not very well educated. But on her application form, she had asked for someone without children who was "tall, good-looking and honest, a college graduate with a high income."

As I left, the man on the couch was still sitting there, looking despondent. A matchmaker urged him to set up another blind date. He shook his head. "I'm giving up. I'm numb," he said. That only goaded the matchmaker into action. "Look, this one's tall and her ex-husband has custody of the child," she said briskly. She showed him a photo of a woman in her early 40s. He looked at it. Then he paid another 15 cents.

Those who were hard up could always buy a wife. In Yunnan, a shifty-eyed man in Ruili's open-air market offered to sell a woman to my *Wall Street Journal* colleague. "Hey, beeg faat maan!" the man said in English, by way of introduction. As the very married father of two, Jim McGregor just shook his head.

"Jim," I hissed. "Ask *how much*."

The going price was $300. Before I could suppress the terrible thought, it flashed across my brain: $300 was a bargain. Juggling work, family and toilet-paper inventories, I'd always complained to Fat Paycheck that what *I* really needed was a wife.

"Me, too," he'd retort.

Perhaps I should have bought one for each of us.

It wasn't funny, of course. With the return of women to chattel status in China, it wasn't surprising that prostitution was also making a comeback. First mentioned in Chinese literature around 500 BC, the trade abruptly ended in 1949. The victorious Communists rounded up prostitutes, arranged marriages for them and sent recalcitrant ones to labor camps. Beijing later announced it had wiped out venereal disease. From the 1950s through the 1970s, students in medical school never saw a patient with syphilis.

"Women hold up half of heaven," Chairman Mao triumphantly declared, after the Communists took power.

Then heaven came crashing down. By 1990, Xiamen (pronounced SIA-mun) had opened a "detention center" for prostitutes.

It was a prison, really, where women who had been sentenced to one-year terms attended political classes and venereal-disease clinics. It didn't work. In 1992, the flesh trade was so blatant in Xiamen that to find a prostitute to interview, all I had to do was sit in my hotel cafe.

Wang Mei, 22, once sold vegetables in the Fujian countryside. Now she was selling her body in the big city. She was pretty, with fine skin and dramatic cheekbones. On her maiden plunge into the post-Mao world of Suzie Wong, she had painted her eyebrows, squeezed into black Spandex and hung around a coffee shop. In no time, two men picked her up. But she had no idea what she was doing. As she got into the taxi, she whispered to the prostitute with them, "How much do we get?"

Wang Mei discovered she could earn as much in one night as six months in her village. She turned her first trick in a single room with the second couple waiting on the other side of a makeshift curtain. "It didn't take long. After we finished, we waited outside while they did it," she said smoothing her pageboy with sturdy hands, the only hint of her peasant past.

Xiamen, once known as Amoy, had been a "treaty port," forced opened by British gunboats after the Opium War. In an echo of that past, Beijing opened Xiamen to foreign investment, designating it a "special economic zone." Businessmen flooded in, especially from nearby Taiwan. "It's okay to eat, drink and be merry. But some Taiwanese businessmen eat, drink, go whoring and gamble," Zhang Zongxu, Xiamen's deputy mayor, told me and Lena Sun of the *Washington Post*.

Outside Xiamen's ubiquitous seafood restaurants, prostitutes beckoned, hoping to lure passersby into private cubicles. Xiamen University students solicited customers at $10 a trick on the beach behind the campus. On the busy highway between Canton and Fuzhou, the provincial capital, low-rent brothels masqueraded as roadside cafes. Prostitutes, sunning themselves, waved to any vehicle that slowed down.

Lena and I hired a taxi and asked the driver to stop at a tiny barbershop at the base of a dirt hill. A leather-jacketed man emerged, still chewing a chicken leg, his face shiny with grease. "We have three girls here, age 19, 21 and 24," he said to the driver, ignoring Lena and me. "Two are plump, one is thin. They cost 65 yuan ($11) each."

We'd primed our driver to pose questions on our behalf. "Where are they?" he asked, helpfully.

The man jerked his head. "The police have been nosing around recently, so it's been tense. The girls work in a shed back there in the orchard."

Many prostitutes were peasants. In Xiamen, false rumors of jobs six months earlier had sparked an influx of 100,000 migrants. Wang Mei was one. She had left a family behind so poor they subsisted on rice and turnips. She agreed to talk to Lena and me when we promised to compensate her for her time. The hotel cafe was bad for an interview because the waitresses knew what she did for a living. So we brought her up to our room. She was still nervous, jumping every time the motor of the mini-bar fridge kicked in. "Everyone is scared to death of getting arrested," she said.

When she first arrived in Xiamen, she worked in a state factory canning pineapple. But the pay was low and the work was hard. "I was a temporary worker. Everybody ordered me around." Wang Mei quit after two months. Within days her money ran out. She remembered overhearing co-workers gossiping about a certain coffee shop and decided to earn some easy money.

"I sat down there with a group of women," she said. "I didn't dare speak. Then one of them called me upstairs to meet some men. We chatted and ate and went away in a taxi."

Wang Mei felt numb after her first customer. "Later I felt sick, because even though I was making a lot of money, I hated it." She didn't start using a condom until after she contracted venereal disease. She said she had since been cured.

About two-thirds of her customers were Taiwanese businessmen, who usually bought her dinner first. Perhaps because she still looked young and pretty, she could charge from 500 to 1,000 yuan for an evening, then 30 times the average daily urban income. She kept it all because she didn't have a pimp. Her dream was to open a hairdressing salon. "I can't rely on this," she said, gesturing to her body. "Looks last such a short time."

A month earlier, at Spring Festival, she had returned home for a brief visit. She brought only some peanut candy and honey so her family wouldn't get suspicious. "People think we have it easy, that we make lots of money, but my life is bitter, very bitter," she said. "I can't go home. I can't make any money at home."

My maternal instincts kicked in. I handed her a room-service menu and asked if she wanted something to eat. She picked one of the cheapest items, a plate of fried rice. Half an hour later, there was a knock on the door. It was the cafe's waitress. She gaped at Wang Mei, then at Lena and me, then back at Wang Mei.

I had made a serious mistake. Wang Mei left immediately. On her way out, I belatedly noticed the surveillance cameras in the hallway. How could we have been so stupid? Through contacts, Lena and I learned that Wang Mei was later picked up by the police and charged with talking to foreign journalists.

When Beijing made Hainan Island into China's biggest special economic zone, it didn't expect the fastest-growing industry there to be sex. But the bustling tropical island soon became the prostitution capital of China. Some cities have tourist shops, displaying stands of postcards. Haikou, the provincial capital, displayed posters of diseased genitals. In stomach-churning color, storefront VD clinics put up photographs showing what would happen if you didn't avail yourself of their services.

"We have lots of venereal disease here," said Huang Mingfu, 30, resplendent in a white cloak, Adidas running shoes and a fake Rolex. In Haikou, a city with an official population of 310,000 and a transient population at least half that, he had no shortage of customers. A former employee of the municipal medical association, he called himself a doctor and charged 300 yuan ($37) for a single injection that he claimed would cure gonorrhea. Unlike a public hospital, which might send a report to the patient's place of work, he promised confidentiality.

I had flown to Hainan Island with Yan Yan, the wife of Julian Schuman. At night, we watched a wan young woman solicit a man under a streetlight. "Can't you pay more?" we overheard her say. "My life is very bitter."

"I won't pay you more than 50 yuan ($6)," he replied.

After more bargaining, the two struck a deal and walked, a yard apart, to a seedy hotel across the street.

The sex trade was everywhere. At the entrance to a neon-lit massage parlor, a uniformed policeman, his cap askew, sat sprawled on a bench. When I dropped by, he was chatting with one of the masseuses, a young woman in a sweater and black stretch pants. Inside were six private rooms, aglow with pink fluorescent lights. A masseuse lay asleep on one of the beds. When I started asking questions, the policeman summoned the manager, who couldn't explain to me why a man would squander a week's pay for an hour in the sauna, which more or less replicated the weather outside anyway. Behind him, the cop snickered at my dumb questions.

Government documents said that masseuses earned in a day what they'd earn in a factory in a month. In one celebrated case, a graduate of Huanan University earned 120,000 yuan ($15,000) in four months. Then she emigrated to Australia.

"Buy a ticket!" urged a young man, sitting under a beach umbrella on the sidewalk. We did. Inside a darkened shack, we joined about 50 others, mostly men, on rough plank benches to watch a soft-porn video called *Lin Liguo's Beauty Contest*. It showed uniformed PLA officers procuring virgins for the sex-crazed son of Lin Biao, Mao's second-in-command. I remembered the chaste "adult-only" movie I'd recently seen in Beijing and laughed. Yan Yan's uncle, who lived in Haikou, told us hard-porn movies were also available, but tickets weren't sold openly.

In Haikou, we found it impossible to walk down the main street at night without being propositioned. Yan Yan, who loved adventure and misadventure, suggested offering herself as bait. That's how we discovered the pickup protocol and prices. If a man was interested, he'd brush you with his shoulder as he passed. If you smiled, he'd start to negotiate. The going rate was 50 to 150 yuan ($6 to $18). Women from Beijing and Shanghai commanded more, peasants less.

Within ten minutes, my news assistant had snagged several customers, escaping each time by raising her price. One thin man in a suit, with alcohol on his breath, was a graduate of the Beijing

Institute of Architecture. His wife and children remained in Beijing, he said, while he had come to Hainan to sell real estate.

I got into the act myself. Brush. Smile. Hello. A man with glasses from Canton proposed going to a nearby hotel. When I began asking too many questions, he realized something was amiss and fled. I decided Yan Yan was better at research.

At a brightly lit sidewalk cafe, four middle-aged men tried to pick up a prostitute. Yan Yan began chatting them up. All were cadres or Communist Party members from Shenzhen, China's most successful special economic zone, on the border with Hong Kong. They frankly admitted enjoying the flourishing prostitution scene in Haikou. "That's the way the whole society is," said one. "Why shouldn't we enjoy it too? We also have feelings and needs." Then they joined two prostitutes at a nearby table.

In my windbreaker, running shoes and glasses, not to mention my backpack, I don't think I looked much like a prostitute. No matter. When I asked for two single rooms at Haikou's Tower Hotel, seven clerks at the front desk stared. Most hotels would be thrilled to rent two rooms instead of one. This one wasn't.

"Single women must share a room," a desk clerk declared. "It's the rule of the Public Security Bureau."

With my usual shyness, I produced my passport, called for the manager and demanded to see the police regulation in writing. After a delay and a huddled discussion, the clerks reluctantly admitted that there was no such rule – and gave us two rooms.

When I saw them, I regretted being so pushy. They were mosquito-infested and mildewed. And Yan Yan's uncle warned us to expect the worst after the front-desk incident. The police would certainly conduct a bed check in the middle of the night, he said, common treatment for Chinese women staying alone in hotels. (Experienced prostitutes avoided this problem by having their pimps register on their behalf.)

So we left and checked back into the Haikou International Financial Center, Hainan's fanciest hotel. We'd stayed there earlier, but left because our phones wouldn't stop ringing. Yan Yan's uncle had already explained to us that when the caller hung up without a word, it was probably a prostitute soliciting business. But when the caller stayed on the line, it was probably a john looking for a prostitute.

I told Yan Yan that this time we might as well get a story out of it. The next time the phone rang, she answered. "Is Miss Li there?" the caller asked. Yan Yan purred, "No, Miss Li isn't in this room. Why?"

The man said he was in room 1708. Would Yan Yan like to *wanr yi wanr* (fool around)? How about a cup of tea in his room?

"Call me in a little while," said Yan Yan, sound a bit like a Chinese Mae West. "I'm busy with a guest right now."

When she hung up, I called the front desk. A moment later, Assistant Manager Wang Wen was at the door. I gave him my business card, and complained about the johns, the prostitutes and the most recent phone call.

"What can we do?" he shrugged. "How do we know they're prostitutes? They don't have a mark on their forehead. We don't have any proof to grab them." As for the phone call, he added, it had to be a misunderstanding. He stood up to leave.

The phone rang on cue. It was the man in room 1708. Yan Yan enthusiastically agreed to go up. The manager turned pale. I instructed my news assistant to stand in the hallway to negotiate a price. Under no circumstances was she to go into his room. Assistant Manager Wang seconded that. Then we took the elevator up together.

Yan Yan, wearing a powder-blue denim mini, rapped on the door. The manager and I hid in a corner next to the stairwell. I heard her chatting merrily with the man for a few moments. Then I heard her walk in. The door closed. My heart sank. Assistant Manager Wang fumbled for his master key. Just as he was about to pound on the door, Yan Yan stepped calmly out, and motioned us inside.

The man was sitting on an unmade bed. He was slim, about 30, with oiled hair. He had already taken off his shoes, and looked slightly foolish in a tie, shirt, pants and white socks. He stared in terror at us as Yan Yan repeated their conversation.

"Let's have a cup of tea. Then let's have fun," the man had said.

"How much will you pay?" Yan Yan countered.

"How much do you want?"

Yan Yan picked a number based on her earlier research. They bargained a bit more. Then she called us in.

The man was now sweating profusely. He looked longingly at the pack of cigarettes on his bedside table, but didn't make a move. He weakly denied the conversation. When I pulled out my notebook, he looked respectfully at me, and I realized he thought I was a plainclothes police officer. Well, why not? As he answered my questions with utter docility, I thought: *I could get used to this.*

His name was Wen Bo, and he was a businessman from Shenzhen. He was in Hainan to hold talks with customs officials, he said. Assistant Manager Wang told Wen Bo he would have to check out the next day. "You know you can't do this in our hotel," he said, sternly. "As a guest, you shouldn't do this."

We left Wen Bo still sitting on his bed, holding his head. Outside in the hall, Manager Wang shrugged again, "We have no proof. We can't do anything."

I shrugged, too. Back in my room, I turned off the ringer on my phone.

A decade later, I was shocked to see that storefront brothels had reached Beijing. I shouldn't have been. Official statistics put the cases of sexually transmitted diseases in 1997 at close to half a million, nearly a hundredfold increase from 1985. And the 1997 figure was probably low – private clinics rarely reported their cases.

Authorities had always kept the tightest lid on the capital, whether it be panhandling or political dissent. So it spoke volumes about the government's loss of control when, on my trip back in 1999, a Chinese friend took me to Hooker Alley in Beijing, in the north end of the city. If blatant prostitution was right here, under the nose of the Central Committee, then it was everywhere.

Hooker Alley – Robin Benger's nickname for it – was a street of stalls selling cheap clothing, plumbing fixtures and snack foods. But every few shops, there was a glass-fronted hairdressing salon. Heavily made-up young women sat facing outward, morning, noon and night. It reminded me of Amsterdam's red-light district, where prostitutes sat, like wares, behind plate-glass windows.

I went into several "salons" to chat and look around. They were identical: bleak rooms with a grimy sink in the corner and a curtained-off bed at the back for massages, or more. My Chinese friend, who lived in the neighborhood, told me the "salons" were run by pimps. The prostitutes usually took clients to nearby apartments, charging 200 yuan to 400 yuan ($25 to $50) a trick.

"Can I get my hair done?" I asked, walking inside one.

An elderly man leaped up from the sofa as if I had cattle-prodded him, and rushed out. The three women inside looked startled, too, but smiled.

"We can wash your hair, but the, ah, stylist is, ah, away today," said one.

They all looked at me as if I were the dumbest creature on earth. But when I didn't leave, they hospitably patted an empty stool beside them. They were wearing cheap coats and platform shoes, and appeared to be in their early 20s. They all had bright red lipstick and penciled, plucked brows. As we sat together, warming our hands over a small coal stove, I told them I was from Canada. They told me they were from Jiangxi Province, which I knew was one of the poorest regions in south China.

I asked how they liked Beijing. They giggled. Then I dropped all pretense. I told them I knew what they did for a living and asked if they were protecting themselves against AIDS. "Do you use condoms?" I asked.

They giggled some more. "How should I say ..." said one young woman. "It's not convenient to talk about that. We can only talk about things on the surface."

Just then, their pimp appeared. He didn't look very friendly. I mumbled an excuse, and beat a hasty retreat.

16

Love Thyself

Deng Pufang, the disabled eldest son of China's late leader, Deng Xiaoping, at a 1989 press conference. After the Tiananmen Massacre, Deng Pufang rarely made public appearances. Photo: Jan Wong

Wang Dan was right. The student activist believed that you needed money to have democracy. At the end of the millennium, it was not a dissident-led revolution, but economic *evolution* that posed the biggest threat to the government. Still, Beijing remained hypersensitive about dissent. As a result of news blackouts many Chinese had never heard of Wang Dan. And ten years after the massacre, some university students were still asking if the Western media had made it all up.

"I have always been curious about the so-called 'Tiananmen Square Affair' ... and wanted to find out the truth," one Chinese student e-mailed a friend in the West in 1999. All he knew was what he had been told: The army had exercised "great restraint" before suppressing the "rioters."

You could see that as a victory for Big Brother. I didn't. The fact that he was asking questions about Tiananmen and e-mailing them around the world was evidence of Beijing's loss of control. Freedom of information was already shaking the very foundations of the Chinese Communist Party.

Half of China's population was now under 25. They didn't see their future tied up with the Chinese Communist Party. Indeed, in 1999 I heard that Beijing University, the most desirable school in China, was so desperate to recruit anyone still willing to major in Party history that it had been forced to set rock-bottom entrance requirements.

There were now 650 million Chinese born after the Cultural Revolution. They had no memory of Chairman Mao, ration coupons or collectivism. And they got scant help from their disillusioned parents, who had squandered their own youth on a Maoist dream. That had only made them doubly determined to give their one and onlies everything they never had. Parents of the Lost Generation indulging kids of the Me Generation – now, that was a toxic combination.

Without an ideology to anchor the country, callousness reigned supreme. A friend of mine named Fang Fang was cycling to work in Chengdu one morning when she saw a crowd gawking at a hit-and-run accident. Nobody was helping the victim. As Fang Fang pressed closer, she saw that it was her own sister-in-law. "If I hadn't taken her to the hospital, she would have died."

For me, the decline of civility crystallized in 1991. All morning long, the tiny corpse lay on the frozen dirt on the edge of a busy Beijing street. It was a baby boy. He was naked except for a strip of cloth around his waist, the traditional dressing for an unhealed umbilical cord. His tiny fists were clenched and his eyes shut, as if to ward off the winds of that bitter December day. His face and chubby arms were red and chapped, his chest blue-white.

Cyclists and passersby paused for a look. Some murmured in horror. More than one was surprised he was a boy, not a despised girl. At the bus stop, a few people made outlandish jokes, perhaps to mask their discomfort. At noon, schoolchildren on their way home for lunch stared at the baby lying on the ground, without even a blanket.

Had no one bothered to call the police? Or had the police simply not bothered to respond? It took a Canadian to prod authorities into action. My friend, Patricia Alexander, passed by in a taxi in the late morning, and refused to leave until something was done. Even then, it was two more hours before police actually removed the body.

"It was so life-like. I was shocked," she said. Pat, who speaks Chinese, ran to the traffic policeman at the corner. "It's not my responsibility," he told her. When she persisted, he called the district station.

The police eventually arrived, but focused on crowd control. Two hours after Pat first tried to get help, the tiny corpse was still there. When Pat wouldn't leave, someone called the special police in charge of foreigners. They arrived in ten minutes. A live Canadian woman posed more of a problem than a dead Chinese baby.

"The most important thing seemed to be to want me to go," said Pat, who finally called me in tears to see if I could help. I arrived just after a third group of police officers, who wrapped the tiny corpse in a man's jacket and took it away.

The incident reminded me of the Kitty Genovese murder in New York City. Some say that, too, marked the decline of civility in a great city. In 1964, 38 law-abiding citizens watched a killer stalk and stab a young woman in three separate attacks. For half an hour, dozens heard her screams, but not one went to her aid or phoned the police. One witness called after she was dead.

The Chinese weren't always so callous, either. But civility disappeared after the Cultural Revolution, the Tiananmen Massacre and a lifetime of political brainwashing. An autopsy revealed the baby had died of exposure. He had been alive and healthy when someone abandoned him on the road in the middle of the night.

The husky man with the bristling brush cut settled into his wheelchair, stared at the assembled media and launched into a diatribe. "The disabled in China have a bitter life. Almost all live in poverty. Many have no jobs. Handicapped children can't go to school." With that, the eldest son of Deng Xiaoping launched a magazine for the disabled at a Beijing news conference.

When he was 24, Deng Pufang had jumped out a window to escape his Red Guard persecutors during the Cultural Revolution. Now he was paralyzed from the waist down. That was a personal tragedy, but a stroke of luck for every disabled person in China. In a society that traditionally despised disability, Deng Pufang used his power and privilege to improve the plight of the handicapped. Chinese talked about the disabled the way we did in the West several generations ago: "idiots," "cripples," "morons" and "imbeciles."

But no one dared talk like that about the eldest son of China's paramount leader.

China had an estimated 60 million mentally or physically disabled people. Only one in four had jobs, according to Deng Pufang. The government had tried fining organizations that refused to hire disabled people. But with so many state enterprises laying off workers, many companies preferred to pay the fine. Beijing's top ten universities even applied for a blanket exemption. They hosted so many foreign visitors, they explained, that they had to consider their image.

"The right to work is a basic human right of the handicapped," declared Deng Pufang, who once eked out a living during the Cultural Revolution weaving wire baskets. At the time he was injured, he was denied proper medical treatment. But in 1979, after his father regained power, he went to Ottawa for an operation to implant three stainless-steel plates in his broken spine. Now, in grand nepotistic tradition, he had become chairman of the China Disabled Persons Association.

"My life, quite frankly, is much easier than that of most handicapped people," he said, puffing his ninth cigarette in two hours. At 45, he had a beautiful, doting wife and was rumored to be carried around at home on the back of a male nurse. At the press conference, I watched several sweating, red-faced aides hoist him in his wheelchair, lit cigarette and all, up a flight of stairs to get him into the meeting room.

Little in China was wheelchair accessible. That included washrooms, streets, buses, restaurants, stores, schools, offices, train stations, airports, apartments and factories. Remember how impressed Wang Dan had been by sidewalk curb cuts in New York? To him, they symbolized the West's respect for human rights.

Deng Pufang must have been lobbying hard. In 1999, I was pleasantly surprised when I visited the new Shanghai Museum. There, beside the main entrance, was the first handicapped ramp I'd ever seen in China. (What also amazed me were the museum's toilets, spotlessly clean, with soap dispensers and hand dryers. The stalls even had rolls of soft white Kimberly-Clark stuff. Alister and Robin couldn't understand why I came out of the ladies room babbling about toilet paper.)

With no social services, parents struggled to care for their disabled children. Many parents simply locked them up at home while they went to work. China had only 100 special schools for four million handicapped children in the cities. In the countryside, another 3.8 million disabled children received no education at all.

When I attended Beijing University in the 1970s, there wasn't a single disabled person on campus. I later found out why. Handicapped people were explicitly barred from higher education. Under Deng Pufang's influence, some disabled were finally allowed to attend university, provided – and this is true – they had the same disability as his, namely lower-body paralysis. The blind, for instance, were not admitted. They considered themselves lucky to be trained as masseurs.

Yang Bingyuan once won an all-expenses-paid trip to Sichuan's scenic Mount Emei. A model worker? A lottery winner? Guess again. Yang Bingyuan gave blood – once – and only under duress.

Chinese considered giving blood a step short of dying. Indeed, the criteria for involuntary "donors" was pretty much what you'd look for when selecting cannon fodder in the West. "I was chosen by my leaders because I'm young, unmarried and have no elderly parents to care for in Beijing," said Yang, a 23-year-old announcer at Radio Beijing. "Everyone is reluctant to give blood, so they had to give us a reward."

He won the ten-day junket after giving the standard 200 milliliters, compared to the 450 milliliters donors give in Canada and the United States. In addition, his workplace gave him a week to recuperate and several hundred yuan in cash. Would he give blood again? He shook his head. "It was my first time, and my last."

Decades of cradle-to-grave collectivism had left everyone convinced it was better to receive than to give. Political campaigns had obliterated religious beliefs. And a decade of Cultural Revolution cruelty, followed by two decades of me-first capitalism, had wiped out the last vestiges of empathy.

China was becoming a selfish society. It had no soup kitchens or homeless shelters, no Salvation Army-style charities. When the Yangtze River overflowed its banks, leaving thousands homeless, so few Chinese were willing to donate anything that authorities simply docked their pay. (Some were worried about corruption, of course, and feared the goods would never reach the victims.)

But nothing illustrated the new callousness more starkly than the huge resistance to donating blood. In 1984, when China began its first regular blood drives, only 19 people gave blood in Beijing, then a city of ten million. And most of the 19 donors were foreigners.

So authorities tackled the problem with their usual finesse. They fobbed the main burden off on the peasants. Then they bribed, browbeat and fined everyone else. Beijing and Shanghai passed laws making "donations" mandatory for all adults between 18 and 50. And each workplace was issued a quota of 3 donors per 100 staff. Any place failing to meet it had to pay five times the normal fee for employee transfusions.

Workplaces ran lotteries, with the winners, I mean, losers, "donating" blood. Managers threatened demotions. Some even resorted to hiring peasant stand-ins. Still others ordered temporary workers to give blood on behalf of the entire office, on pain of dismissal.

At the same time, factories and offices offered junkets to seaside resorts, several months extra pay and up to a month's paid vacation. Cash-strapped companies sometimes forced the rest of the staff to help. At one Beijing high school, the teachers pooled their money as bonuses for their unlucky colleagues.

Most Chinese didn't realize the human body replenishes lost blood within a week or two. Some officials feared all the prizes would only reinforce traditional taboos. The lavish rewards helped convince many Chinese that blood was irreplaceable. "And what happens if next year prices go up? People will demand more and more money," said Xing Lixiang, deputy director of the Beijing Blood Donating Committee. "People are afraid to give blood. Hardly anybody comes voluntarily."

No one volunteered at a military design institute, so everyone drew lots. The unlucky winners all begged off, citing high blood pressure, low blood pressure and heart conditions. So it became Wang Tao's turn. The 25-year-old military technician feared he'd lose out on promotions if he refused. So he gave blood, and in return, got ten weeks pay and a week's vacation. The blood station also fed him five hardboiled eggs on the spot.

In the West, blood donors might get juice and cookies. In China, giving blood was so little understood that everyone stuffed donors with food. A car packed with delicacies trailed Nanny Ma's 19-year-old son to the blood center so he could gorge right afterward. Later, his manager treated him and five other donors to a banquet. That night, the manager visited him at home, bearing a huge basket of cellophane-wrapped fruit.

In Canada, about 4 percent of the population donates blood without payment. Many give a hundred times or more in a lifetime. But in China, voluntary donors accounted for less than 0.2 percent of the population, according to the Chinese Red Cross. Repeat donors were so rare that anyone who gave 14 times got a grip-and-grin photo with a member of the ruling Politburo. (That was invaluable, you will recall in the case of Plum Blossom Lin, as collateral for bank loans.)

The reluctance to donate blood can be partly traced to the Chinese tradition of filial piety. You were supposed to keep your body intact out of respect for the ancestors. Confucius even said, "Blood is a gift from your parents and is not to be lost." But Hong Kong showed that cultural taboos could be overcome. Fifteen years ago, like China, it had a donor rate of only 0.2 percent. But educational campaigns pushed the donor rate up to 3 percent, said Dr. Susan Leong, chief of the Blood Transfusion Service of the Hong Kong Red Cross.

Asked why Chinese on the mainland seem to lack the charitable urge, Xing, the blood-donor official, paused a long moment. "How should I answer this? Socialism means we should have deeper feelings for each other, but Chinese are rather …" She searched for the right word. "Pragmatic."

Even with press-ganged state employees, cities were meeting only 45 percent of their needs. So authorities took advantage of the growing urban–rural gap, and bled the peasants dry. They paid them a fraction of the going rate and extracted twice as much blood per donor. Many state organizations, including the Chinese Foreign Ministry, hired peasants as stand-ins to fulfill their own quotas. Local gangsters, known as "snakeheads," recruited the rural donors in return for a 20 percent kickback.

By the mid-1990s, peasants accounted for 55 percent of China's urban blood supply. At Beijing's Chongwen Blood Station, I found dozens of peasants crowded into a smoke-filled waiting room. "A snakehead told me to come," said Wu Lihua. She and about 80 others had left their village the night before, cramming onto a rickety white bus. When the blood station opened at 7 a.m., they were the first ones through the door.

The snakehead, Yan Zhenxun, was a fast-talking 33-year-old in a Western suit and a grimy white shirt. Ten times a year, he made the 16-hour round trip from Xizhong County. The going rate for 400 milliliters was 120 yuan. That was a huge amount for his clients, who averaged 400 yuan a year working the fields back home.

But at that price, the peasants couldn't afford a transfusion themselves. "They come voluntarily. It's good money," said Snakehead Yan, who had traveled there with several tough-looking bodyguards. All morning, he helped process the busload of peasants through the chest X-rays and simple interviews. The peasant donors never saw who took their blood. They rolled up the sleeves of their padded jackets and thrust their right arms through a hole in a frosted window. Still clutching their bare arms, they ran outside to fight over the 47 seats in the bus. Latecomers had to squat on the trash-strewn floor for the eight-hour ride home. No one offered them a boiled egg.

China stopped importing foreign blood in the early 1990s for fear of AIDS, said Xing, the blood-donor official. But it took years for China to start screening its own blood for HIV, the virus that causes AIDS. The first cities, Beijing and Shanghai, didn't start until the mid-1990s. In late 1998, the government finally banned the sale of blood to stop the spread of AIDS. By then it was estimated that blood transfusions were responsible for 17 percent of AIDS cases in China. Hepatitis B and C had also infected millions through transfusions.

Given how hard-hearted everyone was about blood donations, did Xing hold out much hope for China? And what had happened on June 4, 1989, when the Chinese army shot its way into

Tiananmen Square? She glanced around nervously. "We went out on the street that night and told people we needed blood," she said quietly. "Everybody gave."

As a Montreal Maoist myself, I knew how traumatic it was to break with an ideology. Long after, the thought patterns lingered. You'd catch yourself still thinking that left was morally superior to right, that communism was better than fascism. Elia Kazan, the Oscar-winning film director and one-time Communist, explained why he named names during the McCarthy era. "It's hard for anybody who wasn't a Communist to understand how strong a hold those beliefs had on you. Your emotional commitment keeps overriding everything your intellect and common sense tell you. It's akin to a kind of religious faith."

It was not surprising, then, that religion and superstition made a vigorous comeback in the moral vacuum left by Maoism. Many Chinese began attending church. Others burned incense at Buddhist temples. Millions more turned to *qi gong* (chee goong), derided as witchcraft during the Cultural Revolution. "There's a lot of pressure in our society," said Lin Zhongpeng, an official of the Chinese Qi Gong Society. "This helps us relieve stress."

In its hard version, *qi gong* was a kind of brick-smashing kung fu. In its soft version, it was a traditional breathing exercise like yoga, practised by 50 million Chinese. But at the end of the millennium, a fantastic form of *qi gong* resurfaced that traced its roots to the eighth century BC. Claiming supernatural powers, its practitioners boasted of seeing through walls, hearing conversations thousands of kilometers away, even bending laser beams. They also claimed to emit *qi* (or ch'i: "breath"), vital energy or healing vapors, to treat cancer, AIDS and mental illness. For a fee, of course.

As a former banking reporter, I always followed the money. One famous *qi gong* master charged patients about four days pay for a two-second diagnosis, no questions asked. "I used to repair machines. Now I repair people. It's much more profitable," Zhao Xuezhong, 50, told me. The former repairman in a Beijing electrical-wire factory was rumored to have "treated" some of China's top leaders. In addition to X-ray vision, he also claimed long-distance curing. That is, he could cure an ailing person in Hong Kong or Buenos Aires or Rome, sight unseen, while sitting in Beijing. "If this was the Cultural Revolution, I'd be shot. But this is the new open policy," said Repairman Zhao, who declined to disclose his income.

Fearing a backlash, savvy *qi gong* masters sometimes treated patients for free. I watched a Buddhist monk named Shi Benzhen stop on a street corner to help out a Chinese woman. The monk, who was dressed in flowing gray and saffron silk, hung a necklace of wooden beads around the woman's neck. Then he placed his hands on her belly and back. Bowing his shaved head and furrowing his bushy brows, he said, "If you believe me, I can cure you. If you doubt me, I cannot." After a few minutes, the woman exclaimed that the pain on her right side had disappeared. The monk took no money, uttered a Buddhist blessing and jumped into his chauffeured white sedan.

In 1999, authorities arrested a *qi gong* healer after 146 of his patients died. Helped by glowing stories in the Chinese media, Hu Wanlin had set up licensed hospitals in Shaanxi and Henan provinces. The stories had neglected to mention that Hu had previously served time for manslaughter.

Astonishingly, Chinese authorities endorsed *qi gong*. The government-controlled press routinely published accounts of the magical feats of its master practitioners. Municipal health agencies issued certificates allowing them to treat patients. And the Education Ministry allowed China's first *qi gong* college to open right across the road from Beijing University.

Even the PLA rented out its auditorium at the Beijing Military Hospital for a *qi gong* "healing" session. Intrigued, I went one muggy August morning for a look. I found Liu Guohong, a heap of waxen skin and bones, lying in the front row. He could not speak. His older sister, a sales clerk with a single long braid, told me he had a tumor near his olfactory nerve. "We came here to see if he could be cured."

Suddenly, a Chinese version of Michael Jackson's *Beat It* filled the stadium. A *qi gong* master strode onto the stage. "You must have faith," said Chen Linfeng. "I cannot cure you unless you have faith."

More than a thousand people had paid about two days' pay for a ticket, hoping for some curative vapors from this former electrician. At 27, Master Chen resembled a young Elvis Presley, with greased-back pompadour and ingratiating smile. He ordered them to close their eyes and clasp their hands, prayer-like. Then he taught them some "magic incantations."

"I feel like I'm in church," a middle-aged woman whispered beside me. I agreed. We had the faith healer. All we lacked was the tent and the snake oil. After half an hour of magic incantations, Master Chen announced he would begin emitting his *qi* – or healing vapors. He sat on stage, jerking his arms, moaning eerily into a microphone. A few people began to sway and shake. Others waved their arms above their heads.

At mid-afternoon, Master Chen took a break so his aides could flog cassette tapes of his *qi gong* workout routine. He gave me his business card, which listed 11 titles, when I grabbed him for a quick interview. He said he kept only the profits from his tapes. The 8,000 yuan from ticket sales, he added, went for auditorium rent. That seemed a tad high, so I checked with an army-hospital spokesman. The rent, he said, was 250 yuan.

I backed off to let Master Chen's fans have a chance to meet him. They mobbed him as if he were a rock star, screaming his name and proffering refreshments. A peasant woman carrying a spindly child struggled to get his attention. At first, he ignored her desperate pleas. But as she tugged at his sleeve, he finally listened. She told him that her 11-year-old daughter had been disabled since birth, when her oxygen had been accidentally cut off. "What should I do?" she beseeched.

He glared at her and snapped, "Practice *qi gong*."

I approached the bewildered woman, who told me her name was Jiang Youmei. She and her daughter had journeyed 400 miles from Yantai, a fishing port in Shandong Province, to see Master Chen. By then, he had already returned to the stage, where he resumed his shaking and moaning. We went back to our seats.

At the end of seven hours of this, an overweight woman mounted the stage. She told the audience she had been lame for years, "I'm cured," she screamed, tossing aside her crutch. Then the sister of the man I first saw lying in the front row rushed forward. In a thick rural accent, she shouted, "He's all better. He ate 25 dumplings during the lunch break." To thunderous applause, her brother, still looking waxen, walked slowly about the stage.

Like acupuncture, *qi gong* held that illness resulted when invisible channels in the body were clogged. But while acupuncture was a well-established medical treatment, the revival of *qi gong* split China's scientific community down the middle. Many top scientists endorsed it. Others condemned its practitioners as charlatans.

One science newspaper invited a team of American experts on the paranormal to examine a group of *qi gong* masters. The masters, who claimed magical healing powers, failed every test. But *qi gong* got an unexpected boost from Qian Xueshen, an eminent rocket expert and chairman of the Chinese Scientists Association. Qian opined that *qi gong* was a "sophisticated science."

Driver Jia, who preceded Driver Liu at the *Globe*, was both a believer and a Party member. He tipped me off about a *qi gong* rally at the Beijing Workers Sports Stadium. He was going with his wife, and let me tag along. The three of us went one hot summer night, and found the 13,000-seat stadium nearly full. Smack in the center, where the ringmaster of a circus might stand, a *qi gong* master was slowly waving his arms. As his *qi*, or healing vapors, flew about the stadium, a woman in a white dress started wailing uncontrollably. Another shrieked, then swooned. A young man beat his chest and moaned. I felt nothing. But all around me, people twitched and shook. Others cried. Some laughed hysterically. An old man near me talked in tongues, then screamed that he was cured. Even Driver Jia began rocking violently back and forth.

"Stop it," his wife hissed. "Everybody's looking at you."

"I can't help it," he said.

In April, 1999, more than 10,000 adherents of a *qi gong* sect magically materialized outside the headquarters of the Chinese leadership, then disappeared. They assembled without warning and sat peacefully on the sidewalk, meditating for an entire day. It was the largest public demonstration in Beijing since the 1989 Tiananmen protests.

Called Falun Gong, or Buddhist Law, the group claimed to have more than 100 million followers. That seemed unlikely. But the Chinese government still put the membership of Buddhist Law at a staggering 20 to 70 million. The sect was led by a 48-year-old martial-arts master called Li Hongzhi who, citing political pressure, moved to New York in 1998.

The demonstration was sparked by a magazine article that said the Buddhist Law group spread lies and could cause mental illness. The author was He Zuoxiu, a physicist who helped develop China's nuclear weapons, and who has long crusaded against superstition. The mass protest caught the Chinese leadership off guard. After two days of silence, the official media sternly warned the *qi gong* sect against further actions that "jeopardize social stability."

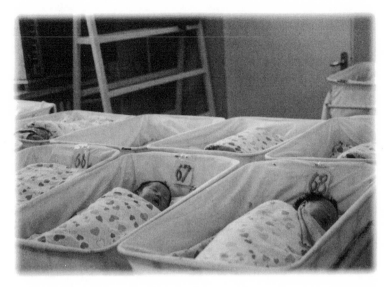

17

China's Little Emperors

Candle-wrapped babies in maternity ward at Haidian Hospital in Beijing.
Photo: Jan Wong

Instead of administering shock treatments to gays, China should have praised them as model citizens. After all, the country's biggest problem was overpopulation. At Beijing's Sun Altar Park, parents lined up with their one and only toddler for the one and only swing. Housing, transportation and schools, not to mention swings, were all overcrowded. Even far off the beaten track, in rural China, it was impossible to find a lonely spot when nature called. Always, always, there would be people around. For someone coming from one of the world's emptiest countries, it was unnerving.

On the other hand, China was a reporter's page-one dream. No matter what the topic – pollution, executions or cellphones – everything was always "the worst," or "the biggest" or "the greatest." But the story where numbers mattered most was population.

The one-child rule, enforced since 1979, had reconciled many urban Chinese to having only one. But in the 1990s, a child was born every 1.5 seconds in rural China, and every third one of these was born to parents who already had a child, if not two or three. "There's a big gap between our policy and reality," admitted Shen Guoxiang, a family-planning official at the National Population Reporting Center in Beijing. "Some cadres themselves don't agree with the birth-control policy. We also have places where no one is watching."

One of those places was Beijing. Chen Ping was a guerrilla mom. For her third pregnancy, she left the capital, went into hiding, then gave birth in another province. Back in Beijing, she and her husband, a button salesman, lived openly with their new baby boy and their six-year-old daughter. The middle child, an unwanted girl, had already been given away at birth.

Chen Ping and her husband were part of the 100 million rural migrants who could flout the one-child rule with impunity. China's vaunted birth-control dragnet, it turned out, had several gaping holes. Beijing family-planning officials weren't responsible for outsiders. Their home province of Zhejiang couldn't keep track of them. And the province where the baby was born didn't care because it didn't have to count the newborn in its quota.

When I arrived in China in 1972, the population was 800 million. By 1999, it had jumped by half a billion. Strenuous measures have slowed the national birth rate to a respectable 1.1 percent, but experts still predict the population will rise from a current 1.3 billion to 1.5 billion by 2030.

To monitor the menstrual cycles of a quarter of a billion Chinese women of reproductive age, China hired 150,000 full-time and 1 million part-time birth control workers. It gave them Draconian powers. But the one-child goal remained elusive in rural China, home to 75 percent of the population. In the Chinese countryside, birth control was a crazy quilt of exceptions and benign neglect. Even in cities, people couldn't keep the regulations straight.

Zhang Zhuangzhi (pronounced Jang Juong-jer), a Beijing architect who designed office furniture for me in the pre-filing cabinet days, dutifully notified her Street Committee when she got pregnant. But instead of congratulating her, it ordered her to get an abortion or be fined a week's pay for failing to seek permission in advance for a first pregnancy. Architect Zhang, 30, hadn't kept up with the ever-changing fine print of China's family-planning rules.

"You should be so happy to be pregnant. Instead, you're mad because you feel you've done something wrong," she said. She paid the fine and later had a baby boy.

■

Banning anesthetic during childbirth, I'm convinced, was a diabolical plot to ensure China's one-child policy. That way, you wouldn't even *think* about coming back twice. After preliminary research into the subject, I fled to a lovely hospital in Hong Kong to have Ben and, later, Sam.

In China, anesthetic was never given for vaginal deliveries. Childbirth classes were non-existent. Many women went into labor equipped only with fear. "They want to make it so horrible people won't have another baby," said Sabina Brady, a technology-transfer consultant who had two babies in Beijing. "I was in California with a warm, loving doctor and then I came back to whips and chains. They believe in *au naturel*. It is hellishly painful."

The three-bed delivery room at the Haidian Maternity Hospital did indeed resemble a scene from Dante's *Inferno*. At one bed, a doctor sewed up a woman who had just given birth. In the next, a woman in labor screamed with pain and chewed on her nightgown for relief. In the third, a woman lay in tears; her baby had been stillborn.

For many, the most searing memory was not the lack of anesthetic, but the degrading bedside manner of the doctors and nurses, who were always female. "They treated her just like an animal," said Gu Yuanmin, recalling his wife's experience. "Even today, I still feel like crying when I think about it." His wife had been forced to share a gurney with another woman in labor, with her feet next to the other's head. As the two women lay there moaning in pain, a doctor had snapped, "You both should have thought of that nine months ago when you were having such a good time."

At the Beijing Maternity Hospital, considered the best in China, I watched a class of medical students crowd around a woman about to undergo a difficult forceps delivery. All of a sudden, the doctor screamed at the hapless woman: "Stupid, what are you doing with your legs?"

What Nanny Ma remembers most clearly about giving birth to her only son was the nurse berating her for not pushing correctly during contractions. "She yelled at me, 'You idiot. You know how to defecate, don't you?'"

Husbands were typically barred from delivery rooms. "There's too many Chinese, so we're not treated like people," said Architect Zhang. At Haidian Hospital where she had her baby, the husbands had to wait in a drafty stairwell. Each time a baby was born, a nurse appeared behind a glass door, yelled the father's name, held up the infant for a moment, then disappeared. "We let the father have a glance. We don't let him touch it," Wang Yun, the hospital's director, confirmed.

The mothers rarely got to hold their babies, either. "They gave me a glimpse – just enough for me to see it was a boy," said Architect Zhang. "I didn't even have a chance to see his face." She was allowed to peek at her son only once more – through a nursery window – before she left the hospital. Even then, she had to beg a nurse for the privilege.

Maternity hospitals didn't bother to help mothers breastfeed. Instead, the nurses fed the infants sugar water. Many women, unaware that suckling stimulates milk supply, concluded they didn't have enough. By the 1990s, less than 10 percent of Chinese babies were breastfed, down from 81 percent in the 1950s. Formula-makers such as Gerber stepped into the breach. The Chinese, who already believed Western products were superior, happily splurged on imported formula for their one and only.

The seeds of China's runaway population problem were sown in the 1950s. Chairman Mao, himself a peasant, disparaged expert warnings to control the birth rate. The more people, the better, he declared, especially in the event of nuclear war.

After the Great Helmsman's death in 1976, Deng Xiaoping, himself the father of five, decreed the one-child policy. But it never took firm hold in rural China. Increased mobility, a free-wheeling economy and the end of the Maoist agricultural collectives all diluted Communist controls. With tradition continuing to make daughters beholden only to their in-laws, peasants knew they had to have a son if they didn't want to starve in their old age. With a population still longing for feudal-sized families, the result was a demographic disaster.

"They're nowhere close to a one-child policy," said Aprodicio

Laquian, deputy representative in Beijing for the UN Population Fund.

The failure rate of China's stainless-steel ring IUD also spawned huge numbers of "out-of-plan" pregnancies. The ring can be blamed for half of China's 10.4 million annual abortions, or nearly one for every two live births. The steel ring, manufactured in China since the late 1950s, easily slipped out of place. It failed about 10 percent of the time. But China inserted it in more than 50 million women because it cost 2 cents, compared to the more reliable, copper T-shaped IUD, which cost 22 cents and had a 99 percent reliability rate. Abortions cost $4, but the ministry that paid for IUDs didn't pay for abortions.

"It's penny-wise and pound-foolish. They're not counting the cost of an abortion or the pain and anguish to the woman," said Laquian. "We're telling them this is false economy."

About 40 percent of Chinese couples used the steel-ring IUD, compared to fewer than 5 percent for condoms. Authorities pushed IUDs because they eliminated free choice. "We won't take out an IUD unless the woman has a special certificate from her workplace," said Lei Zhixian, who ran a private abortion clinic.

I showed up unannounced one day in 1990 at Dr. Lei's tiny clinic, down a narrow alley in east Beijing. Outside, half a dozen young men, banished from the waiting room, smoked cigarettes. Inside, privacy was non-existent. The consulting room and waiting room were one, separated by a stained white sheet hanging down the middle. When I explained I was a Canadian reporter, Dr. Lei invited me to sit in while she interviewed patients.

At 68, she looked like a bespectacled grandmother but was actually a retired state gynecologist. She peered at Li Huizhen, who already had a year-old baby, complained of nausea and swollen breasts.

"You're pregnant," said Dr. Lei. "Will you do it today?"

The 30-year-old, her face impassive, reached into her pocket, and handed over several days pay. Dr. Lei tucked the money into her white lab coat.

"Do you want anesthetic? It's one yuan extra," she said. "If you've had a baby, don't worry. You can handle it." The young woman decided against anesthetic.

Next, Dr. Lei examined Miao Chunxiang, a pony-tailed waitress who claimed she was 20. "Child, you're pregnant," said Dr. Lei. Then she asked her address. Blushing and stammering, the young woman said she lived with her sister and didn't know the address.

"Don't worry, we'll keep your secret," Dr. Lei assured her.

The young woman shook her head.

"You misunderstand my intentions," sighed Dr. Lei. She agreed to perform the abortion anyway, but harrumphed to me, "All the addresses they give are phony. Everyone says they're married, too." She guessed two-thirds weren't.

Abortions were free at state hospitals, but patients preferred paying Dr. Lei. "The married ones don't dare go to a hospital," she explained. "They'll get fined for not having an IUD in place. The unmarried ones are afraid of losing their jobs."

In fact, some state hospitals had already stopped reporting the procedure to the woman's workplace. At Beijing's Haidian Maternity Hospital, doctors had even stopped checking identification. "They don't ask too many questions now," said Laquian, the UN Population Fund representative. "They just think: one baby less."

Dr. Lei estimated she had performed 4,000 abortions since opening her clinic five years earlier. She was so busy that two patients sometimes shared the clinic's only bed. For an extra 10 yuan ($1.25), she would also insert a steel-ring IUD. About half the women asked for one.

"Would you like to see me perform an abortion?" she asked. I followed her into an inner room with a concrete floor and no running water. A 28-year-old woman named Wang Yanrong was sitting on a sheaf of old newspapers, her splayed legs stuck in metal stirrups. Her period was eight weeks late. (Dr. Lei said she only performed abortions within the first ten weeks.)

Noting it was the patient's third abortion in two years, Dr. Lei briskly donned a pair of latex gloves. Using a pump and clamp, she suctioned out the fetus. The old newspapers soaked up the blood. Then Dr. Lei inserted a steel-ring IUD. The young woman moaned and wept. Right after, she hobbled a few yards to a narrow bed, where another young woman was already lying, also in tears.

■

State hospitals performed abortions up to the eighth month. "Sometimes it takes a long time to persuade them," explained Shen, the Beijing family-planning official. "We don't consider this forced abortion. Every year, we give birth to a whole new Canada. If people understood our problem, they would be less critical."

The wife of a truck driver in Changping county, near Beijing, tried to tough out her second pregnancy. Officials fined the couple the equivalent of five months income. They paid. So the officials raised the fine to four *years* income. The couple paid that, too. Then officials threatened to cancel the husband's license. They agreed to that, too. When the couple still would not abort – they had a daughter, but wanted a son – authorities threatened to cancel the licenses of the woman's brother and brother-in-law, who also drove for a living. The couple finally caved in.

Seven months into her pregnancy, the woman tearfully arrived at Haidian Hospital. A doctor induced labor, then smothered the fetus. "It was a son, but they didn't tell the mother," said Architect Zhang, who had her baby there at the same time. She didn't know whether the woman was ever reimbursed for the fines.

In many parts of rural China, the one-child policy was effectively a "one-son policy." Peasants often bribed local clinics for ultrasound test results, then aborted female fetuses. If the first child was a girl, a couple was often allowed to try again. By 1999, the male/female ratio in China was 120 to 100, according to the Chinese Academy of Social Sciences.

Plum Blossom Lin, the hard-driving factory owner, told me her adopted child was the second daughter of a peasant family. "Her mother considered drowning her," Plum Blossom said. The woman went on to have a third baby. But it was another daughter, who was also given away at birth.

Female infanticide, which virtually disappeared after the Communist victory, was back. William Hinton, author of *Fanshen* and Joan Hinton's brother, happened across a tiny corpse when he stopped to picnic by a stream in Shaanxi Province. "She was just a beautiful little girl, about one month old. Every feature was perfect. There were little white strands of mold across her eyelids and her nostrils," he recalled. "It was early spring. If she had died of ill-ness, she would have been buried. I suppose she just died of hunger and exposure. Her little hand was just perfect, but purple. It looked like she had fallen asleep there, but you can imagine the suffering she went through before she died."

No one really knew how many infant girls were smothered or drowned or exposed to the elements. The luckier ones were aban-doned near police stations or in hospital waiting rooms. Sometimes, tucked in the blanket would be a slip of paper with the baby's date of birth. To its credit, China set up orphanages in nearly every city.

When Marc Pelletier and Carole Noel went to Beijing, they packed some odd items for a childless couple: baby formula, diapers and a stuffed pink kitten named Tutu. But when they left two weeks later, the Montrealers had an extra bundle, their four-month-old Chinese daughter. "We've been very lucky. Usually it takes nine months to have a baby. This whole thing took five months," said Marc Pelletier, 36, cuddling Jasmine, who had tufts of coal black hair and dark, shiny eyes.

In the past decade, Westerners have scooped up tens of thou-sands of Chinese infants, virtually all girls. China's latest export pleased everyone. Unwanted babies found a home, foreigners got a child and cash-strapped orphanages earned a steady income. When I remembered my own abandoned grandmother, I was so happy to know that these despised baby girls could fly away, all expenses paid, to a brand new life in the West.

The flood of foreign adoptions was so great that one enterpris-ing Beijing hotel, the Kunlun, bought 15 cribs and a fleet of strollers. The staff was enthusiastic, if puzzled. "Is it because of the climate that you don't have many children in Canada?" asked Zhang Xihui, the hotel manager in charge of the families awaiting Canadian visas.

Chinese adoptive parents paid nothing, but foreigners were required to make "donations" ranging from $4,000 to $10,000 per baby. "We give you a cute baby. It's free. But Canada is a developed country, so we ask for a donation," said Cao Jun, the grandfatherly director of the Yangzhou Children's Welfare Institute, near Shanghai.

For each of the first 16 girls he placed with Canadians, he charged $4,800 to $6,000, payable by cash, Visa or American Express.

Several orphanage directors told me they consciously chose the prettiest babies for foreign adoption. Just as Beijing weeded out defective goods for export, it believed handicapped babies lost face for the motherland. Well-meaning officials even reassured a shocked Carole Noel that she and her husband could exchange Jasmine if they found a defect.

"After ten hours with her, she was ours," said Noel, 35, smiling at her sleeping daughter. "We would never take her back."

Jasmine was significantly underweight, despite last-minute attempts to fatten her up. Nutritious food, cuddles and kisses were all in short supply at Chinese orphanages. Those left behind sometimes didn't even attend school because no one would pay their tuition fees.

But were conditions as horrific as a British documentary called "The Dying Rooms" alleged in 1995? It depicted a "dying room" at the Shanghai No. 1 Orphanage, where infants were supposedly left to perish of neglect. If true, I wondered, why could no other journalist, even those based in China who spoke Chinese, ever match the story – in Shanghai or elsewhere? And why, if the orphanage was as callous as described, would it hire a staff *doctor* – the documentary's key source? (The doctor leveled the charges after moving to the United States.)

Certainly, Chinese orphans were no one's priority. They were underfed and understimulated. Sometimes they still had trouble walking at two. At the Nanchang Social Welfare Institute, a handful of attendants coped with 70 infants. A Canadian couple, who adopted a baby from there at the same time as Marc Pelletier and Carole Noel, said their four-month-old daughter's neck muscles were so undeveloped she couldn't raise her head. "Her bottom was the color of a deep-red sunset when we got her," said her new father. "It was the worst case of diaper rash I've ever seen."

With stories of corruption filling Chinese newspapers, many feared the much-needed "donations" never filtered down. But the Changsha No. 1 Social Welfare Institute used the $200,000 it received from Canadian couples to install new wiring and ventilation fans, buy wheelchairs and a van, and build new quarters for an adjacent old-age home. The Yangzhou orphanage spent the $85,000 it received in "donations" on a new building, medical supplies, toys and furnishings, including wallpaper for the new playroom. "We use all the money for the orphans," insisted Cao, the director. "The state doesn't take a cent."

Marc Pelletier and Carole Noel, who owned a translation agency in Montreal, completed the adoption paperwork in three months. After two more months, they learned they had a daughter named Wu Yang in Nanchang, a city of 1.1 million in central China. They flew there 11 days later and met her the next morning. They renamed her Jasmine and obtained her adoption certificate within a day. A Chinese passport, a Chinese exit permit and a Canadian visa took another week.

Marc Pelletier, a little dazed by jet lag, several nights of broken sleep and the wonder of fatherhood, sat by the window in his Kunlun Hotel room, cradling Jasmine in his lap. "See, that's Beijing," he cooed to her in French. "It's the capital of your country. See over there? That's the Canadian embassy. It's your new country. We're going there. And when you're older, we're going to take you skiing."

To celebrate Jasmine's new Canadian visa, Marc and Carole took her shopping for souvenirs in Silk Alley, an outdoor market near their hotel. After some gentle bargaining, a merchant capitulated on the price of two cloisonné boxes. Motioning to Jasmine, who was completely bundled up, he said, "I give you a good price because of the baby." When told she was Chinese – and newly adopted – his eyes widened. "Adopt me," he begged.

Some parents didn't completely abandon their children, not permanently, at least. Six months after Huang Jianxing and his wife had a baby boy, they moved to Beijing – without him. They left their only child behind in Suzhou, 600 miles away, to be raised by Huang's mother. "It's better for him this way," said Huang, 28, a prosperous tailor. When I expressed surprise, he bristled. "I send my parents money all the time."

Many Chinese parents chafed at the one-child policy, but a surprising number didn't see the point of actually living with their offspring. No statistics were available, but Chinese child-care experts estimated that between 5 and 10 percent of urban couples abdicated parental duties for years on end. Considering China's 1.3 billion population, absentee parenthood affected millions.

"In Western culture, everybody knows you don't take a child away from the primary caregiver. In China, that's what they sometimes do, several times, between zero and five years," said Dr. Kirsten Herh, a Danish child psychologist who had a private practice treating foreigners in Beijing.

In Yang Dongsong's case, she didn't live with her first-born for the first 14 years of his life. Instead, she left him with her parents in Beijing after her 54-day maternity leave ended. Then a struggling English teacher in Qinhuangdao, 200 miles away, she reasoned that food, heating and education were better in the capital. Twice yearly, she and her husband visited their son. "I thought it would be easier on me because there was no nursery at my workplace," she said. "But I was miserable. He knew I was his mother only because my mother often spoke of me."

Experts say such separation traumatizes both children and parents. "It's a terrible deprivation for the parents. They miss out on a chance to nurture their own children," said Dr. T. Berry Brazelton, a child-development expert at Harvard Medical School.

In 1978, Yang gave birth to her second son (just before the one-child policy kicked in). Again, she wanted to fob the baby off on her parents. But they were already busy taking care of her first-born *and* her brother's only child. Yang had no choice but to raise her second son herself.

She and her husband and their second son eventually moved back to Beijing. But for five more years, their first son continued to live with his grandparents. "The school was better in their neighborhood. I saw him on weekends," recalled Yang, 46, who found a job at the Ford Foundation in Beijing.

By the time I met her, the family was finally reunited under one roof, but it wasn't exactly a Hallmark moment. The older son felt jealous that she favored the second son. Yang, however, felt no guilt. "We feel closer to the younger one because we brought him up. I don't think there's anything to regret. My eldest was not harmed. My parents took good care of him."

Communist ideology put politics before family. During the Cultural Revolution, millions of urban families were split when parents, children or both moved to various farms in far-flung provinces. Diplomats assigned abroad were not allowed to take their offspring. "The feeling was that children shouldn't interfere with the revolutionary cause," said Isabel Crook, a Lifer who raised three children in Beijing.

In the 1950s, President Liu Shaoqi urged that children be sent to state-run boarding nurseries. The idea was to instill them with socialist values and quarantine them from their parents' bourgeois ideas. In the 1980s, as revolutionary ideas waned and the West beckoned, parents who went abroad also left their children behind. Architect Zhang planned to leave her toddler with her parents so she could go with her husband to France for several years. "If I find work, I may bring him over," she said. And if not? She shrugged.

The Chinese reporter who interviewed me for the "yellow banana" article seemed most impressed that I kept Ben and Sam with me in Beijing, instead of shipping them back to Canada to fend for themselves. (I didn't point out that I had a nanny, a housekeeper, a chauffeur and a cook, not to mention one very tired husband.)

Some parents even opted to put their children in boarding nurseries in the same city. At the one run by the health ministry, the tears would come after dinner when parents arrived to take home the day children. "We tell those who stay the night that their mommy and daddy have to work," said Ren Shuling, head of the nursery.

Two Beijing friends of mine, Yang Xinya and his wife, Wang Jin, put their twin sons in a boarding nursery for years. They picked the boys up Saturday afternoons and returned them Monday mornings. Later, when the nursery began urging parents to take the children home on Wednesdays for mid-week family sleepovers, the couple sometimes demurred. "We wanted to work at night," said Yang Xinya, who was teaching himself English. The couple also found it inconvenient because they both had to pick up the boys: Each parent could take only one child on a bike. In 1989, when the couple had a chance to study in Canada, they left their preschoolers behind. The twins remained in the boarding nursery and the grandparents picked them up on weekends. After a year of this, the family was reunited in Montreal.

Mary Claire, a newly arrived three-year-old American, came over one day to meet Ben, then four. She was surprised to see both Nanny Ma and me. Settling into the same stuffed armchair as Ben, she turned to him and said, "So, you have two moms."

To outsiders, it certainly seemed like kids were indulged in China. Not surprisingly, the new generation of spoiled brats was dubbed "Little Emperors." In the cities, the one-child culture was so strong that sibling rivalry had become an unknown. Nanny Ma was herself the mother of an only child. When Sam arrived, her reaction was to segregate him from Ben. To avoid squabbles, she simply didn't allow them to play together. (Back in Canada, they do everything together now, including squabble.)

Yet child-rearing in China also stressed discipline, obedience and conformity. From the first moments of life, thumb-sucking and security blankets were prohibited. Toilet-training began at one month and was usually completed at one year. Left-handedness was banned. Crawling, the main way infants explore their environment, was discouraged by parents who feared the concrete floors were too dirty. Instead, babies were carried until they walked.

A joint study by the University of California and Beijing's Institute of Child Psychology found that at eight months Chinese babies were behind American babies in motor development. Chinese babies also crawled one or two months later. And they lagged in sitting skills and the ability to grasp objects while crawling, said Dr. Dong Qi, vice-director of the Institute of Child Psychology.

Some believed that rigid rules were the only way 1.3 billion people could live in harmony. "Chinese people are afraid of softening up their child for a world that isn't very soft. Unfortunately, they miss the point. Children need inner strength," said Dr. Brazelton, who has studied China's one-child phenomenon.

A Chinese baby entered the world kicking and screaming. But within minutes, the midwife would straighten its arms and legs, roll it in a blanket and tie the bundle with a piece of rope. For Chinese, it was the first taste of freedom lost. The "candle wrap," so-called because the finished product resembled a fat candle, was a full-body straitjacket. Crying usually stopped because even breathing was difficult. "I saw them unwrap one," said a UN health specialist in Beijing. "The baby took a deep breath."

Many parents kept their babies swaddled this way for months, in the belief it kept the infant warm. "It limits a child's movement, so there isn't enough stimulation," said Dr. Wu Fenggang, a psychologist at the Child Development Center of China. Candle-wrapped babies were sometimes so tightly wrapped their blood couldn't circulate, causing hypothermia. Infants also had trouble clearing their lungs of mucus, prompting experts to blame the candle wrap for acute respiratory infections, a leading killer of infants in China.

Occasionally, a version of the candle wrap was taken to a tragic extreme. Some peasants in the poorest parts of north China stuck their babies in sandbags, which acted as both anchor and "baby" litter. Starting as early as ten days after birth, bare-bottomed infants spent their first year in sandbags, freed only for feedings or a change of sand. The peasants, who needed to work in the fields, bagged the children even when they were old enough to walk, tying them to a bed with rope. Chinese newspapers reported that some children spent five years in a sandbag. Owing to the lack of stimulation, "sandbag babies" had abnormally low IQs, according to Dr. Wu, who participated in a study of 400 such children. He also found that parents who used sandbags felt that children raised this way were more docile and filial.

Comfort habits were considered both a character flaw and terribly unhygienic. Ben would be left open-mouthed in astonishment when complete strangers walked up and yanked his thumb out of his mouth. There was no point in fighting 1.3 billion Chinese. I'd just wait until they left, then hug him and whisper, "It's okay with me, Ben, if you suck your thumb." And his thumb would go straight back in.

At Three Mile Village Nursery in Beijing, toddlers who hugged stuffed animals or chewed on quilts were kept under surveillance. "We watch them the whole nap," said Xie Shuling, the vice-principal, with a benign smile. "We tell them, 'Look at the other children. They don't need anything to go to sleep. Why can't you be like them?'" At another nursery, teachers confiscated cuddly toys that the one-year-olds had brought from home. "These are bad habits. We just tell them we lost it," said Ren Shuling, the director.

With disposable diapers unavailable, parents began toilet-training babies at one month. They would *ba* them, which meant hoisting a baby over a potty and whistling to mimic the sound of running water. Most Chinese toddlers were toilet-trained by one year and wore pants split open at the crotch, making it easier to squat down and pee whenever they felt the urge.

Nurseries stressed conformity. During morning calisthenics at Ren Shuling's nursery, toddlers fanned out into four neat lines from a single one – and back again. In art class, four-year-olds copied a painting of a bear, with a sun on the left. The teacher noted proudly that out of 32 children, only one "goofed," and drew the sun on the right.

No one considered self-esteem, or even basic tact. One Chinese friend asked me, in front of Ben, who I loved more, Ben or Sam? When I said nothing, she repeated the question. "Both. The same," I finally said, which was true.

As for self-esteem, teasing children to the brink of tears was considered an adult prerogative. Parents often dangled toys in front of toddlers – and snatched them away, again and again, until the children screamed in frustration. "It's considered very amusing to bait the kids into crying. Then everyone laughs and says, 'How funny, we finally got them to break down,'" said Michael Crook, who ran a school in Beijing.

Psychologists condemned such behavior. "It teaches children to be dishonest themselves when they grow up," said Dr. Wu. Repeated taunts also taught children early on to suppress their emotions, added Dr. Herh.

At Sun Altar, the single-swing park, I noticed a tearful toddler, shakily calling out, "Papa, Papa." I was about to help when I realized the father was quietly stalking him, a few yards away. After what seemed an eternity, the father finally revealed himself, laughed with pleasure, gathered his distraught son in his arms and gave him a kiss.

China's last Mao Generation had hatched China's first Me Generation. This was the unintended result of the one-child policy. Li Xiaodong, a Communist Party cadre in the Ministry of Agricultural Machinery, told me he had no idea how to stop his 12-year-old son from slashing the furniture with scissors. "I've tried slapping him, but it doesn't do any good," he said. "When I was 12, I cooked, washed and cleaned for my family. But my son doesn't know how to do anything."

For generations, the big, extended family defined each person's place in the hierarchy. Chinese had no clue how to raise an only child. There was no indigenous Dr. Spock to guide them on their way. While parents still candle-wrapped their infants and enforced taboos against thumb-sucking, they often surrendered in the face of antisocial behavior.

"It's the one-child policy," agreed Architect Zhang. "We all want the best for our child." She bought her son expensive giant prawns for dinner but would not eat any herself. In the summer, I saw grandmothers chasing after their grandchildren on the sidewalk, bowl and spoon in hand, begging them to take another bite. In a land of scarcity, love was expressed through food. Child obesity, unheard of a decade ago, became so common that hospitals in Beijing held "fat reduction camps." My housekeeper's ten-year-old son was so overweight that she had to sew all his clothes. When he was 11, she still bathed him each night and dressed him each morning. She even tied his shoes.

You could bemoan China's little emperors who didn't know how to tie their own shoes. But I saw a ray of hope. For the first time in Chinese history, the individual was more important than the collective. Pampered onlies were growing up to be strong-willed, spoiled, self-centered types who reminded me of, well, Americans. When you have a nation of little emperors, you can't have a nation of little slaves, and maybe, just maybe, China will get democracy. With its one-child policy, the Communist Party may have unwittingly sown the seeds of its own destruction.

Epilogue

With Nanny Ma on my secret visit back to China in 1999.

Photo: Beatrice Pinosa

To the West, China seems remote. But just as faxes, phones and the Internet have brought the outside world to China, the world's most populous country is at our doorstep, too. Whatever happens there will affect us sooner than we think. So it matters that China has 650 million little emperors. It matters that China is searching for a spiritual glue to hold itself together. And it matters whether China evolves peacefully and democratically, or disintegrates into chaos.

The world has shrunk. If Beijing cannot provide a stable environment, the Chinese people will vote with their feet. And they will be coming soon to a neighborhood near you. President Jimmy Carter once lectured Deng Xiaoping on human rights and Beijing's restrictions on emigration. "How many would you like?" Deng interrupted. "Ten million?"

Let my people go. This is China's new approach to a whole array of domestic problems. Pesky dissidents won't stop making trouble? Fly them to America at U.S. State Department expense. Unemployment getting uncomfortably high? Issue a million passports. Peasants getting restive down on the farm? Turn a blind eye when snakeheads smuggle them out.

China is stable for the moment. The economy is strong. Yet even under these optimal circumstances, people are trying to get to our shores. For reasons of geography, economics and tradition, many illegal immigrants to North America come from coastal Fujian. In recent years, New York's Chinatown has sprouted a whole new Fujian quarter. Police figure about 100,000 of them are legal, maybe 200,000 more aren't.

I wanted to see the jumping-off point for myself. One late winter day in 1992, I went to Changle County in Fujian Province. The rocky, deeply indented coastline provided hundreds of natural harbors. For more than 1,000 years, the Fujianese have looked to the sea for their livelihood, and part of that livelihood has always been smuggling. With the opening of China to foreign trade, Fujian quickly reverted to its clandestine ways. Fishermen smuggled in American cigarettes and smuggled out heroin, guns, antiques – and humans. Even the son of a local Communist Party Secretary resurfaced in Japan. "He was smuggled there," said a lone fisherman, who was repairing his boat on the deserted white sand beach.

Human cargo was highly lucrative. By the late 1990s, local gangsters were charging about $40,000 to transport a peasant to North America, a new twist on the old head tax. Unlike pampered city folk, peasants were willing to slave away in sweatshops or restaurants to repay their debts. Snakeheads also preferred peasants because they left behind a secure web of clan relations, otherwise known as knee-capping collateral.

Like Migrant Worker Zhao in Big Mound Village, these illegal immigrants are terribly, sometimes criminally, exploited. Yet they keep coming, because a terrible life abroad is better than what they had back home. Some peasant women end up in hellish New York brothels, turning $22 tricks. But if they turn 17 or 18 tricks a night and keep half for themselves – not an uncommon arrangement – they can make two to three times more than Wang Mei, the Xiamen prostitute. At that rate, they can repay their debt to the snakehead in just seven months. And they don't get sent to labor camps for talking to a reporter.

My friend, Great Leap, who was fired for befriending the Pakistani tourist, upped and left China a few years ago. She managed to get to the United States legally, where she eked out a living operating a video store in Queens, New York. But her goal always was to go back to school. And she did. In May, 1999, she graduated with an MBA in international business from a university in Providence, Rhode Island.

The exodus, legal and illegal, is a safety valve for China. Tiananmen revealed desperate anger at the government. Ten years later, the basic contradictions have not been resolved. To attain capitalism, you must shutter inefficient state enterprises, which means throwing millions out of work. Market-Leninism – Communist controls *and* a capitalist economy – can't work. They are like two tectonic plates, shifting and grinding against one another. In the 21st century, can China absorb the shocks, or will there be a quake?

China is now plugged into the rest of the world. The Internet, faxes, cellphones and computers have already created that fundamental pillar of democracy: freedom of information. Despite Communist Party controls, dissidents, gays, entrepreneurs, *People's Daily* reporters, are all talking to one another – and to the outside world.

Some experts think that Beijing's rapid economic growth gives it the same stake in peace and stability as the West. China wants to compete, they say, not on military might, but on economic strength. I agree that trade fosters human rights and democracy, but only indirectly. Indeed, the more the West engages Beijing's leaders, the more harshly they seem to treat their dissidents. The Communist Party's priority is power. But the dilemma facing China's leaders is this: If the economy grows fast enough, they will become peacefully irrelevant, but if it slows down too much, they will be made violently irrelevant.

The question is no longer whether China *will* change, but *who* will change it? The tiny, brave band of dissidents is pushing for democracy, but I don't see them taking China by storm. I believe that the most dangerous anti-Communists may be risk-taking entrepreneurs like Plum Blossom Lin. The Me Generation of little emperors won't take kindly to cattle-prods, either. Visualize a businesswoman in an Armani suit with a cellphone and a Mercedes. Or a young man addicted to Starbucks caffeine and cyberspace. Now imagine a Communist cadre telling them what to do. You can't, right? That's because the new capitalists and the little emperors and the Internet will make the Communist Party irrelevant.

At the end of the millennium, the basic contradiction of the Middle Kingdom is change with no change. China is trying to combine breathtaking economic upheaval with a permafrost political system. Despite its embrace of capitalism, China remains a totalitarian dictatorship. That contradiction sparked the 1989 demonstrations at Tiananmen Square and the subsequent massacre. It could spark another. Today the pace in China is so fast, the changes so earth-shaking, that anyone who claims to know what will happen next, really doesn't. Some China watchers predict a descent into chaos. With corruption and unemployment on the rise, perhaps the peasants and workers will revolt. And, in the endless cycle of Chinese history, those in power might crush them once again.

But I think China has a chance. In 1999, I felt a country moving toward freedom, democracy and unprecedented prosperity. China is racing through a telescoped Industrial Revolution, creating more wealth than ever before in its 4,000-year-old history. In 1957, in a ruse to encourage people to speak their minds about the Communist Party, Mao called on everyone to "Let a hundred flowers bloom, let a hundred schools of thought contend." Today, a more apt slogan might be: "Let a billion fortunes bloom." No matter who is right, the doomsayers or the optimists, the reverberations are certain to ripple outward to the rest of the world.

On my last day in China in 1999, I went back to see Nanny Ma. She cried, at first, because I hadn't brought Ben with me. The hurt of losing him had made her resolve never to take another job as a nanny. She still worked for the *Globe*, but as a housekeeper. She missed Ben so much, she told me, that she could hardly stand to look at other foreign children.

I'd been thinking about babies, too. I thought about Root Shen's adopted daughter in Waterdown Village, about that tiny corpse abandoned on a frozen Beijing road, about my own grandmother, offered to any passerby in Canton. I asked Nanny Ma about the Ten Minute Baby. Her maid, it turned out, had gotten married and quit. Nanny Ma had no idea what had become of that unwanted little girl or even what her name had been. She shrugged, puzzled at why I seemed so fixated on that particular baby girl. "You can get one anywhere," she said. "*Duo de hen*" (there's so many).

For the sake of that Ten Minute Baby, and so many others like her, I hope China will change, soon, for the better. And deep down, I have a feeling it will.

INDEX

A

abandoned children (*see also* infanticide), 3, 4, 5, 47–8, 300, 308–11, 320–1
abortion, 17, 63, 221, 300, 303–5
acupuncture, 294
Adler, Pat, 145, 146, 147
Adler, Sol, 143, 145–6, 147, 153, 154
adoption, 3–5, 44, 47–48, 204, 220, 306–8
affluence, 12, 13, 26, 39, 42–3, 45, 46–7, 53–6, 69–70, 86–7, 104–5, 189, 190–2, 204–8, 211–5, 234
agriculture, 37–9, 46, 55, 62, 65, 66–7
AIDS, 200, 235, 241, 247–50, 251, 279, 290, 291
airlines, 112–4
Alexander, Patricia, 284–5
Anhui Province, 214
arms dealing, 21, 135
art, 262–3
Auden, W.H., 225–6
Avon Products Inc., 187–90

B

Baskin-Robbins, 186
beggars, 58–62
Beijing, 56, 58, 59–61, 278, 288, 290
Beijing Military Command, 19
Beijing No. 2 Prison, 25
Beijing University, 11, 25, 73, 183, 283
Bell, Alister, 6–7, 46, 47, 160, 202, 235, 286
Benger, Robin, 6–7; 46, 202, 235; 253, 278, 286; photo credits, 10, 140, 194
Bethune, Dr. Norman, 143–4
Big Mound Village (Da Qiu Zhuang), Hebei, 53–56, 67–8, 318
Big Red Door (Zhejiang Village in Beijing), 56–58
birth control (*see also* one-child policy), 16, 17, 18, 44, 47, 58, 63, 116, 249, 261, 299–304
blacks, 132–6
blood donations, 287–91
Brady, Sabrina, 301
Brazelton, Dr. T. Berry, 309, 311
Bright Asia Primary School, 69–70
Britain, 151, 243, 250
Brouwers, Hans, 20
Buddhist Law religious group, 294–5
Burma, 241–4, 247–50

C

Canada, 102, 286, 287, 289, 305, 306–8
Canadian Embassy, 62, 63
"candlewrap" babies, 312, 314

Canton, 76, 187–90, 272

capitalism, 38, 53–58, 68, 74, 151, 186–90, 202, 203–8, 287, 319

cars, 12, 13, 95, 208, 211–6, 218, 222

Cernetig, Miro, 6, 11

Chai Ling, 203

Chen, Gerald, 147–8

Chen, Kathy, 79

Chen Mei, 73–4

Chen Yi, 73–4, 213

Cheng Xingguo, 74–5

Chengdu, 102, 118–123, 160

Cheung, Tai Ming, 19

child rearing, 311–4

childbirth, 301–2

Chinese Communist Party, 14, 16, 24, 30, 59, 64, 66, 74, 187, 202, 203, 215, 219; 283, 314, 319; and foreigners, 142, 147; in Tibet, 170, 173, 175; and gays, 228, 231; and mentally ill, 252, 256; and divorce, 268, 269; and marriage, 270; officials, 38–9, 70, 73, 205, 276; 318,

China Democratic Party, 33

Chinese Women's Journal, 80–81, 267

Chinoy, Mike, 85

CNN, 20

Chongqing, 219, 220–1

Chou En-lai, 66, 115, 147, 149

Coca Cola, 76, 111, 264

Coe, Frank, 143

communist controls, 15–8; 19–20, 22, 23, 24; in Tibet, 163–4,

168–9; and phones and Internet, 196–203; and AIDS, cancer, 250; and population, 302; and capitalism, 319

computers, 74, 97, 131, 198, 201–3

conformity (*see also* candlewrap babies) 313

corruption, 48–9, 70, 75–6, 97, 190–1, 199, 206, 214

Cosmopolitan, 93

crime, 16, 17, 54, 58, 94, 134, 219, 242–3

Crook, Isabel, 310

Crook, Michael, 313

Cultural Revolution, 5, 13, 59, 69, 104, 116, 141–5, 147, 150, 204, 206, 219, 220–2, 236, 267–8, 284, 285, 286; and end of civility, 285, 287; in Tibet, 166–7; and *qi gong*, 291, 292; and split-up of families, 310

Cui Zi'en, 224, 234–5

cuisine, 28, 40, 43, 67, 74, 105, 107–8, 114–123, 161, 162; in Tibet, 172

D

Dairy Queen, 186

Dalai Lama, 163, 164, 166, 176, 178

Dalian, 98

Davies, Peter, 85

democracy, 26, 27, 32, 33, 199, 200, 204, 283, 319; and one-child policy, 314, 320

Democracy Wall, 27, 33

Deng Pufang, 285–7

Deng Xiaoping, 14–5, 27, 42, 54, 64, 68, 80, 94, 129, 212, 250, 285, 302, 317

dentistry, 111–2

disabled, 285–7

dissent, 21–34, 68, 77, 79, 98, 319–20; and "medical parole" 28–29, 30, 31, 34

divorce, 116, 185, 253, 267, 268, 269–71

Doje, 166–7

Dragon Pool Village, Gansu, 65

drugs, 241–50

D'Souza, Michael, 101

Dunkin Donuts, 186, 192

E

economic development, 12, 38–9, 44, 45, 46, 53–8, 67–8, 320

education, 43–5, 62, 63, 69–70, 95, 156, 204; of disabled, 287; in Tibet, 168–9, 176, 292

emigration, 317–9

English language, 11, 29, 32, 44, 70, 151, 162, 204, 227, 229, 232, 264, 268, 310

Engst, Sid, 140, 144–5, 155–6

Electrolux, 187–8

e-mail, 32, 198–203, 283

Epstein, Israel, 141, 142, 143, 150

Ermenegildo Zegna, 190

Esprit, 192

etiquette, 40–1, 132, 197

executions, 60, 75, 106, 183, 241–2, 243, 245

F

family planning (*see* birth control)

fax machines, 32, 33, 74, 203, 317, 319

Ferragamo, Salvatore, 190–92

films, 261–2, 275

firefighting, 216

foreigners, attitude to, 78–81, 113, 127–137; Lifers, 141–156; fake 137, 205

Fu, Charlene, 79

Fujian Province, 203, 261, 272–4, 318

G

Gansu Province, 62–6

Gates, Bill, 201, 202

gays, 200, 224–237, 254, 299 (*see also* toilets, gay sex in)

Gere, Richard, 28, 176

Globe and Mail, 3, 4, 6, 83; and staff, 251, 294

Great Leap Forward (1958), 149, 155

Gu Weiming (Future Gu), 97–8, 163, 215

Guangdong Province, 56, 58, 118, 187

Guanxi (cronyism, nepotism), 73–6, 84, 205, 207, 268, 286

gulag, 25, 27, 29, 31, 33, 34, 60, 94, 95, 105–6, 142, 146, 147, 206, 243, 245; and prostitutes, 271–2

Guo Bin, 236–7

H

Häagen-Dazs, 186
Haikou, 274–9
Hainan Island, 274–9
Han Dongfang, 98
Hangzhou, 7, 37, 56, 77, 98, 133, 198
Harrer, Heinrich, 177
Hatem, George, 142
health, 63–5, 66, 95–6, 156, 218, 250–2, 291–4
Herh, Dr. Kirsten, 309, 313
Hinton, Bill, 305–6
Hinton, Joan, 94–5, 140, 144, 155–6, 305
homeless, 58–62
Hong Kong, 6,7, 38, 78, 184, 276, 289, 301
Hope, Bob, 81
hotels, 19–20, 40, 100, 105–7, 276–7, 306
housing 12, 54–5, 56, 57, 64, 66–7, 75, 84–5, 97, 189, 204, 205, 236
Hu Yaobang, 14, 21, 22, 220
Hui, Saiman, 140, 173, 225
human rights, 14, 27, 33, 77–8, 106, 129, 200, 317, 319; in Tibet, 163–4, 168–9, 176–78; and mental patients, 255
humor, 81, 219

I

Ikea, 93, 186
infanticide, 284–5, 305–6
inflation, 40, 65, 68, 98, 152, 264
Internet, 198–203, 236, 317, 319

Isherwood, Christopher, 225–6
Israel, 152–4

J

Japanese, 131, 132, 153, 216, 220
Jews, 141, 152–4
Jiang Zemin, 19, 199
Jiangsu Province, 118
journalists, controls on 37, 62, 76–80, 159–60, 178, 198, 274; and ethnic Chinese foreign correspondents, 79

K

Kaifeng, 153–4
Kazan, Elia, 291
Kentucky Fried Chicken, 58, 181–2, 186
Kiln Pit, 59–62
Koko Nor, 107
Koreans, 131–2
Kroll, Christian, 243, 244, 248
Kunming, 242, 245, 246

L

labor camps (*see* Gulag)
Laquian, Aprodicio, 302–4
Lee Kuan Yew, 75
Lee-Young, Joanne, 191–2
left-handedness, 121, 311
Lei, Zhixian, Dr., 303–4
Leibowitch, Max, 153
lesbians, 225, 235–7
Leys, Simon, 142
Lhasa, 159, 160, 161–2
Li Honghu, 169–70, 176
Li Peng, 199, 207

Li Xiaohua (Ferrari Li), 211, 212
Li Xiuxian (Fairy Li), 188–90
Li Yanhe, 226
Lin Biao, 275
Lin Hai, 201
Lin Mei (Plum Blossom Lin), 204–6, 289, 305, 319
Lin Shutao, 110, 115–6
little emperors (spoiled brats), 69–70, 104, 311–4, 317
Liu Nianchun, 33, 77
Liu Qing, 33
Liu Shaoqi, 310
Liu Xinyong (Driver Liu), 82–3, 87–89, 100, 251
Louis Vuitton, 190–2
Lu Maoguo (Chef Lu), 120–3
Luo Family Mill Village, Gansu, 63–4

M

Ma Naiying (Nanny Ma), 3, 5, 111–2, 127, 251, 289, 301, 311, 320
Mao, Madame (Jiang Qing), 144, 146, 147, 148
Mao Zedong, 5, 13, 29, 64, 66, 68, 98, 101, 129, 141, 147, 148, 177, 275, and cars 212; and foreigners, 143; and nostalgia; 117, 156; and opium, 243; and personality cult, 207; and *Selected Works*, 59; and slogans, 94, 111, 125–6, 143, 150, 271, 320; and youth, 284; and population control, 302

Marsh, Dr. David, 256
Marx, Karl, 38, 53, 94, 145–6, 153, 187, 208, 267
McDonald's, 93, 130, 156, 186
McGregor, Jim, 242, 244, 247, 248, 249, 255, 271; photo credit, 240
mental illness, 151, 228, 244, 245, 252–7, 291
mental retardation, 63–64
Mickleburgh, Rod, 27, 191
migrants, 3, 43, 53–62, 67–8, 95, 98, 300, in Tibet, 165–6
Miles, James, 77, 80
Mok, Ben, 187
Montreal West High, 197
Mou Qizhong (Middleman Mou), 206–8
MSG, 121–2, 123
MSG Club, 79

N

Nanking, 56, 133, 197, 198
New York Times, 27
Nike Inc., 186, 187
Ningxia, 99
Noel, Carole, 306–8
Norinco, 19, 103–4

O

Obesity, 117, 314
One-child policy, 43, 44, 47–8, 204–5, 221–2, 284, 299–304, 311–4
Opium Wars, 243, 252. 272
Orphanages, *see* adoption
Overseas Chinese, attitude to, 79–81, 130, 136–7

P

Panchen Lama, 173

peasants, 37–49, 62–8, 197, 288, 289–90, 293

Pelletier, Marc, 306–8

People's Armed Police, 19

People's Daily, 199

People's Liberation Army, 14–5, 18–21, 24–5, 95, 101–4; 105–7; in Tibet, 162–3, 173; and phones, 196; and car theft, 212; and death rally, 241–2

Pepsi Cola, 185

phones, 17, 32, 38, 46, 49, 54, 74, 83, 160, 189, 195–203, 204, 235, 269, 317, 319

Pinosa, Beatrice, photo credit, 316

pirating CD ROMs, 202

Pitt, Brad, 176

Pizza Hut, 186

police, and business, 19; and dissent 22, 23, 24, 25; and order, 57, 60–61; and stealing *Globe*'s car, 77; and journalists, 79; and repression, 129; and corruption, 214; and gays, 228, 230, 234; and drugs, 242–7; and prostitution, 275, 276, 278; and abandoned baby, 284–5; and *qi gong*, 292

pollution, 217–9

population (*see also* birth control; one-child policy), 299–300

post office, 82–3, 196

poverty, 41–2, 54–5, 58–68, 220

Prada, 191

prison, (*see* gulag, also Qincheng Prison)

prostitution, 33, 248, 249–50, 271–9, 318

protest (*see also* Tiananmen Square), T-shirts 23–25

Public Security Bureau (*see* police)

Q

Qian Xueshen, 294

qi gong (breathing exercises and "cures") 268, 291–5

Qincheng Prison (*see also* gulag), 25, 141, 144, 148, 150

Qinghai Province, 105–8

Qiu Hai, 198

Qiu Ming, 266–8

quotas, 17, 93–6, 163, 169, 288

R

Red China Blues, 4, 6, 14, 15, 77, 79, 155

residence permits, 58, 268

religion, 47, 74, 234; in Tibet, 163–4, 166, 169, 175, 291–5

Rittenberg, Sidney, 141, 146–8, 150

Ruili, Yunnan, 243, 247–50, 271

S

Safire, William, 75

Sampson, Catherine, photo credit, 260

"sandbag" babies, 312

Schell, Orville, 30–31

Schmidt, Werner, 20

Schuman, Julian, 151–2, 153, 154–5

Scorsese, Martin, 176

seder, 152–4

service, 87–9, 99–101, 111–7, 187, 198

sex (*see also* prostitution, gays), 97, 183, 186, 192, 214, 254, 267–9, 274–9; or lack thereof, 29, 31, 54, 104, 129, 184, 185, 254, 261–2, 265, 266–7

sexually transmitted diseases, 217, 271, 272, 273, 274, 278

Shaanxi Province, 66

Shalhevet, Yoseph and Sheila, 153–4

Shandong Province, 118, 293

Shanghai, 56, 58, 100, 118, 121, 151, 153, 199, 203, 231, 233, 256, 286, 288

Shattuck, John, 27

Shen, Agen (Root Shen) 35–6, 42–3, 46–8

Shen Aying (Noble Shen), 41–2, 48

Shulman, Ben, 3, 4, 7, 80, 81, 127, 161, 216, 217, 218, 301, 310, 311, 313, 320

Shulman, Norman (Fat Paycheck Shulman), 3–5, 140, 143, 144, 152, 155, 156, 161–2, 163–4, 172–3, 176, 218, 228, 271

Shulman, Sam, 3, 4, 80, 97, 161, 218, 301, 310, 313

Si Wai Lai, 32

Sichuan Province, 68, 69, 76, 98, 99, 118–123, 207, 208, 219–221

smoking, 29, 76, 236, 250–2, 286

Soviet Union, 102, 135, 206, 251, 254

state-owned enterprises, 96–108, 188–9, 219, 319

State Security, Ministry of, 19, 77–9

stock market, 193–4, 203

Straathof, Caroline, 106–7

Street Committees, 15–18, 229, 300

stress, 253

Su, Jane, 75

suicide, 253–4, 256, 267

Sun, Lena, 30, 33, 77, 78, 79–80, 159–60, 164, 168, 172, 178–9, 272–4

Sun Yat-sen, 225; Madame Sun Yat-sen, 115

Sunshine Village, Shaanxi, 66–67

T

Taiwan, 102, 272, 273

Tampax, 186

Tang Dynasty, 16

Tang Libin, 229–30

television, 67, 69, 167, 183–6, 199

Terrill, Ross, 20

Tiananmen Square, 13, 215,

Tiananmen Square Massacre and protests, 14–5, 18, 20, 25, 26, 30, 32, 66, 77, 79, 130–1, 142, 291, 295; 320; and Yan Yan, 152; and Lifers, 156; and Tibet, 168; and phones, 196; and Middleman Mou, 206, 207, 285; and gays, 231, 232–3; (1990, first anniversary) 21–23;

(1991, second anniversary)
22–3, 25; (1999, tenth anniversary), 200; 283; and Most-Wanted List, 15, 16, 25
Tianjin, 131, 198
Tibet, 76, 98, 106, 157–179
Three Gorges Dam, 219
toilets, 12, 38, 40–1, 43, 45, 46, 47, 48, 69, 85, 107; gay sex in, 227, 228, 231, 233, 286
tourism, 104–8, 120

U

unemployment, 96–8, 99, 156, 221
UNICEF, 66
United Nations, 244, 249, 250, 303, 304
United States, 21, 27, 28, 84, 102, 129–30, 135, 144, 151, 183, 187, 217, 250, 287, 317–9

V

Viagra, 269

W

Walker, Donna, 152
Wan Li, 207, 220
Wang Ce, 33, 34
Wang Chunrong (Springtime Wang), 41–3, 45, 48–9
Wang Dan, 25–7, 30–2, 200, 283, 286
Wang Mei, 272–4, 318
Wang Ruoshui, 199
Wang Xiaobo, 226
Wang Xizhe, 34
Wang Yulin, 147, 148

water, 38, 40–1, 46, 48, 54–5, 61–2, 62–66, 85–7, 133, 167, 217
Waterdown Village (Gaobei Village), Zhejiang, 37–49
Wei Jingsheng, 27–30, 32–3, 38
women (*see also* prostitution; birth control; abortion), 55, 113, 192, 204; and suicide rate, 253; and beauty contests, 263–5; and weddings, 267–8; and advice columnist, 266–9, 269–79; and matchmaking, 269–71; and preference for male children, 305–6
Wong, Jan (Bright Precious Wong), background, 5; 27, 114; family, 3–5, 306; Maoist days, 11, 12; 136, 142, 147, 183, 184, 216; and Chinese government, 6; 79; and ethnicity 80–1; kidnapping attempt, 79; and staff, 96; treatment in Tibet, 171–2; and perils of Tibetan yak tartar, 179
Wong, Mary, 79
workers, 96–101, 131–2, 188, 218
World Bank, 63, 66
Wu, Stella, 137, 259–60
WuDunn, Sheryl, 79
Wu'er Kaixi, 200
Wuhan, 252–3, 256

X

Xiamen, 204, 271–4
Xiao Yang, 98, 219–222; photo 209–210

Y

Yan Guanlong (Dragon Yan), 38–40, 48
Yan Yan, 152, 153, 259–60, 274–9; photo credit, 10
Yanan, 66
Yang Dongsong, 309–10
Yang, Gladys, 149–51
Yang Tao, 231–3
Yang Xianyi, 148–51
Yang Xinya, 310
Yangtze River, 217, 219, 287
Yao Yuexiu (Elegance Yao), 37, 40, 42, 43, 45, 97
Ye, Kippy, 127
Ying Ruocheng, 60, 81
Youth, 39, 43–5, 283, 284
Yu Lihua, 79–80
Yunnan Province, 76, 241–50, 252
Yuppies, 190–92
Yves Saint-Laurent, 191

Z

Zhang Congmi, 12–13
Zhang Hong (Scarlet Zhang) 11–13, 215
Zhang Lin (Zhang, Forest) 29, 33–4, 77
Zhang Yamei, 213–4
Zhao Ziyang, 14–15, 207
Zhejiang Province (*see also* Big Red Door), 300
Zhou Yue (Great Leap Zhou), 129, 318
Zhu Rongji, 176, 198
Zhuang Zedong, 136–7
Zhuang Zhangzhi, 300, 302, 305, 310, 314

About the Author

Jan Wong was the much acclaimed Beijing correspondent for the *Globe and Mail* from 1988 to 1994. She is a graduate of McGill University, Beijing University, and Columbia University's Graduate School of Journalism. The recipient of a National Newspaper Award, among other honours, Wong has also written for the *New York Times* and *Wall Street Journal*. Her first book, *Red China Blues*, was named one of *Time* magazine's top five non-fiction books of 1996. It remains banned in China. Jan Wong lives with her family in Toronto, where she is a columnist for the *Globe and Mail*.